# INCOMPLETE WORKS

By the same author:

Books:
HICKSVILLE
SAM ZABEL AND THE MAGIC PEN

Periodicals:
PICKLE
ATLAS

Cartoon collections:
BETTER LUCK NEXT CENTURY

# DYLAN HORROCKS

# INCOMPLETE WORKS

ALTERNATIVE COMICS

ALTERNATIVE COMICS
21607B Stevens Creek Blvd.
Cupertino, CA 95014
IndyWorld.com

First Northern Hemisphere Edition 2015

ACKNOWLEDGEMENTS
Many thanks to the original publishers and editors of these stories. For more information see the notes on pages 188-191.

Author photo on inside back cover by Grant Maiden.

ISBN: 978-1-934460-54-2
Printed in Hong Kong

for

Terry
Louis
Abe

# CONTENTS

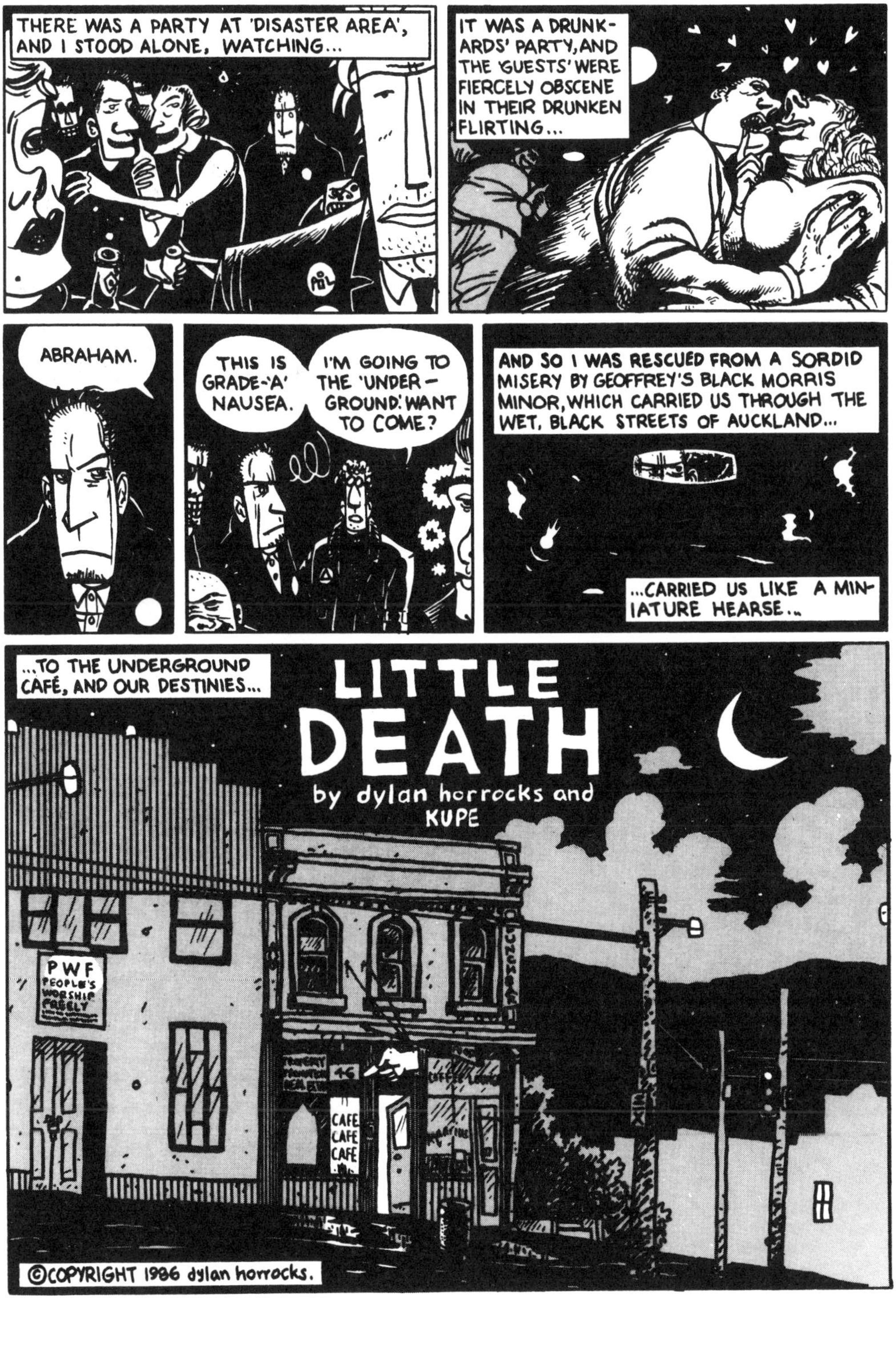
THERE WAS A PARTY AT 'DISASTER AREA', AND I STOOD ALONE, WATCHING...
IT WAS A DRUNK-ARDS' PARTY, AND THE 'GUESTS' WERE FIERCELY OBSCENE IN THEIR DRUNKEN FLIRTING...
ABRAHAM.
THIS IS GRADE-'A' NAUSEA.
I'M GOING TO THE 'UNDER-GROUND.' WANT TO COME?
AND SO I WAS RESCUED FROM A SORDID MISERY BY GEOFFREY'S BLACK MORRIS MINOR, WHICH CARRIED US THROUGH THE WET, BLACK STREETS OF AUCKLAND...
...CARRIED US LIKE A MIN-IATURE HEARSE...
...TO THE UNDERGROUND CAFÉ, AND OUR DESTINIES...
LITTLE DEATH
by dylan horrocks and KUPE
PWF
PEOPLE'S WORSHIP FREELY
CAFE
CAFE
CAFE
©COPYRIGHT 1986 dylan horrocks.

AH, THE TRAUMA OF PHILOGONY! EACH ENTRANCE, EVERY MEETING, THE EYES (& BODY) STRAIN TO CATCH EVERY WOMAN'S FACE AND EVERY SMILE...

THE MIND WITH HOPE YEARNS FOR MORE INTIMATE CONTACT - THE SLOPE OF A NECK, A WHISPERED SMILE — AND *ALWAYS*, ALWAYS DISAPPOINTMENT..!

BUT IN THIS INSTANT — THE HOPE, THE SIGHT TAKES MY BREATH AWAY.

I AM IN LOVE A HUNDRED TIMES IN A SINGLE MOMENT.

HI, ONE COFFEE AND A HOT CHOCOLATE, PLEASE.

AND I COULD SEE GEOFFREY'S EYES SLIDE ACROSS THE ROOM, AND THEN STICK.

JAMES. JAMES "DEAN" MILLS.

'HEART-THROB' JAMES.

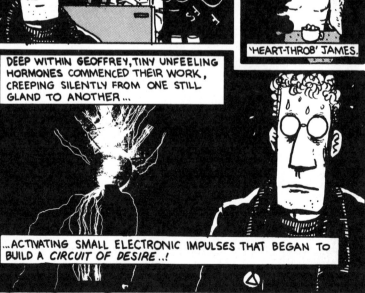

DEEP WITHIN GEOFFREY, TINY UNFEELING HORMONES COMMENCED THEIR WORK, CREEPING SILENTLY FROM ONE STILL GLAND TO ANOTHER...

...ACTIVATING SMALL ELECTRONIC IMPULSES THAT BEGAN TO BUILD A *CIRCUIT OF DESIRE*..!

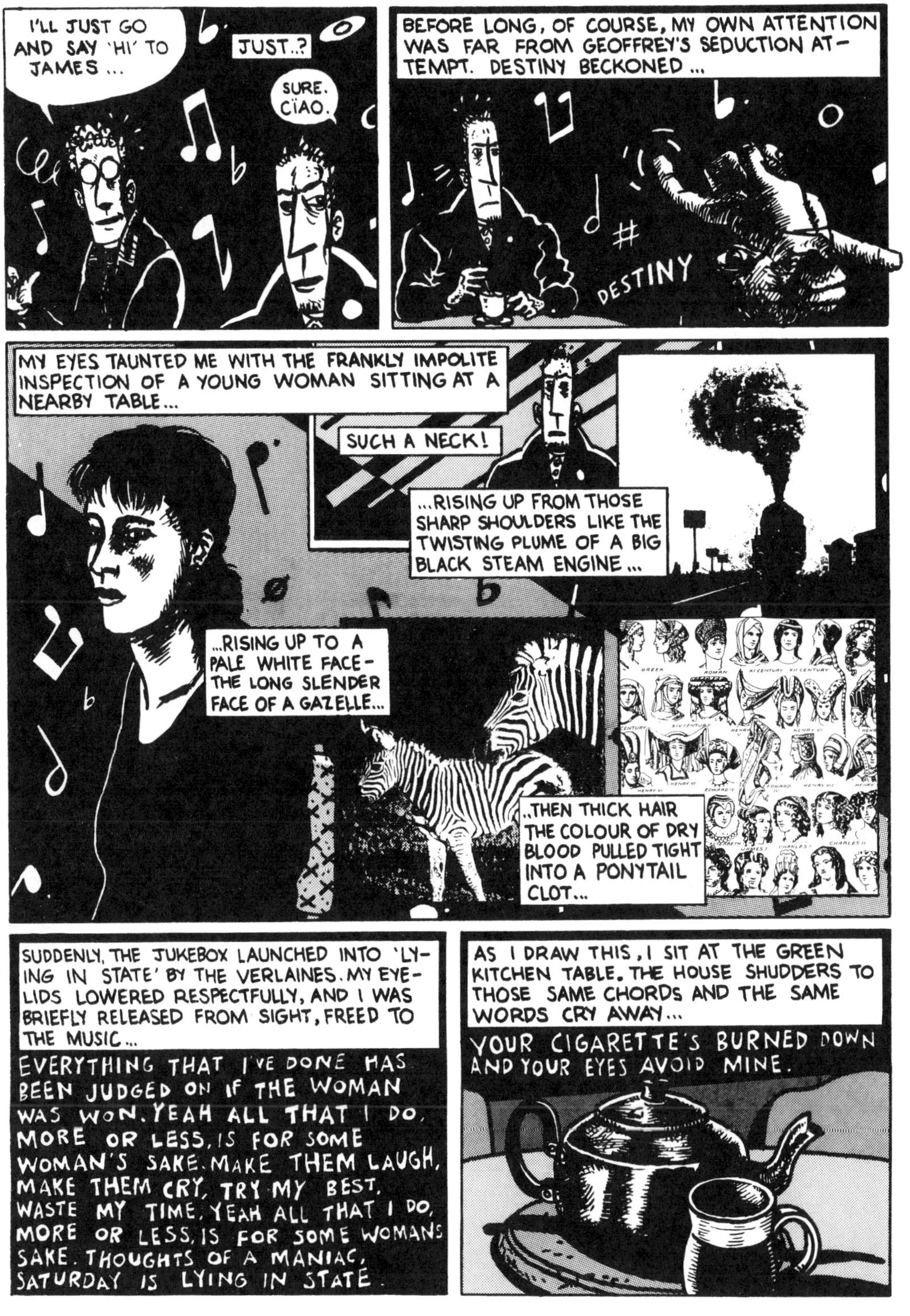

I'LL JUST GO AND SAY 'HI' TO JAMES ...
JUST..?
SURE. CÏAO.
BEFORE LONG, OF COURSE, MY OWN ATTENTION WAS FAR FROM GEOFFREY'S SEDUCTION ATTEMPT. DESTINY BECKONED ...
DESTINY
MY EYES TAUNTED ME WITH THE FRANKLY IMPOLITE INSPECTION OF A YOUNG WOMAN SITTING AT A NEARBY TABLE...
SUCH A NECK!
...RISING UP FROM THOSE SHARP SHOULDERS LIKE THE TWISTING PLUME OF A BIG BLACK STEAM ENGINE ...
...RISING UP TO A PALE WHITE FACE- THE LONG SLENDER FACE OF A GAZELLE...
..THEN THICK HAIR THE COLOUR OF DRY BLOOD PULLED TIGHT INTO A PONYTAIL CLOT...
SUDDENLY, THE JUKEBOX LAUNCHED INTO 'LYING IN STATE' BY THE VERLAINES. MY EYELIDS LOWERED RESPECTFULLY, AND I WAS BRIEFLY RELEASED FROM SIGHT, FREED TO THE MUSIC...
EVERYTHING THAT I'VE DONE HAS BEEN JUDGED ON IF THE WOMAN WAS WON. YEAH ALL THAT I DO, MORE OR LESS, IS FOR SOME WOMAN'S SAKE. MAKE THEM LAUGH, MAKE THEM CRY, TRY MY BEST, WASTE MY TIME, YEAH ALL THAT I DO, MORE OR LESS, IS FOR SOME WOMANS SAKE. THOUGHTS OF A MANIAC, SATURDAY IS LYING IN STATE.
AS I DRAW THIS, I SIT AT THE GREEN KITCHEN TABLE. THE HOUSE SHUDDERS TO THOSE SAME CHORDS AND THE SAME WORDS CRY AWAY...
YOUR CIGARETTE'S BURNED DOWN AND YOUR EYES AVOID MINE.

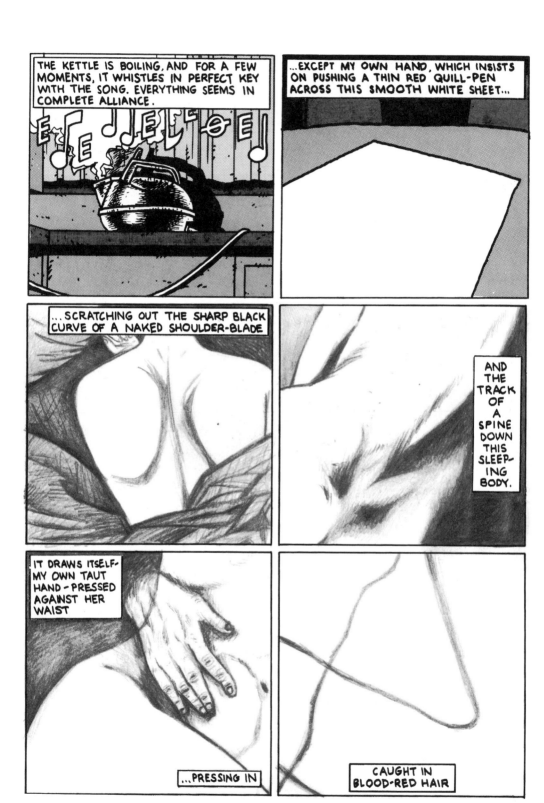

THE KETTLE IS BOILING, AND FOR A FEW MOMENTS, IT WHISTLES IN PERFECT KEY WITH THE SONG. EVERYTHING SEEMS IN COMPLETE ALLIANCE.

...EXCEPT MY OWN HAND, WHICH INSISTS ON PUSHING A THIN RED QUILL-PEN ACROSS THIS SMOOTH WHITE SHEET...

...SCRATCHING OUT THE SHARP BLACK CURVE OF A NAKED SHOULDER-BLADE

AND THE TRACK OF A SPINE DOWN THIS SLEEPING BODY.

IT DRAWS ITSELF- MY OWN TAUT HAND - PRESSED AGAINST HER WAIST

...PRESSING IN

CAUGHT IN BLOOD-RED HAIR

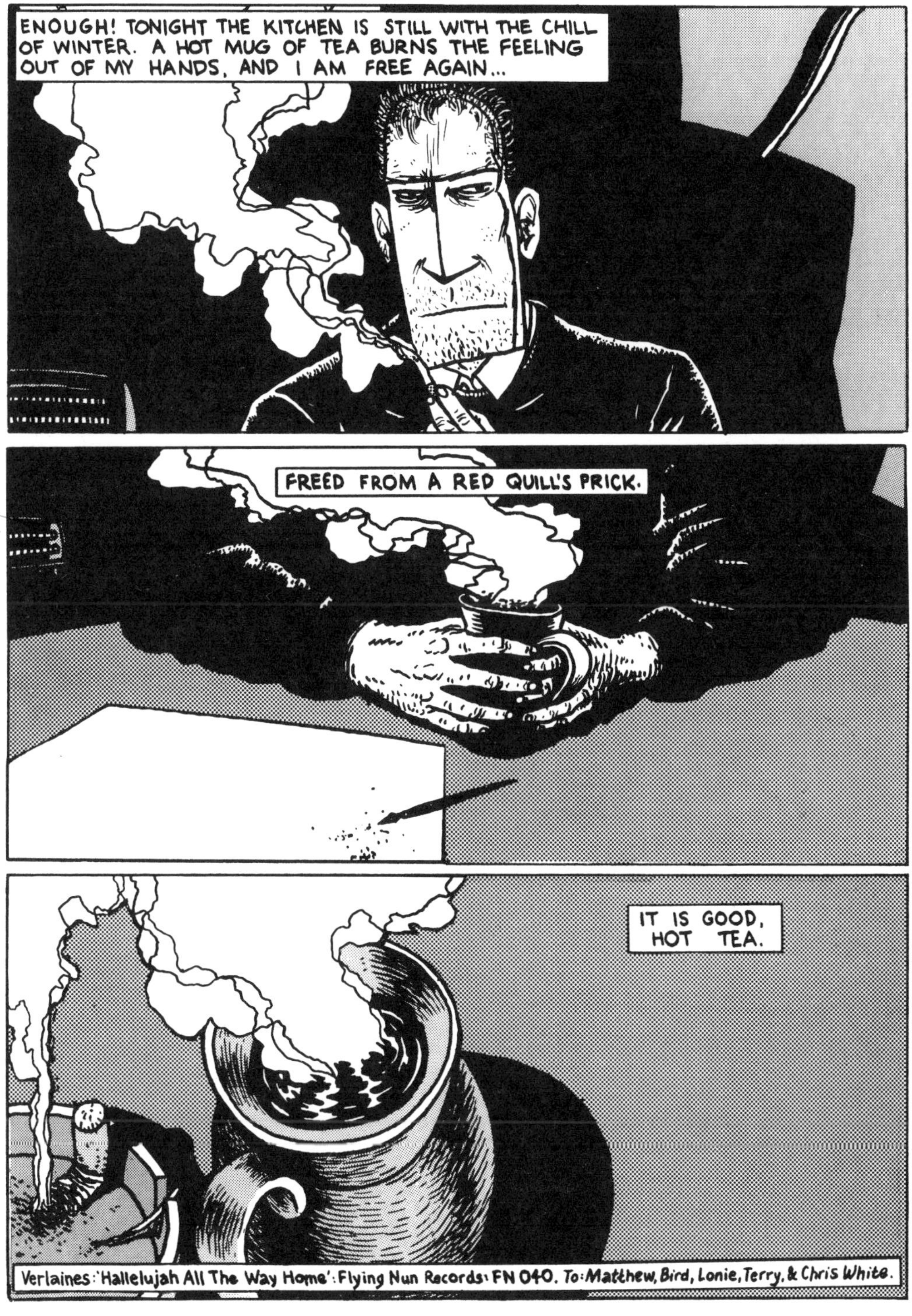
ENOUGH! TONIGHT THE KITCHEN IS STILL WITH THE CHILL OF WINTER. A HOT MUG OF TEA BURNS THE FEELING OUT OF MY HANDS, AND I AM FREE AGAIN...
FREED FROM A RED QUILL'S PRICK.
IT IS GOOD, HOT TEA.
Verlaines: 'Hallelujah All The Way Home': Flying Nun Records: FN 040. To: Matthew, Bird, Lonie, Terry, & Chris White.

# UNWRITTEN STORIES.

SADNESS IS BECOMING SO COMMON IT APPALS ME.

IT MAY JUST BE THE DARK INCESSANT RAIN AND THE VIOLENT COLD WIND, BUT I DON'T THINK SO.

THE FACES OF MY FRIENDS SLACKEN WITH THE PASSING OF TIME, THEIR GESTURES ARE LIMP AND DISMISSIVE...

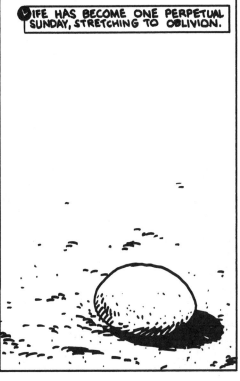

THE MUSIC BEING PLAYED IS SLOW SONGS WITH TRAGIC THEMES...

MANY HAVE FLED TO OTHER COUNTRIES...

AND BLEAK AND LONELY POSTCARDS ARRIVE, WITH SPRING DAFFODILS ON ONE SIDE.

LIFE HAS BECOME ONE PERPETUAL SUNDAY, STRETCHING TO OBLIVION.

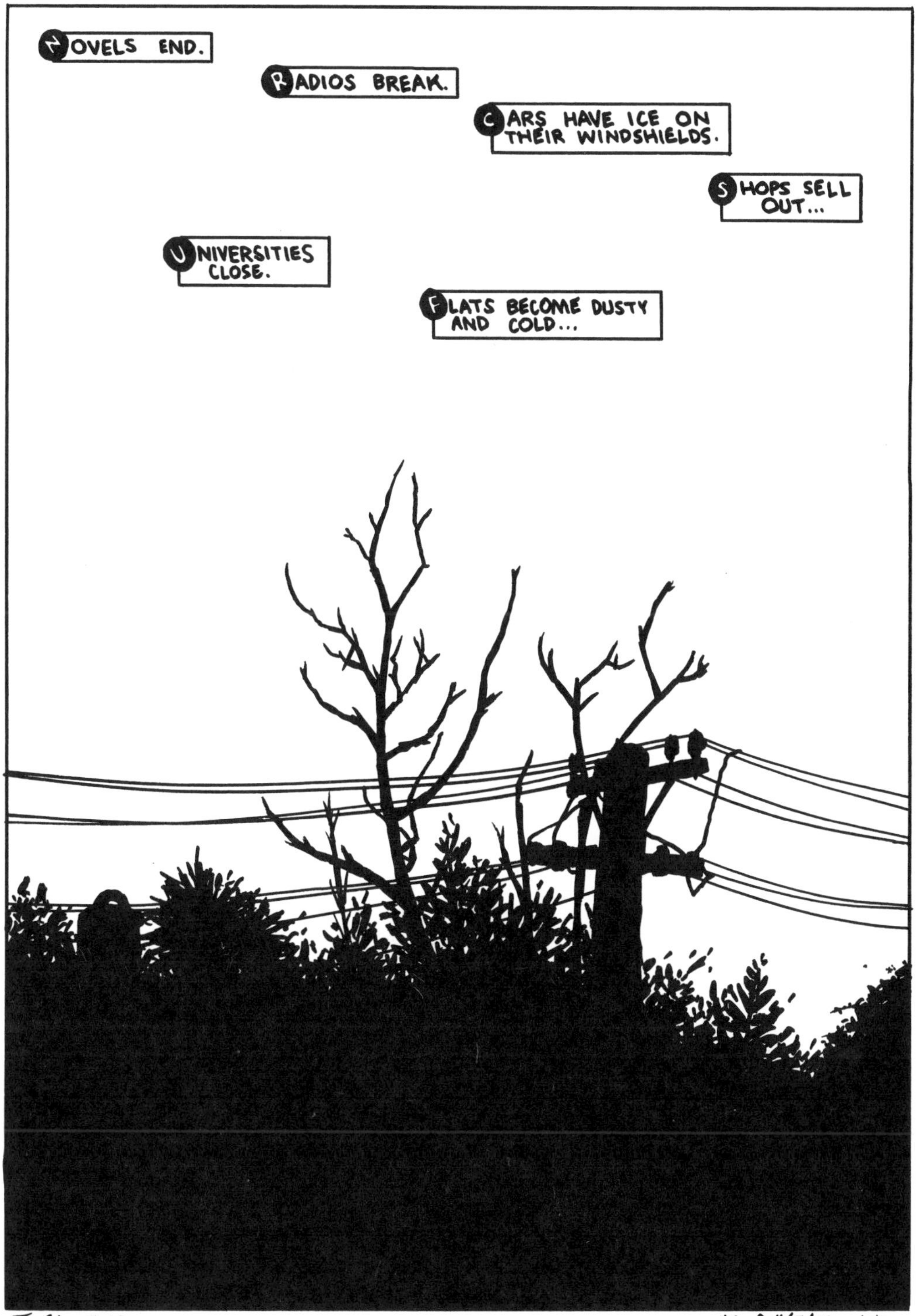
NOVELS END.
RADIOS BREAK.
CARS HAVE ICE ON THEIR WINDSHIELDS.
SHOPS SELL OUT...
UNIVERSITIES CLOSE.
FLATS BECOME DUSTY AND COLD...

To Glenn Dakin.

#1. 9-11/5/87. - dylan.

## Men that Perish.

'Supple and turbulent, a ring of men
Shall chant in orgy on a summer morn
Their boisterous devotion to the sun,
Not as a god, but as a god might be,
Naked among them, like a savage source.
Their chant shall be a chant of paradise,
Out of their blood, returning to the sky;
And in their chant shall enter, voice by voice,
The windy lake wherein their lord delights,
The trees, like serafin, and echoing hills,
That choir among themselves long afterward.
They shall know well the heavenly fellowship
of men that perish and of summer morn.
And whence they came and whither they shall go
The dew upon their feet shall manifest.'

'Sunday Morning' (VII), Wallace Stevens.

© 1989 By KUPE/DYLAN HORROCKS. TO TIM.

Today my lover draws me as the sky, spread above, pale grey then bright emerald, then burning crimson, flecked with clouds of snow or fire, dropping rain or sunlight to the earth.

Today my lover draws me as a piece of driftwood, veined and cracked, smoothed by the sea.

Today my lover will draw me as a drop of sperm - warm, then cooling, drying like a web - against her skin.

Today my lover draws me as a raised fist, made of stone, defiant.

Today my lover draws me as a beautiful curve, and soft skin, warm to touch.

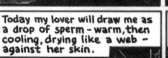

16

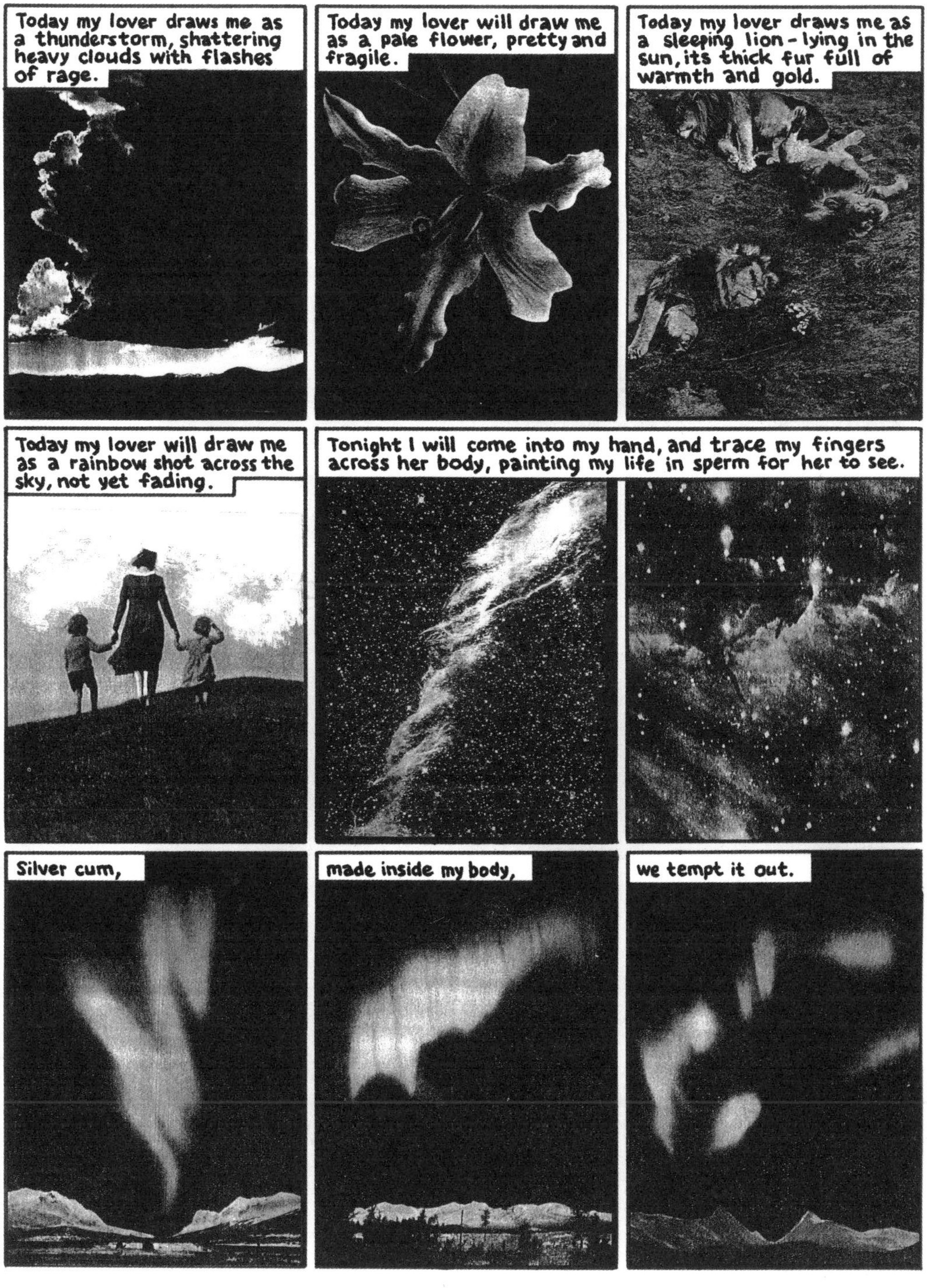
Today my lover draws me as a thunderstorm, shattering heavy clouds with flashes of rage.
Today my lover will draw me as a pale flower, pretty and fragile.
Today my lover draws me as a sleeping lion - lying in the sun, its thick fur full of warmth and gold.
Today my lover will draw me as a rainbow shot across the sky, not yet fading.
Tonight I will come into my hand, and trace my fingers across her body, painting my life in sperm for her to see.
Silver cum,
made inside my body,
we tempt it out.

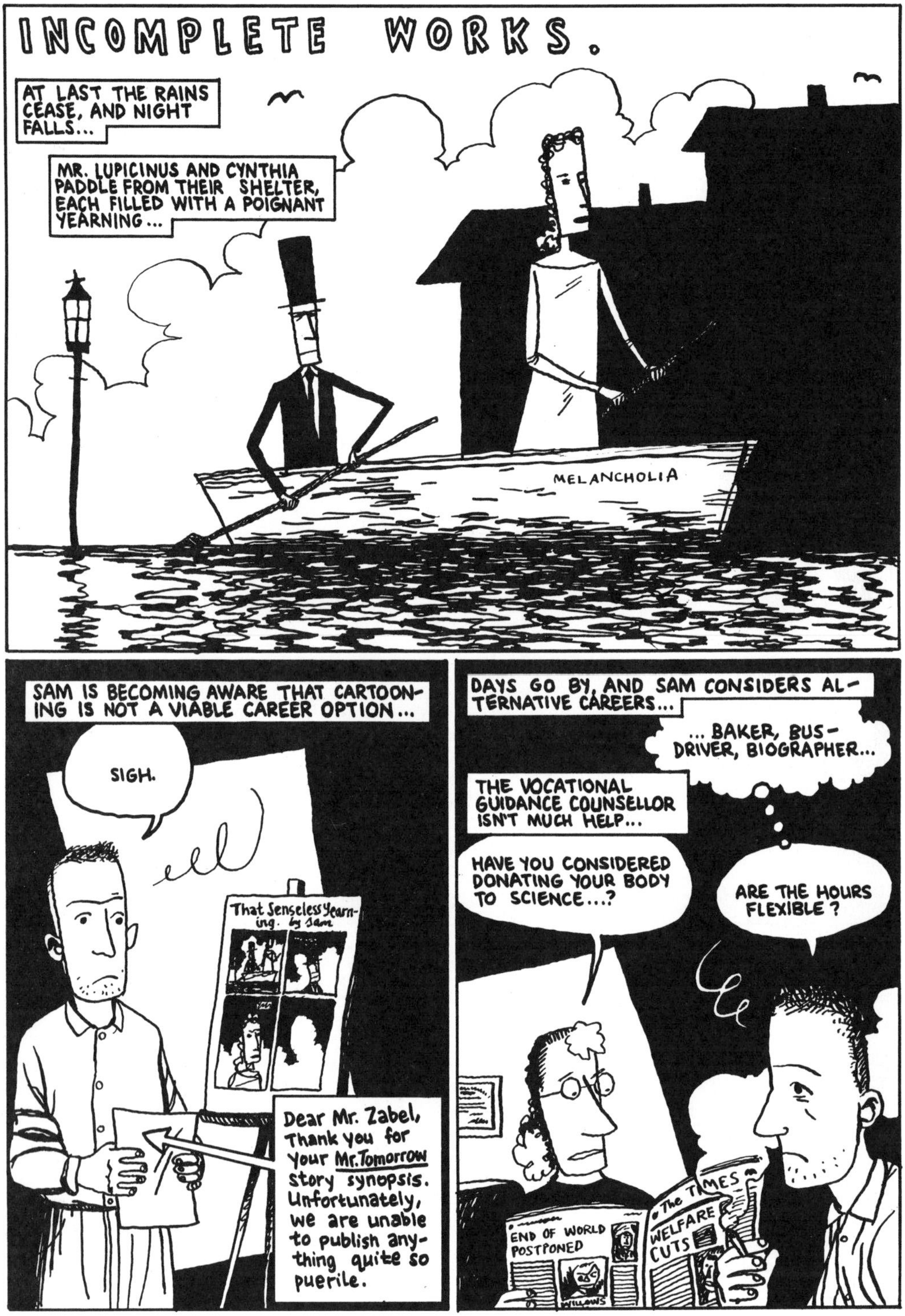
INCOMPLETE WORKS.
AT LAST THE RAINS CEASE, AND NIGHT FALLS...
MR. LUPICINUS AND CYNTHIA PADDLE FROM THEIR SHELTER, EACH FILLED WITH A POIGNANT YEARNING...
MELANCHOLIA
SAM IS BECOMING AWARE THAT CARTOONING IS NOT A VIABLE CAREER OPTION...
SIGH.
That Senseless Yearning. by Sam
Dear Mr. Zabel, Thank you for your Mr. Tomorrow story synopsis. Unfortunately, we are unable to publish anything quite so puerile.
DAYS GO BY, AND SAM CONSIDERS ALTERNATIVE CAREERS...
... BAKER, BUS-DRIVER, BIOGRAPHER...
THE VOCATIONAL GUIDANCE COUNSELLOR ISN'T MUCH HELP...
HAVE YOU CONSIDERED DONATING YOUR BODY TO SCIENCE...?
ARE THE HOURS FLEXIBLE?
END OF WORLD POSTPONED
The TIMES
WELFARE CUTS

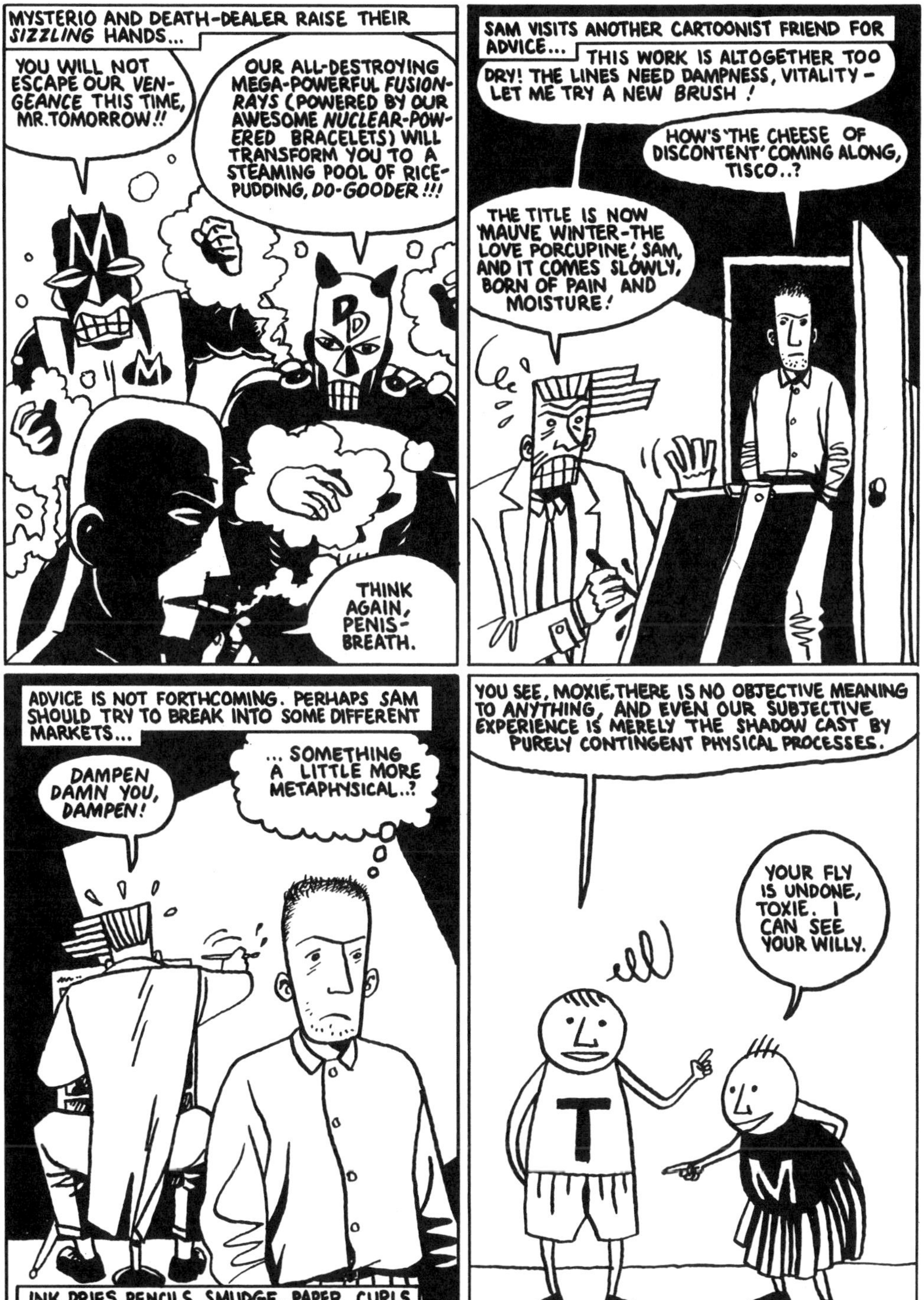
MYSTERIO AND DEATH-DEALER RAISE THEIR *SIZZLING* HANDS...
YOU WILL NOT ESCAPE OUR VEN-GEANCE THIS TIME, MR. TOMORROW!!
OUR ALL-DESTROYING MEGA-POWERFUL *FUSION-RAYS* (POWERED BY OUR AWESOME *NUCLEAR-POW-ERED* BRACELETS) WILL TRANSFORM YOU TO A STEAMING POOL OF RICE-PUDDING, *DO-GOODER*!!!
THINK AGAIN, PENIS-BREATH.
SAM VISITS ANOTHER CARTOONIST FRIEND FOR ADVICE...
THIS WORK IS ALTOGETHER TOO DRY! THE LINES NEED DAMPNESS, VITALITY - LET ME TRY A NEW *BRUSH*!
HOW'S 'THE CHEESE OF DISCONTENT' COMING ALONG, TISCO..?
THE TITLE IS NOW 'MAUVE WINTER-THE LOVE PORCUPINE', SAM, AND IT COMES SLOWLY, BORN OF PAIN AND MOISTURE!
ADVICE IS NOT FORTHCOMING. PERHAPS SAM SHOULD TRY TO BREAK INTO SOME DIFFERENT MARKETS...
DAMPEN DAMN YOU, DAMPEN!
... SOMETHING A LITTLE MORE METAPHYSICAL..?
INK DRIES, PENCILS SMUDGE, PAPER CURLS AND YELLOWS...
YOU SEE, MOXIE, THERE IS NO OBJECTIVE MEANING TO *ANYTHING*, AND EVEN OUR SUBJECTIVE EXPERIENCE IS MERELY THE SHADOW CAST BY PURELY CONTINGENT PHYSICAL PROCESSES.
YOUR FLY IS UNDONE, TOXIE. I CAN SEE YOUR WILLY.

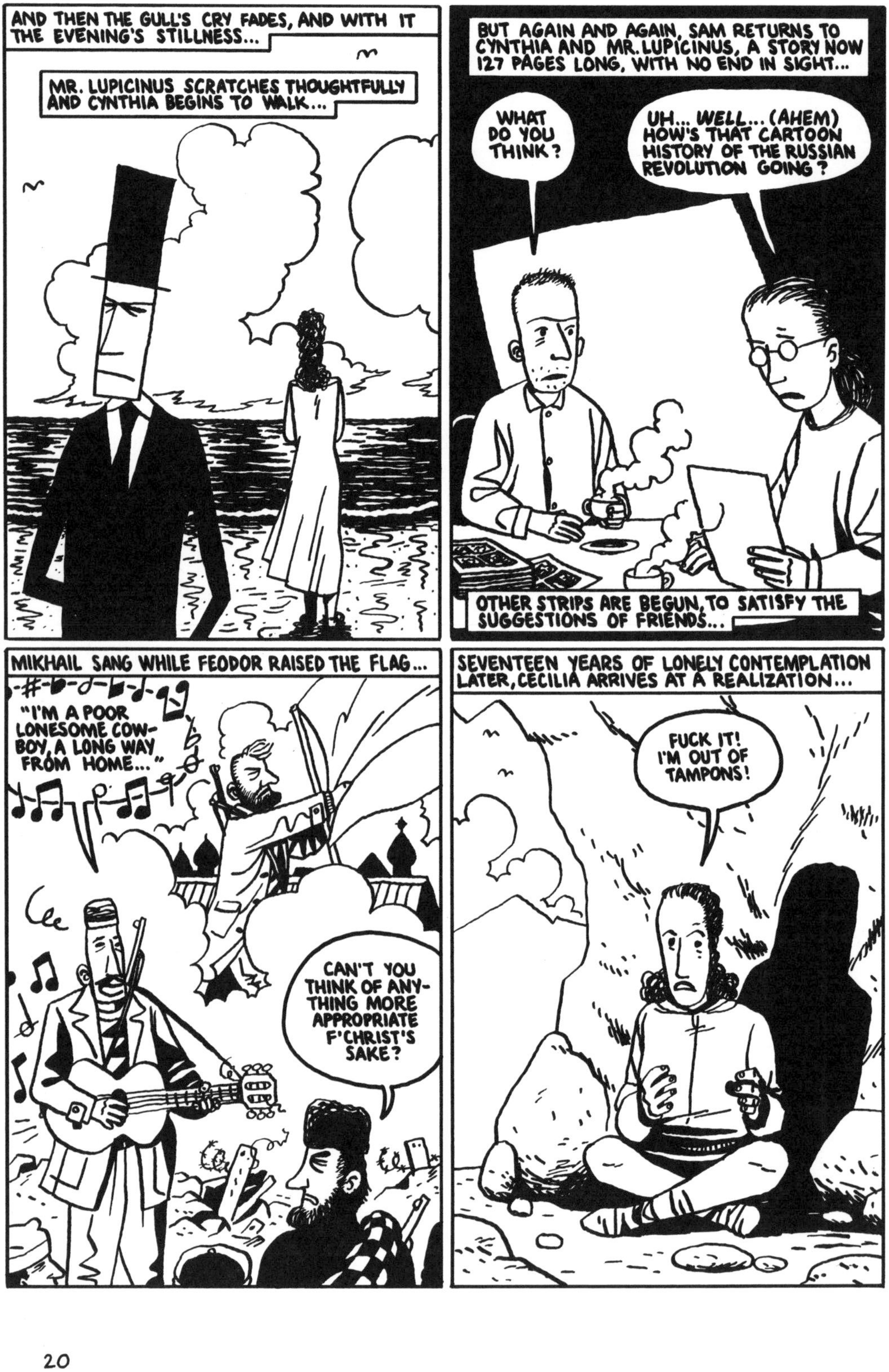
AND THEN THE GULL'S CRY FADES, AND WITH IT THE EVENING'S STILLNESS...
MR. LUPICINUS SCRATCHES THOUGHTFULLY AND CYNTHIA BEGINS TO WALK...
BUT AGAIN AND AGAIN, SAM RETURNS TO CYNTHIA AND MR. LUPICINUS, A STORY NOW 127 PAGES LONG, WITH NO END IN SIGHT...
WHAT DO YOU THINK?
UH... WELL... (AHEM) HOW'S THAT CARTOON HISTORY OF THE RUSSIAN REVOLUTION GOING?
OTHER STRIPS ARE BEGUN, TO SATISFY THE SUGGESTIONS OF FRIENDS...
MIKHAIL SANG WHILE FEODOR RAISED THE FLAG...
"I'M A POOR LONESOME COWBOY, A LONG WAY FROM HOME..."
CAN'T YOU THINK OF ANYTHING MORE APPROPRIATE F'CHRIST'S SAKE?
SEVENTEEN YEARS OF LONELY CONTEMPLATION LATER, CECILIA ARRIVES AT A REALIZATION...
FUCK IT! I'M OUT OF TAMPONS!

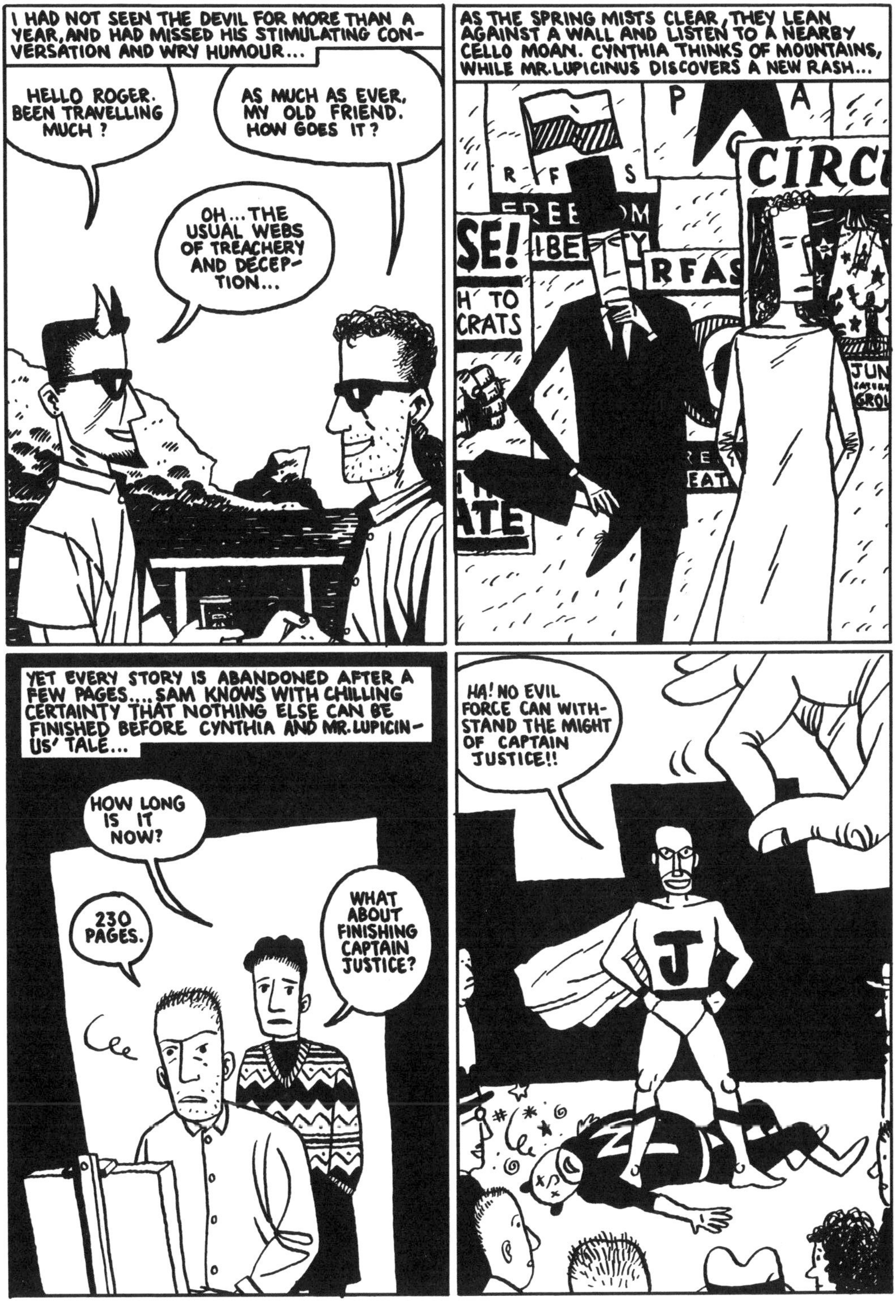
I HAD NOT SEEN THE DEVIL FOR MORE THAN A YEAR, AND HAD MISSED HIS STIMULATING CONVERSATION AND WRY HUMOUR...
HELLO ROGER. BEEN TRAVELLING MUCH ?
AS MUCH AS EVER, MY OLD FRIEND. HOW GOES IT ?
OH... THE USUAL WEBS OF TREACHERY AND DECEPTION...
AS THE SPRING MISTS CLEAR, THEY LEAN AGAINST A WALL AND LISTEN TO A NEARBY CELLO MOAN. CYNTHIA THINKS OF MOUNTAINS, WHILE MR. LUPICINUS DISCOVERS A NEW RASH...
CIRC
FREEDOM
LIBERTY
RFAS
SE!
H TO
CRATS
ATE
YET EVERY STORY IS ABANDONED AFTER A FEW PAGES.... SAM KNOWS WITH CHILLING CERTAINTY THAT NOTHING ELSE CAN BE FINISHED BEFORE CYNTHIA AND MR. LUPICINUS' TALE...
HOW LONG IS IT NOW?
230 PAGES.
WHAT ABOUT FINISHING CAPTAIN JUSTICE?
HA! NO EVIL FORCE CAN WITHSTAND THE MIGHT OF CAPTAIN JUSTICE!!
J

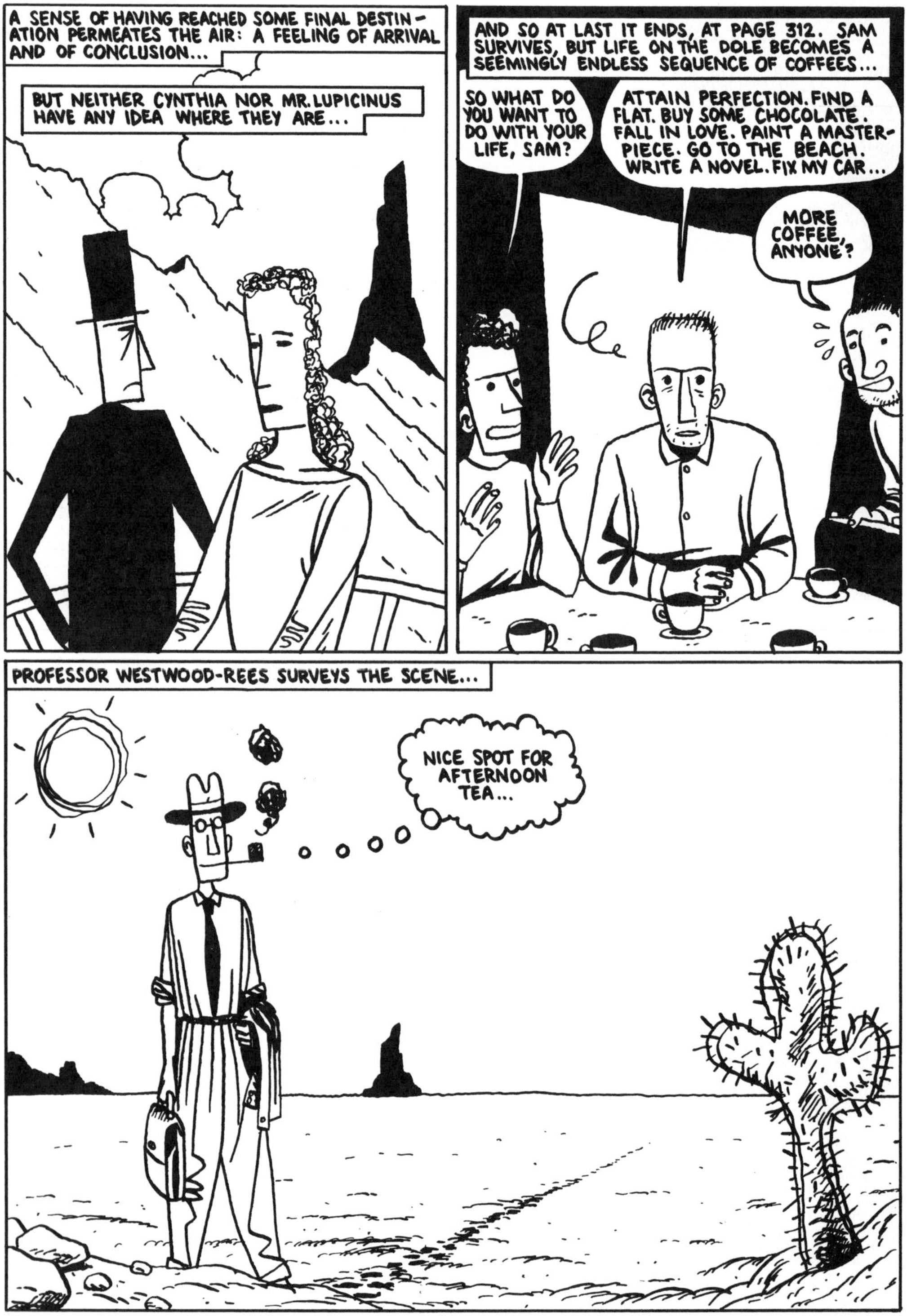
A SENSE OF HAVING REACHED SOME FINAL DESTINATION PERMEATES THE AIR: A FEELING OF ARRIVAL AND OF CONCLUSION...
BUT NEITHER CYNTHIA NOR MR. LUPICINUS HAVE ANY IDEA WHERE THEY ARE...
AND SO AT LAST IT ENDS, AT PAGE 312. SAM SURVIVES, BUT LIFE ON THE DOLE BECOMES A SEEMINGLY ENDLESS SEQUENCE OF COFFEES...
SO WHAT DO YOU WANT TO DO WITH YOUR LIFE, SAM?
ATTAIN PERFECTION. FIND A FLAT. BUY SOME CHOCOLATE. FALL IN LOVE. PAINT A MASTERPIECE. GO TO THE BEACH. WRITE A NOVEL. FIX MY CAR...
MORE COFFEE, ANYONE?
PROFESSOR WESTWOOD-REES SURVEYS THE SCENE...
NICE SPOT FOR AFTERNOON TEA...

# Pickle

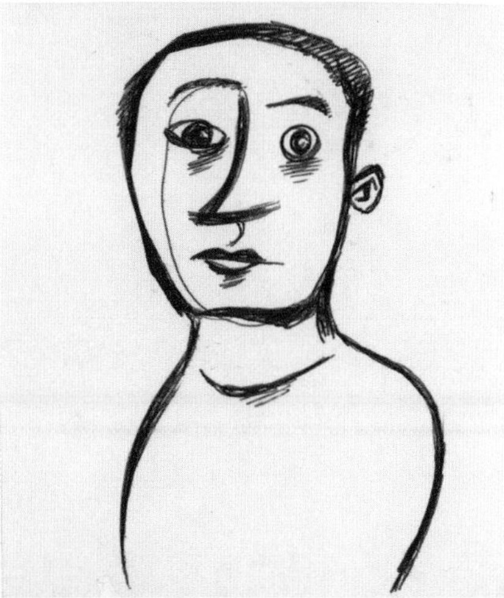

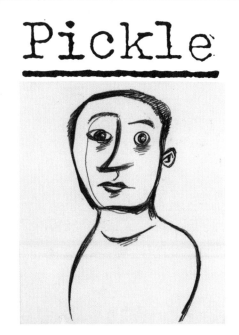

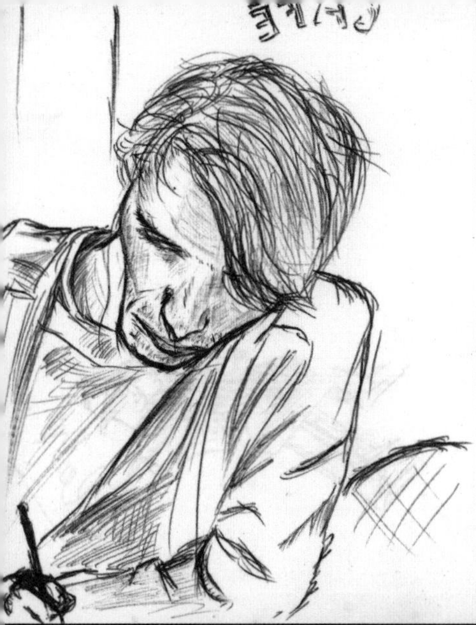

# The Last Fox Story.

— dylan horrocks.
1990.

I crack this story one night while familiar friends sing familiar songs in my room, after an evening of talking about the Poll-Tax in a Harringay pub.

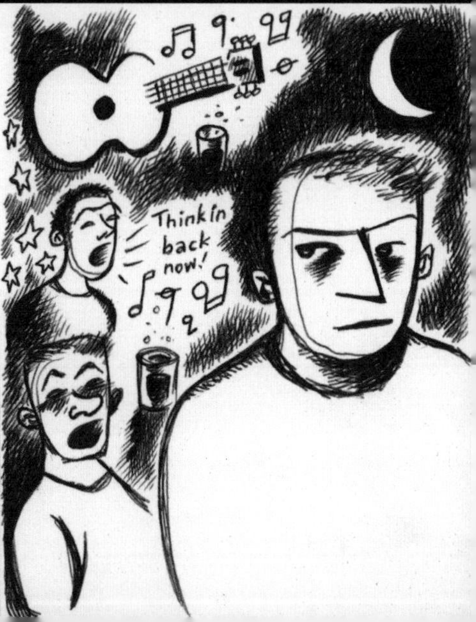
Thinkin back now!

( Looking out the bathroom window, I catch a glimpse of a bright room, filled with red flowers and green plants ).

This strip is for friends & for <u>Fox</u>. Written in a time of strange feelings and late nights.

It goes like this:

The Last Fox Story

or:
'How I Became Afraid of Comics.'

It all began with England, where I arrived in autumn; the skeleton-trees still wore their last leaves like an old skin.

I arrived with drawing-board & a half-drawn story, & plans for many more. My first night here I talked til late of net-working & page-rates, when I really wanted to be asleep.

I drew 8 pages in a week, & bought as many comics.

In a fortnight I'd seen cartoonists, publishers, and, of course...

... comic-shops.

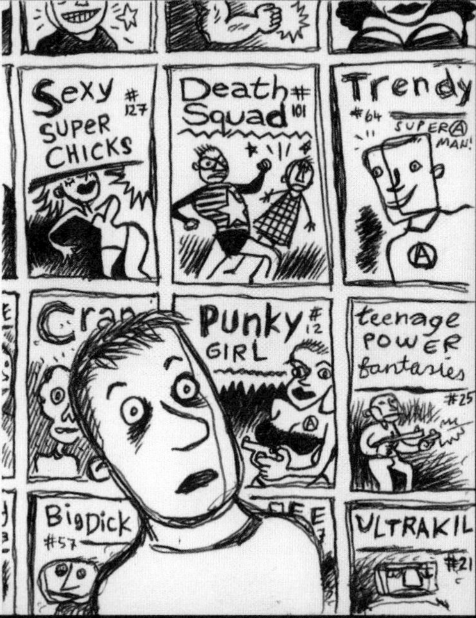
Sexy #127
SUPER CHICKS
Death Squad #101
Trendy #64
SUPER(A)MAN!
Punky #12
GIRL
teenage POWER fantasies
#25
BigDick
#57
ULTRAKIL
#21

Big shops, small shops, shops like supermarkets & shops for eclectic tastes; french shops, japanese shops, bookshops with comics & comic-shops with books. None were as good as the one old shop in Auckland, but all wore the same smells – the smell of old paper in plastic bags. The smell of adolescence. The smell of artificial *hip*, and the smell of latex costumes over mutant muscle sweat.

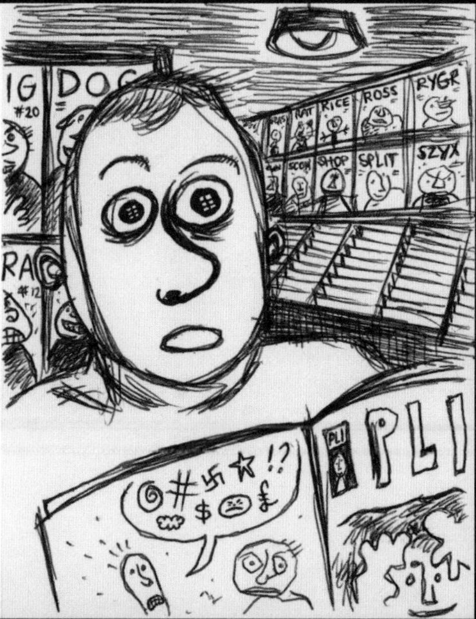
DOG
#20
RICE
ROSS
RYGR
SHOP
SPLIT
SZYX
PLI

And the leaves
began to fall...

As the stresses of emigration
set in, I began to falter – I
longed for home & a simple life,
and the task of building a career
began to seem too huge.

Old projects sat stilled inside
the cupboard, while new stories
took on a melancholy – a
creeping doubt about what I
was doing...

# The Translator.

(working-title).

—I am in London, alone & without much money. I aim to become a professional cartoonist, but so far no-one seems able to understand my work.

—Then a sympathetic publisher* commissions me to translate a graphic-novel by a french cartoonist I've never heard of before: Claudine LeBlanc. The money is meagre, but I enthusiastically accept the job & take the book home to read.

*  I LIKE YOUR WORK, BUT I DON'T THINK IT'S PUBLISHABLE...

—Les Nuits du Soleil.

(a knight lies dead in the snow, while his murderers loot his body)

I have never known such silence as when snow covers our valley.

Then there is no sound: no birdsong, no animal's cry, no music, no voices calling nor sounds of work or play.

Only the crunch of one's own feet in the snow; and then when one halts, there is nothing: only silence.

And then, so heavy is that stillness; so heavy and so terribly sad.

—It reads much better in french, but the book has me caught in its grip. I read it 4 times & then make the first draft in a small red notebook.

—The story:

—A knight is returning from the crusades & invites a friend to spend the winter in his family's castle. The friend has people to see first in a nearby town, & so the knight goes on ahead, eager to see his home again after so many years amid the horrors of war & the desert.

—But when he is only a mile from the castle, he is ambushed by thieves & murdered, & the gifts he had brought back are stolen. The thieves break a hole in the ice of a lake and dump his body into the deep water, where it is soon covered again by new ice.

- A week or two later, the friend arrives & is surprised that the knight is not there. Worried, the castle mounts a search, but the wintry countryside reveals nothing.

- As winter deepens the friend becomes involved with the knight's sister, & they share their growing love and also their growing sadness at the knight's disappearance.

- Throughout, the dead knight's voice describes his longing for his home & family, and his memories of the crusades, as the scene of his murder is buried with snow, and then - slowly - the winter melts into spring.

- The ice is gone, & the lake is fresh and clear. Flowers blanket the grass where the knight died. He has left no sign. The lovers court & the world turns ...

- But there at the end, the author has repeated a phrase used once before in the book, which I do not quite understand. Or rather, I understand the _phrase_, but not its _meaning_, & I cannot think how to translate it into english.

- I try to ignore it, and begin work on the second draft. The work is much slower now. And always I keep returning to that phrase.

- I mention it one day to the publisher, whose french is even worse.

- "You can ask Claudine yourself if you like," he says. "She is visiting London in a week; I'll introduce you."

Nervous

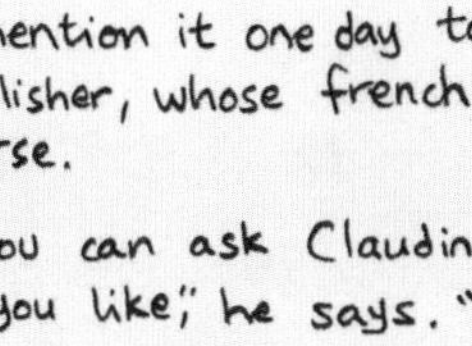

- And so we meet. She is twice my age, and reminds me of an Italian movie, but she's friendly and laughs at my french without making me feel stupid.

- I avoid saying how much I like her work, & she seems to appreciate it. She asks to see mine, but I'm too embarrassed.

- I wonder whether we'll have an affair, like in the Italian movie.

- When I ask about the phrase, she can't think how to explain it, and says she will think about it.

—In the meantime, we become friends; I show her London, & she spends hours in the museum & the manuscript room at the Library. We go for day-trips to the country...

There the story faltered; I began to feel unsure of their relationship.

I had envisaged an affair: superimposed maps of London, Paris and Auckland; postcards from France; comics written for one-another. But now I wondered whether to keep things platonic...

Worse, though, was that problematic phrase. How could I find a phrase in french that was relevant, spoke some subtle wisdom, and yet could not be translated, nor explained by its author ?

I wracked my brains, but it was no good. I asked french people & they made hopeful suggestions. But nothing worked.

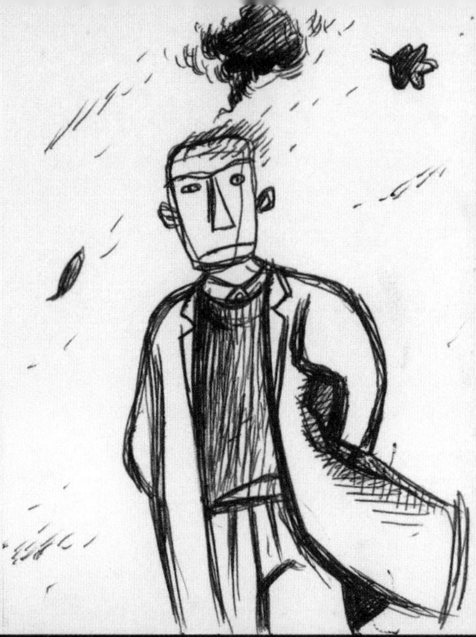

Into the cupboard !

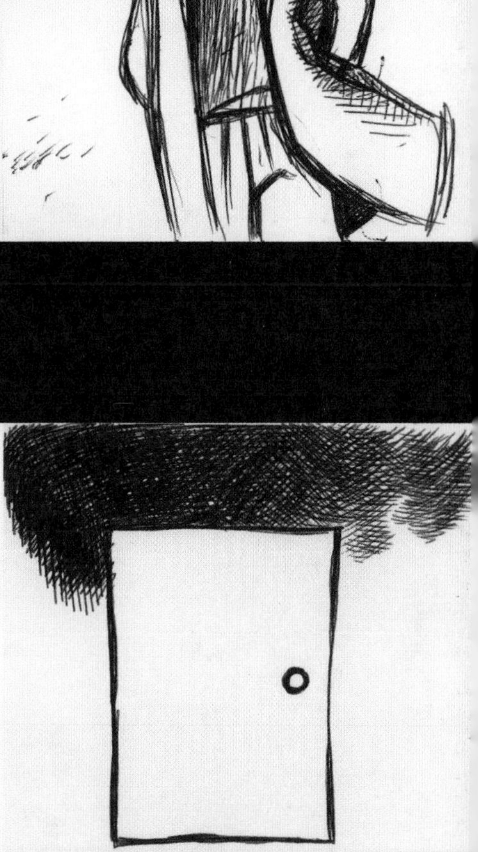

Other stories crawled along, never getting far.

My portfolio underwent three months of constant reorganisation before joining everything else...

...in the cupboard.

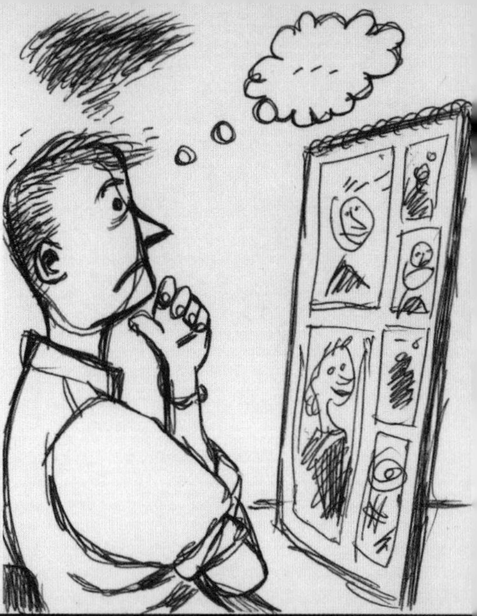

...

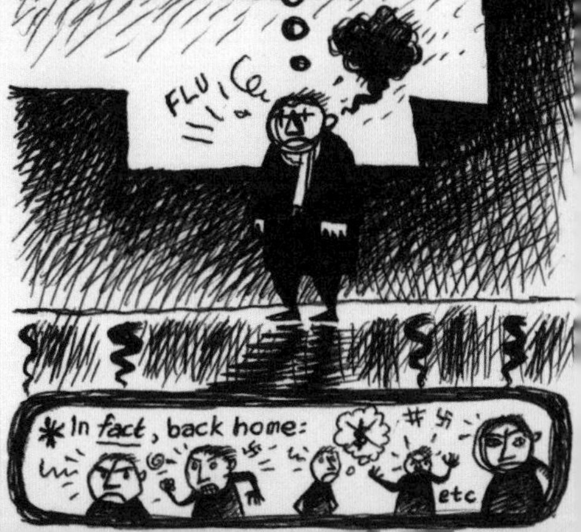

Meanwhile, back home:*
FLU
*In fact, back home:
etc

Time passed too quickly.

Money evaporated.

I got another job in a bookshop.

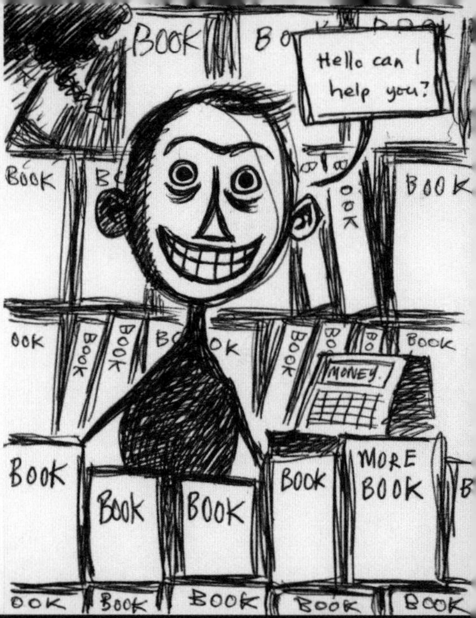
Hello can I help you?
BOOK
BOOK
BOOK
BOOK
BOOK
MONEY
BOOK
BOOK
BOOK
BOOK
MORE BOOK
BOOK
BOOK
BOOK
BOOK

Maybe I'm not a cartoonist, I wondered.

Maybe I'm a bookseller?

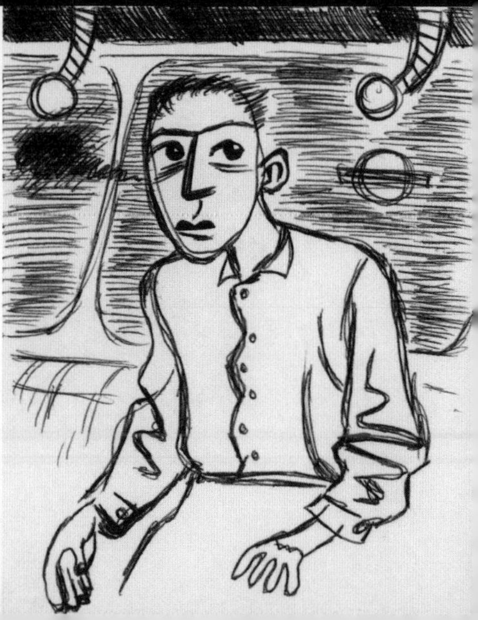

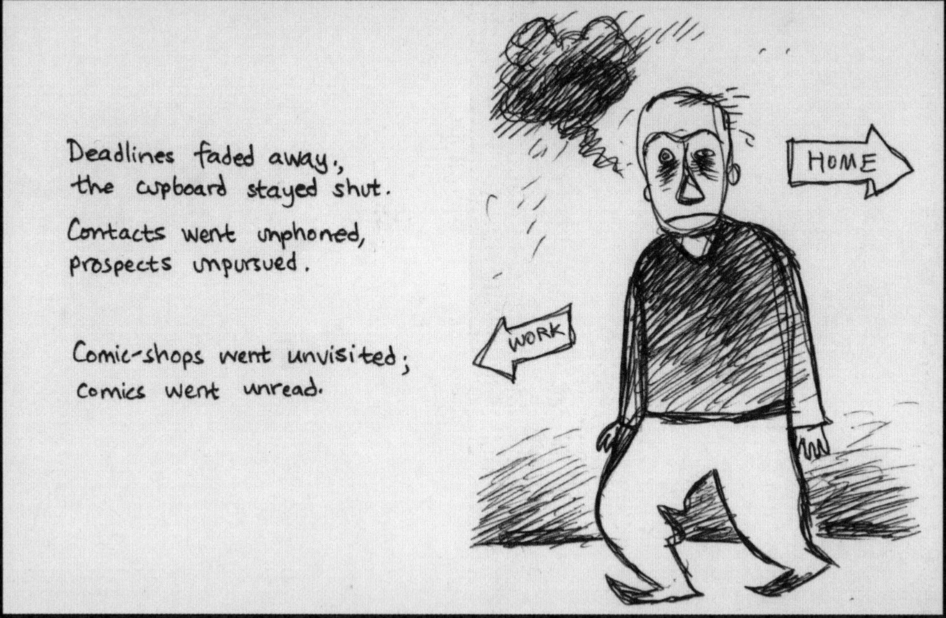
Deadlines faded away.,
the cupboard stayed shut.
Contacts went unphoned,
prospects unpursued.
Comic-shops went unvisited;
comics went unread.
HOME
WORK

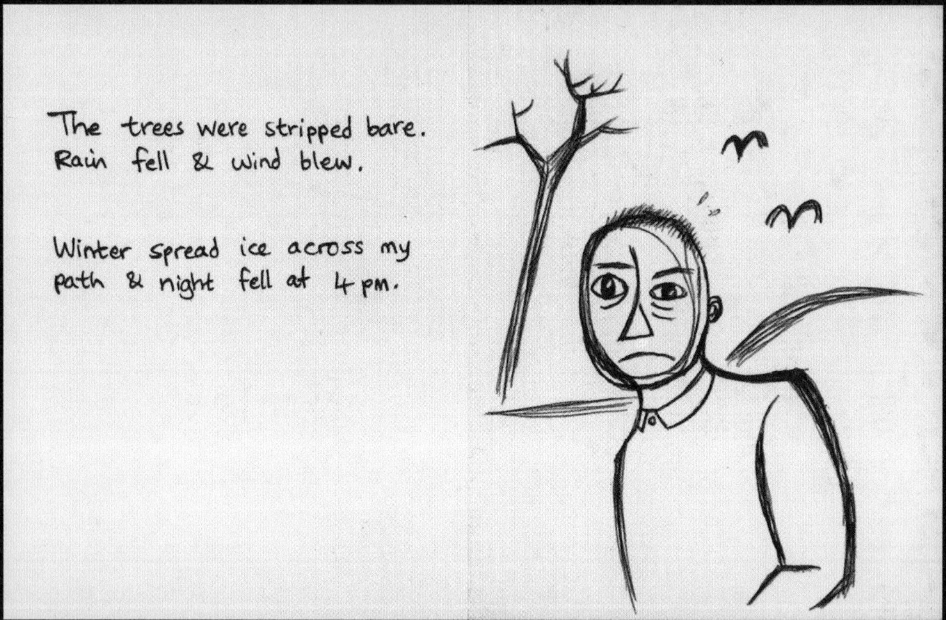
The trees were stripped bare.
Rain fell & wind blew.
Winter spread ice across my
path & night fell at 4 pm.

For a few months I read nothing but children's books and the only story I managed was a picture-book for my neice's first birthday.

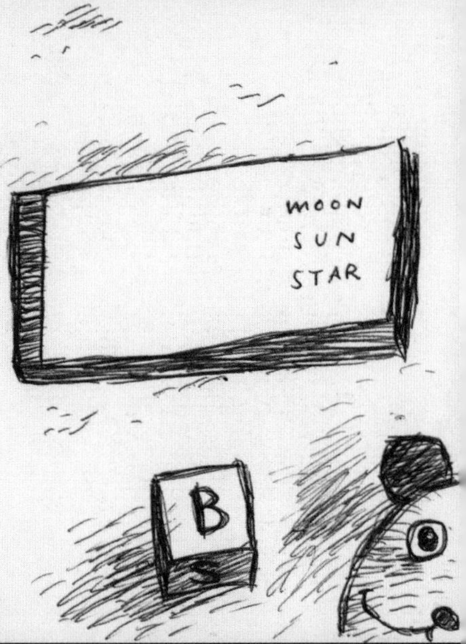
MOON
SUN
STAR
B

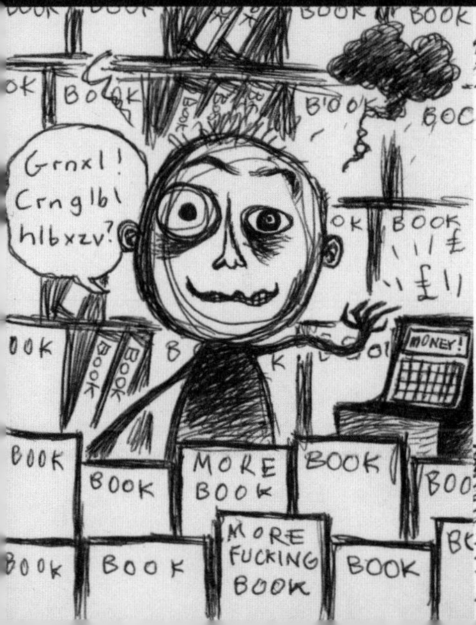
Grnxl! Crnglbl hlbxzv?
BOOK
MONEY!
MORE BOOK
MORE FUCKING BOOK

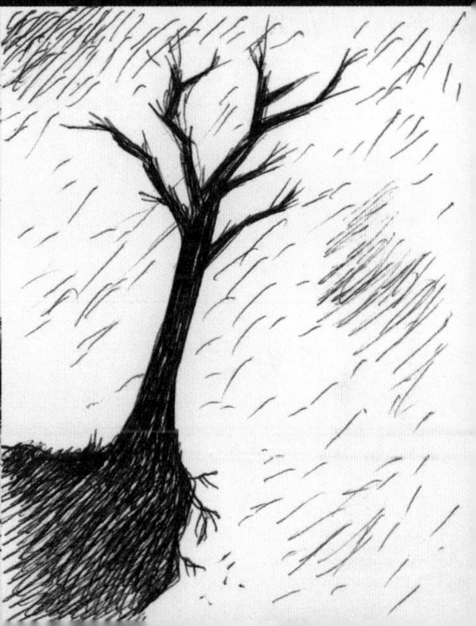

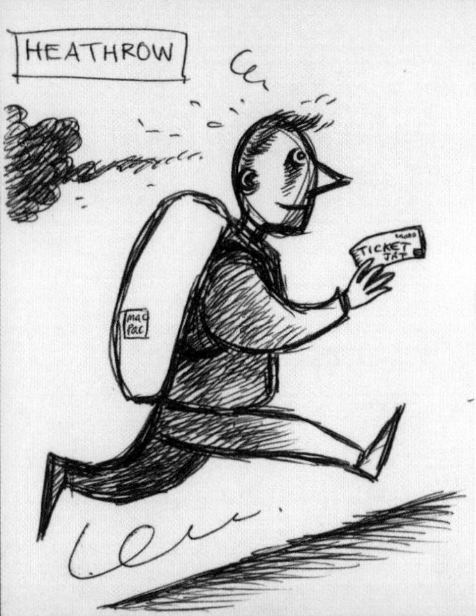
HEATHROW
mac pac
TICKET
JAT

And then I went to Yugoslavia to meet my Best Friend !

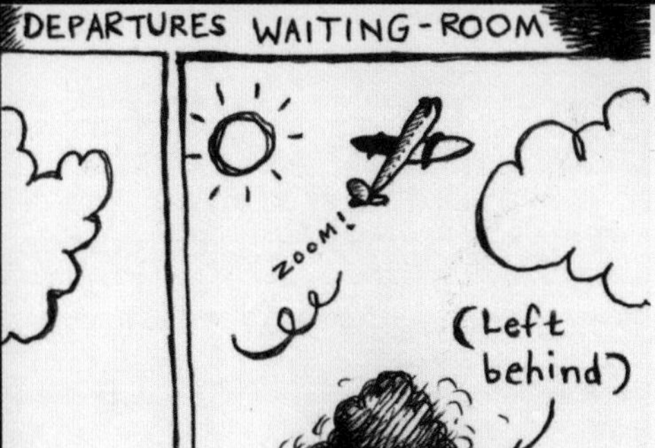
DEPARTURES WAITING-ROOM
ZOOM!
(Left behind)

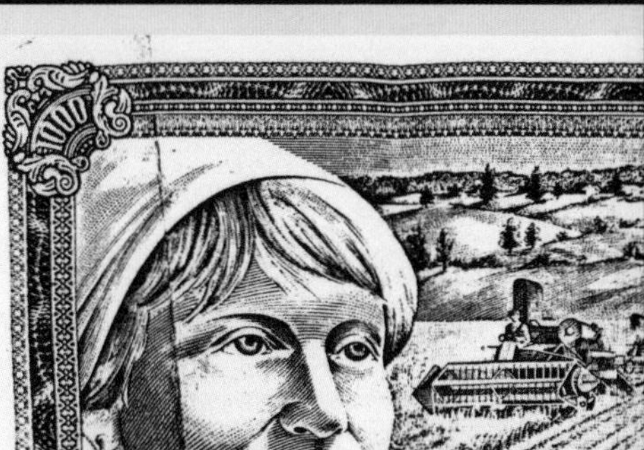

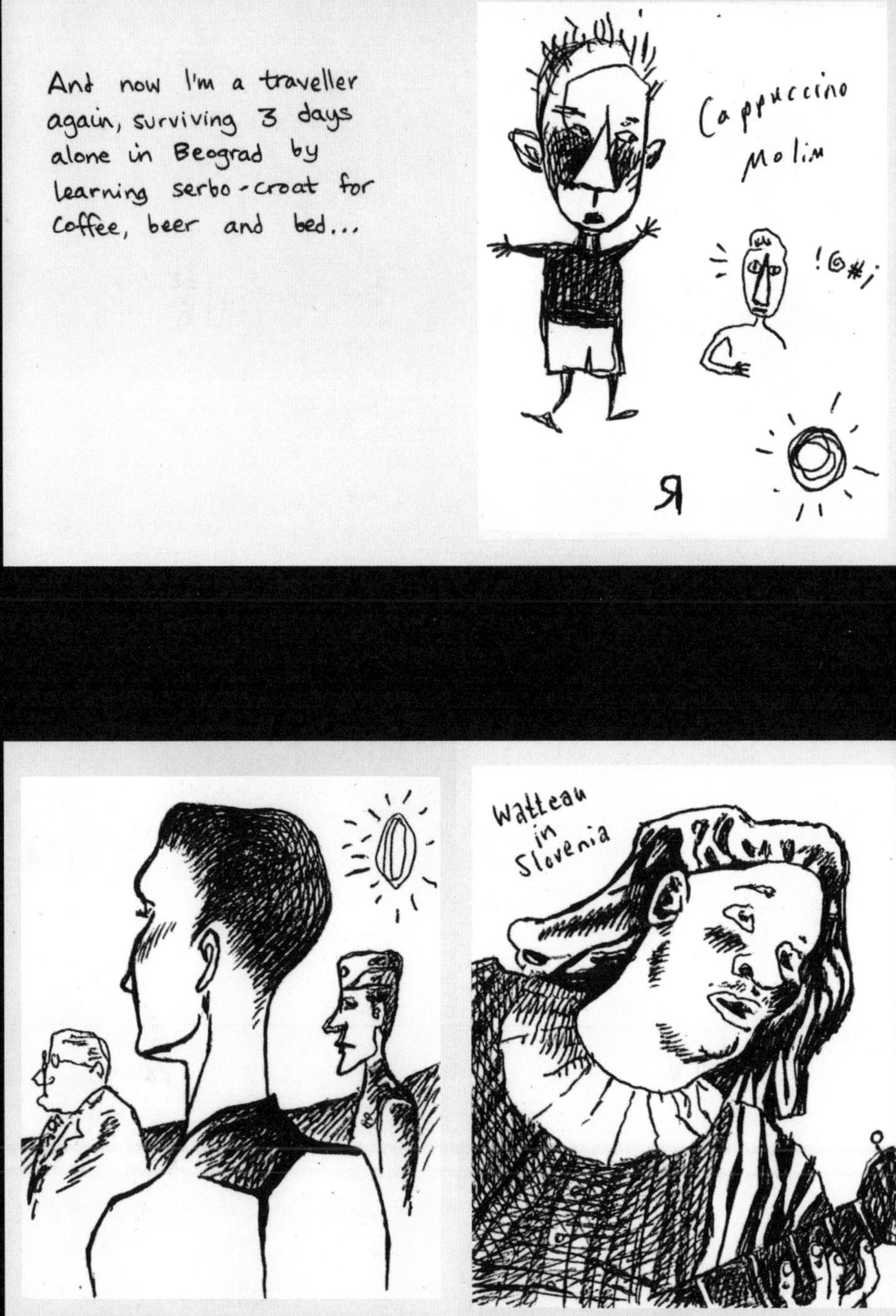
And now I'm a traveller again, surviving 3 days alone in Beograd by learning serbo-croat for coffee, beer and bed...
Cappuccino Molim
Я
Watteau in Slovenia

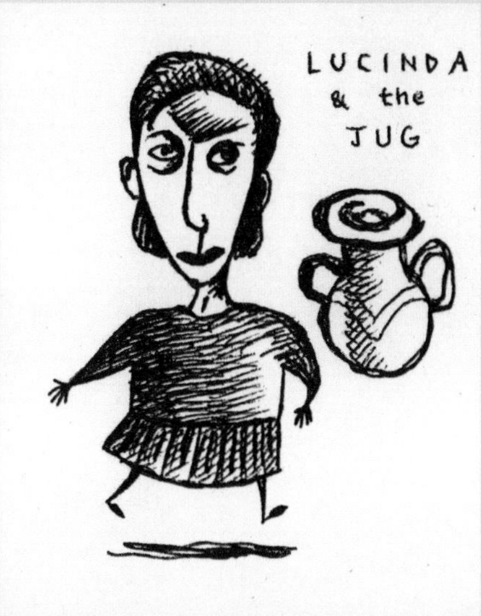
LUCINDA
& the
JUG

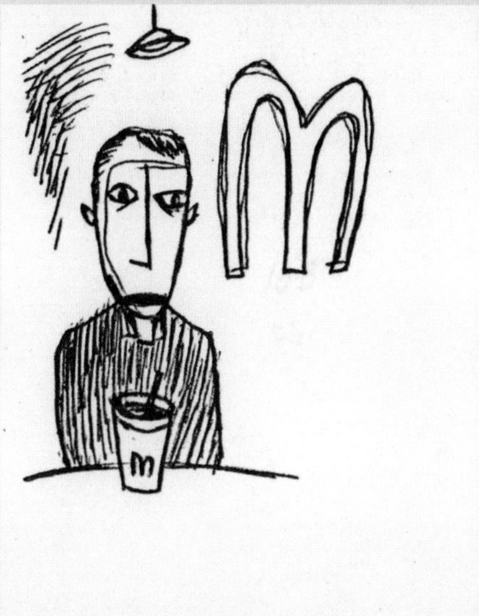
M
m

(countless adventures later:)

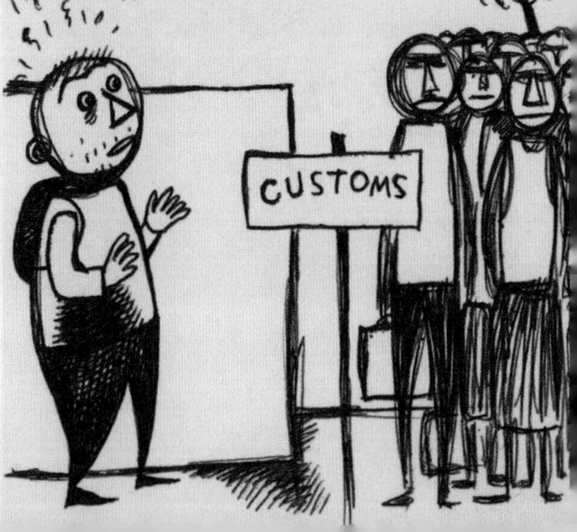
AIRPORT
WORRY
FRET
familiar wave
CUSTOMS

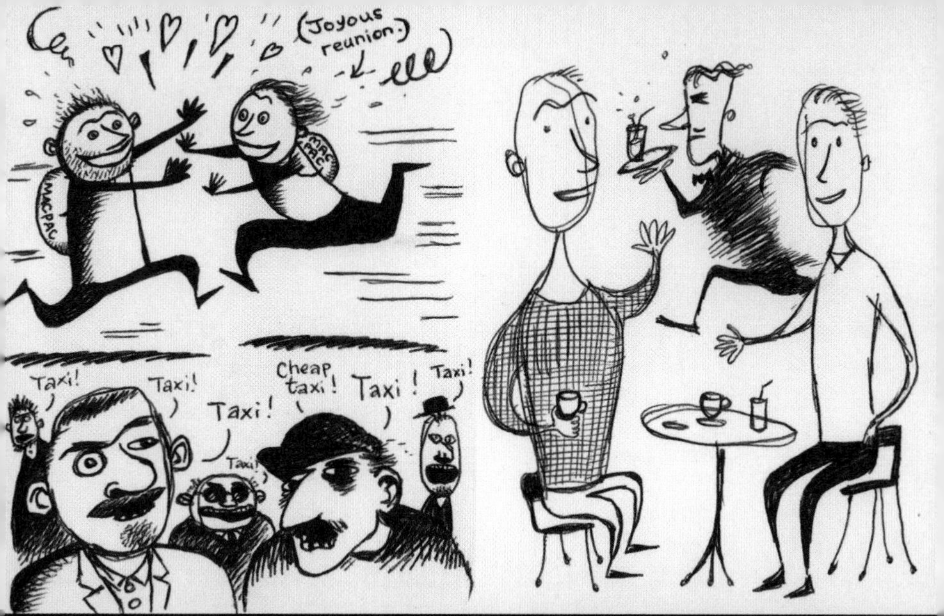
(Joyous reunion.)
MACPAC
MACPAC
Taxi!
Taxi!
Taxi!
Taxi!
Cheap taxi!
Taxi!
Taxi!

Then:

Sitting in a bar in Trogir, surrounded by tiny medieval streets, the sea to one side, Terry reads my notes for the Translator's story:

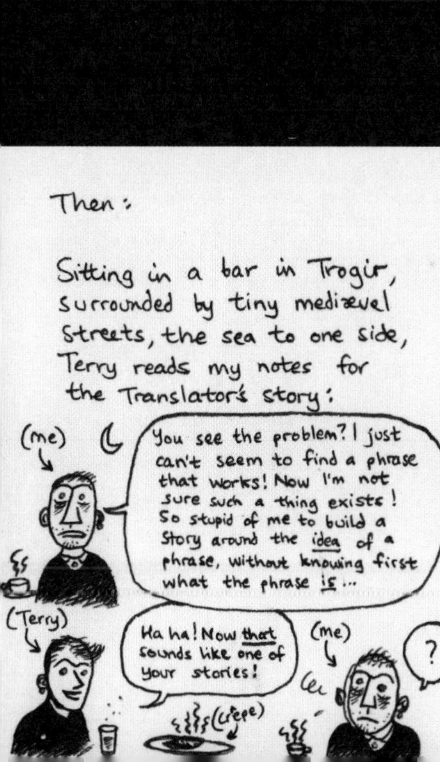
(me)
You see the problem? I just can't seem to find a phrase that works! Now I'm not sure such a thing exists! So stupid of me to build a story around the *idea* of a phrase, without knowing first what the phrase *is*...
(Terry)
Ha ha! Now *that* sounds like one of your stories!
(me)
?
(crêpe)

And she's right, of course.

That *is* the story.

(*Nb*: The waitress spoke english, & told us she spent a year in Perth.

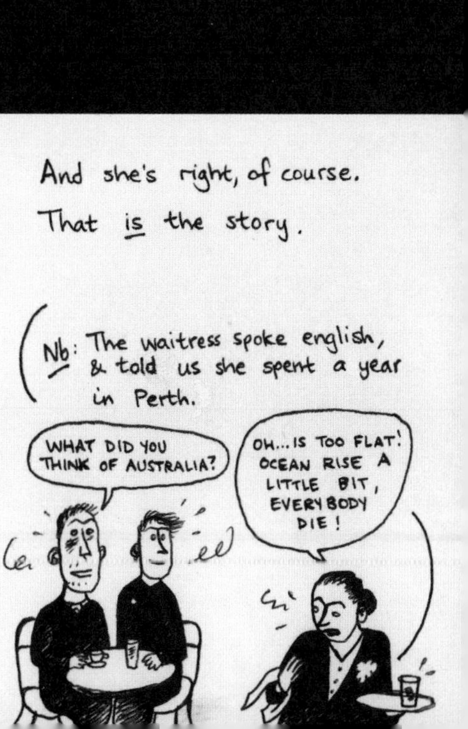
WHAT DID YOU THINK OF AUSTRALIA?
OH... IS TOO FLAT! OCEAN RISE A LITTLE BIT, EVERYBODY DIE!

# ARRIVALS

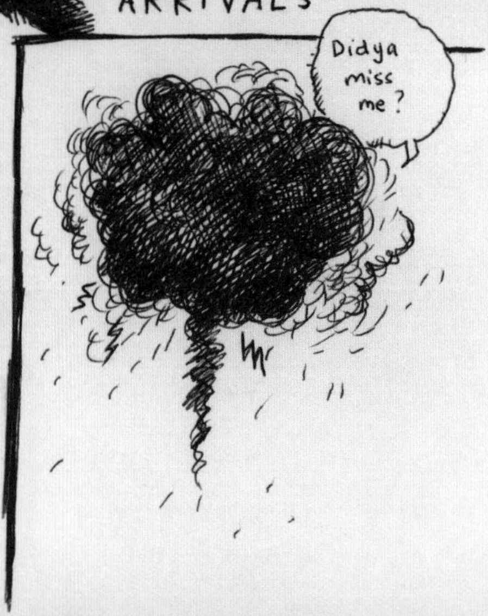
Didya miss me?

Then back to England alone, because I have to be back at work, while she will follow soon.

The moneymachine eats my card at Heathrow in an utterly unprovoked act of malice, & I have to talk my way on to the Tube.

I'm back, alright.

It's after this that I first notice the fear.

I idly wander into a comic-shop for the first time in months.

Halfway in, I realise I'm sweating. By the time I reach Love & Rockets I'm dizzy & have a pain in my gut. I stagger outside, wondering if I caught something weird in Yugoslavia.

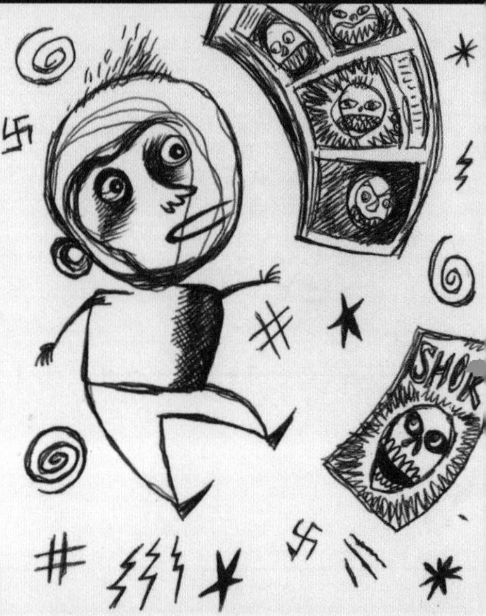
SHOK

But no. A few simple experiments confirm the worst:

I have become terrified of comic-shops,

& - in fact - of comics.

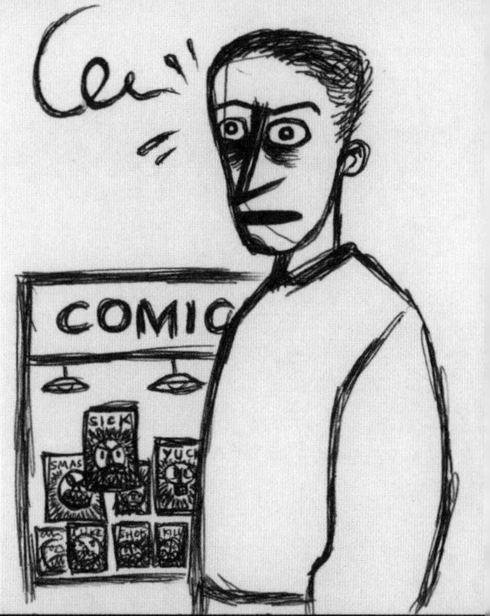
COMIC
SICK

It persists for months. I can't even look at my own work without the room spinning.

I can find no explanation. Doctors are at a loss. Friends are astonished. Comics arrive in the post but remain unopened ...

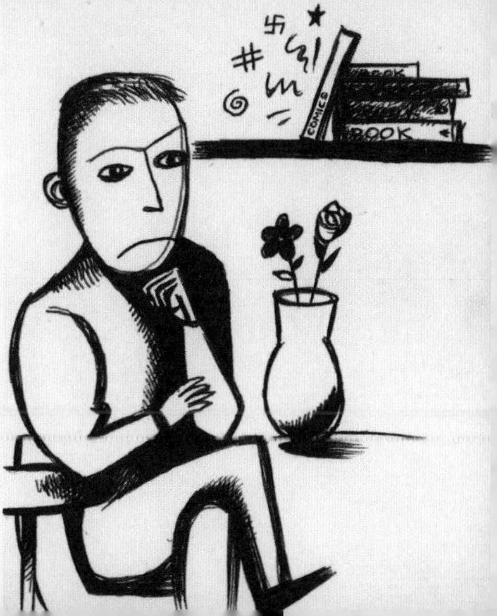
COMICS
BOOK

What can I do, I wonder?
When Terry arrives, she suggests I ignore it & enjoy other things. I toy with the idea of writing novels or illustrating children's books.

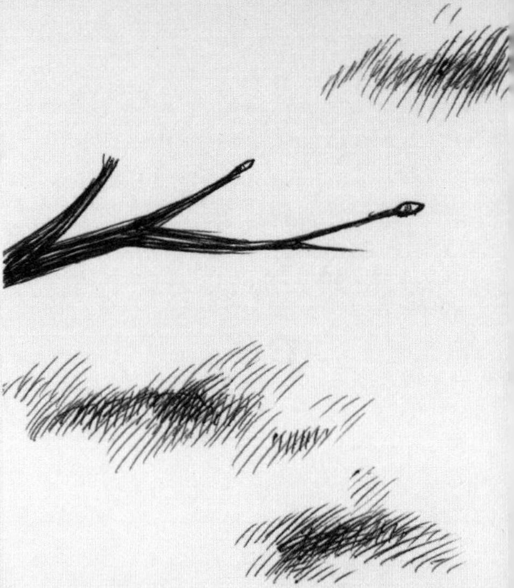

(Tiny green buds appear at the tips of branches).

Then I notice another strange thing: I feel drawn to french bookshops, where I pore over the Bandes-Désinées. I tell people it's good practise for my french, but actually my french isn't good enough to read them properly. I simply look.

One day Paul Gravett lends me a book by a Japanese cartoonist, & it obsesses me. I don't even try to guess the stories, & I delight in not knowing the cartoonist's name.

But what a book!

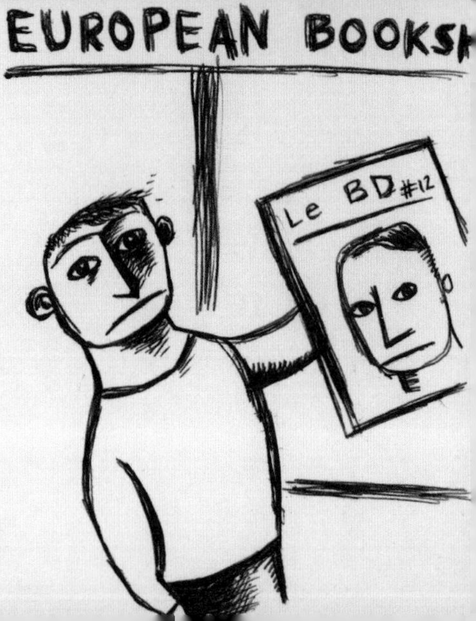
EUROPEAN BOOKS
Le BD #12

This confuses me for a long time.
I try french comics in translation,
but after a page I'm dizzy and
my teeth chatter. Only the
originals will do.

So I stay away from comic-shops
& go on day-trips to the countryside. The hills are the freshest
green I've ever seen, and everywhere
there are new leaves, flowers &
buds.

One day while no-one's
watching, I strengthen
my resolve & finish a
long-overdue strip for
someone.

And spring hits England.

Now I'm back at work, & have finished chapter 1 of a graphic-novel (though the mere words still make my stomach twist). I enjoy it again. I'm ready to face publishers & am not overly worried what they'll say. I've even started putting out a mini-comic, mixing up old strips & new work in progress, courtesy of the bookshop's photocopier. Summer has been hot but now I'm enjoying the slide into a golden autumn. I secretly hope for a fierce & snowy winter, & plan trips to France & Wales & Italy.

But I can't claim to be entirely cured. When someone says a strip of mine has come out, I can't bring myself to go into a shop to see it. Even when the magazine arrives in the post, I flick through it apprehensively & then lay it aside, unable to give it more than a cursory inspection.

I'm looking forward to scouring a BD-shop in Paris, but I'll avoid the english translations.

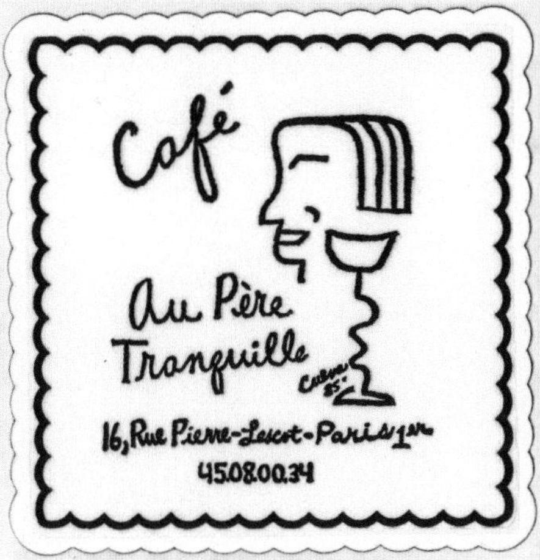
Café
Au Père Tranquille
16, Rue Pierre-Lescot - Paris 1er
45.08.00.34

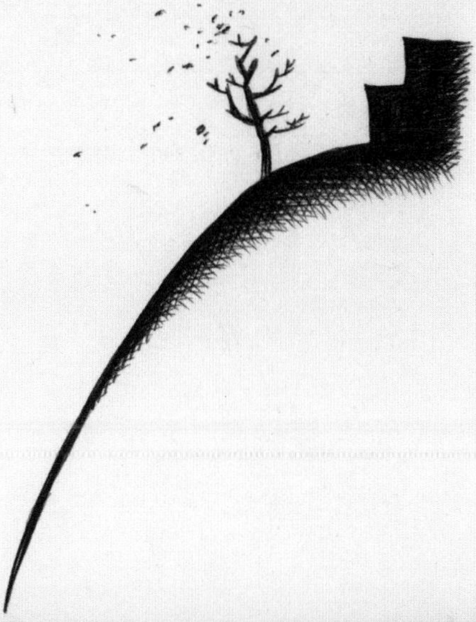

And now outside the leaves are falling, & the cupboard is open. Friends are singing while I write. The story's cracked.

(The red flowers & the green plants

The bright room framed by the bathroom window)

Next, a story about evening...

(written & drawn on location in London, Belgrade & Paris.
Pages 2, 101 & 103 drawn by Terry Fleming.
Dedicated to the usual crowd:
Terry, Matt, family & friends, etc, etc,
& to:
Chloë Brookes-Kenworthy
Eddie Campbell
Glenn Dakin
Paul Gravett
Edward Pinset
&
Fox Comics.



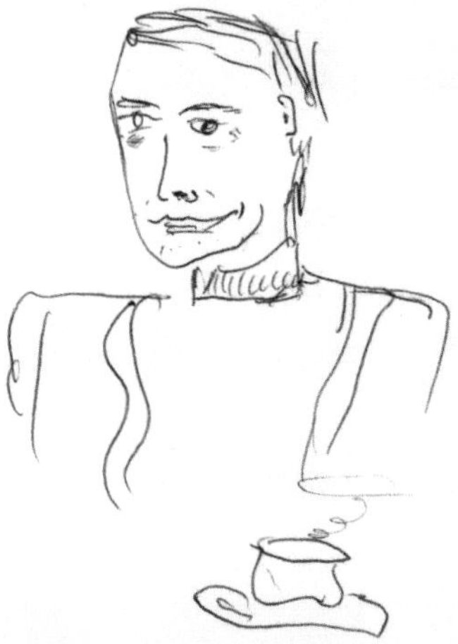

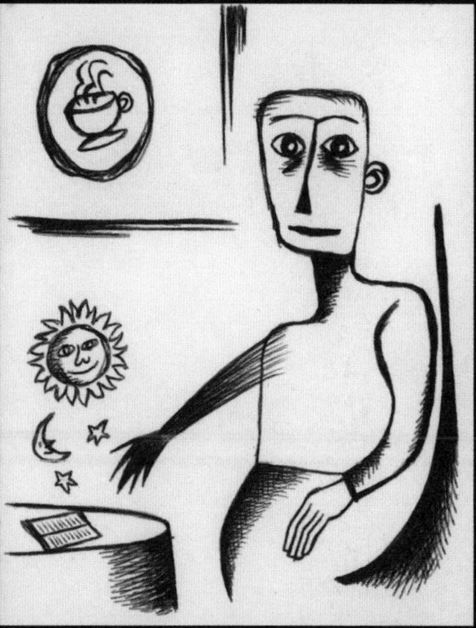

This is Beata.
She is my guardian angel, the voice of my ancestors, my spirit-guide, karma, kismet, conscience incarnate.
She tells me to pay more attention to being whole.

She tells me I eat the wrong food.
I don't get any exercise. I neglect my work.

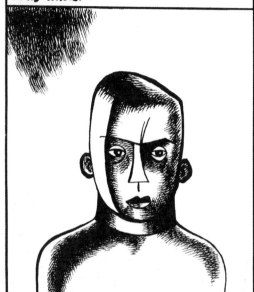

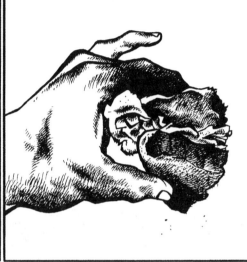

She tells me to stay out of strong winds, stop listening to Arvo Pärt, and cheer up.

This is Lucy.
She always visits when the sun is shining.
Or vice versa.

London 1/91 - Auckland 7/92

to Eleanor. — dylanhorrocks

# Pickle

It was one of those days when the sky is a brilliant blue- clear and cold.

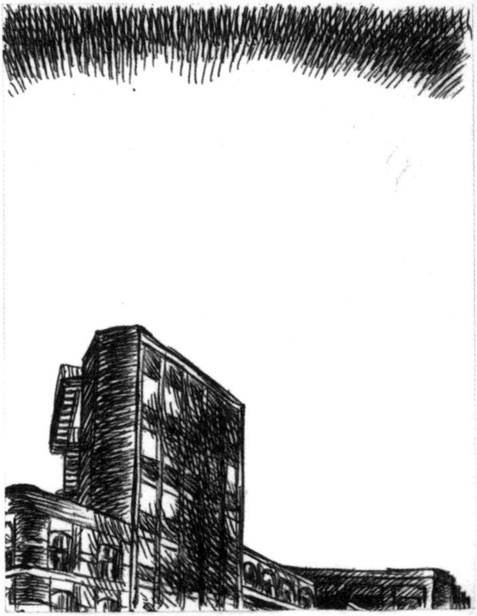

Shining blocks of sunlight moved slowly and silently through the streets, and people crossed the road to walk within one.

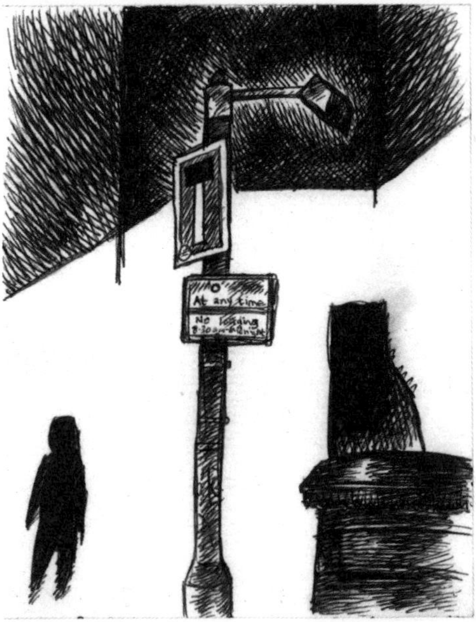
At any time
No loading

When night came the moon hung like a ball of antarctic ice, reminding me of home.

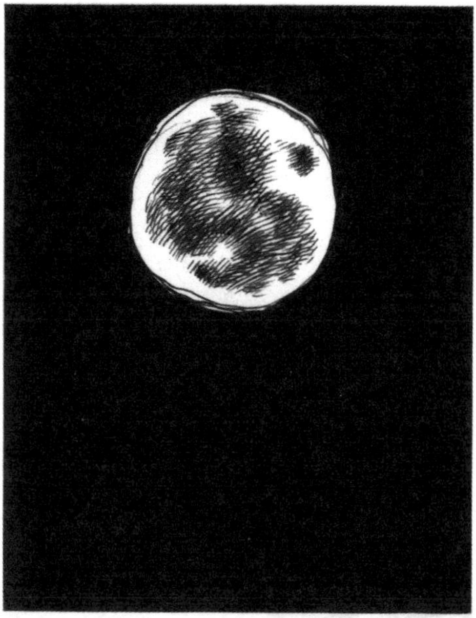

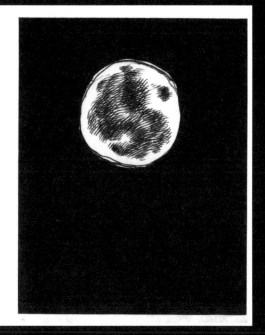

Home was on the phone at midnight, our conversation overlapping and pausing according to the delay.

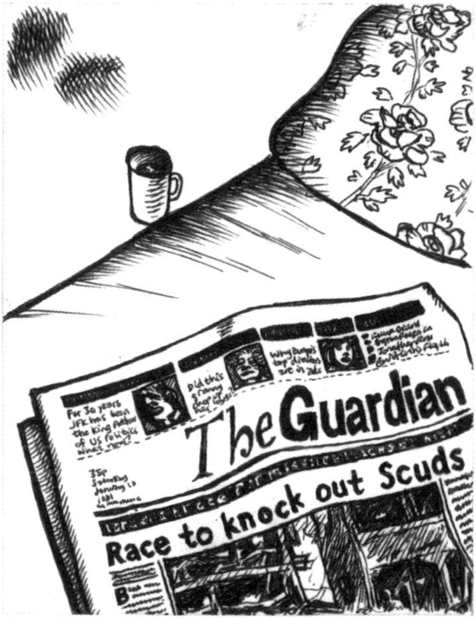
The Guardian
Race to knock out Scuds

Twelve hours apart,
12,000 miles away,
at opposite equinoxes.

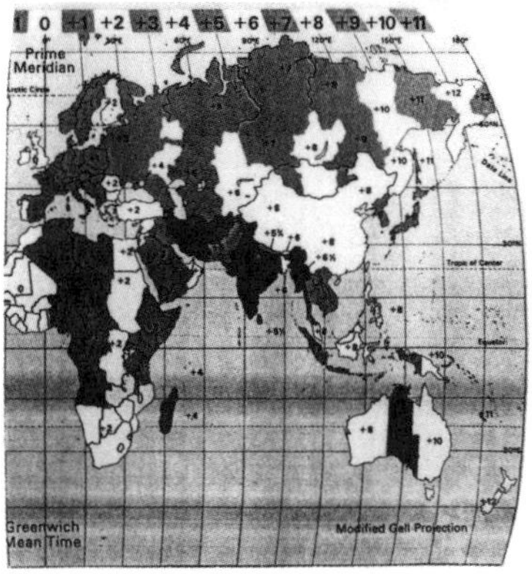
0 +1 +2 +3 +4 +5 +6 +7 +8 +9 +10 +11
Prime Meridian
Greenwich Mean Time
Modified Gall Projection

In a fit of
melancholy,
I dig out the
tarot.

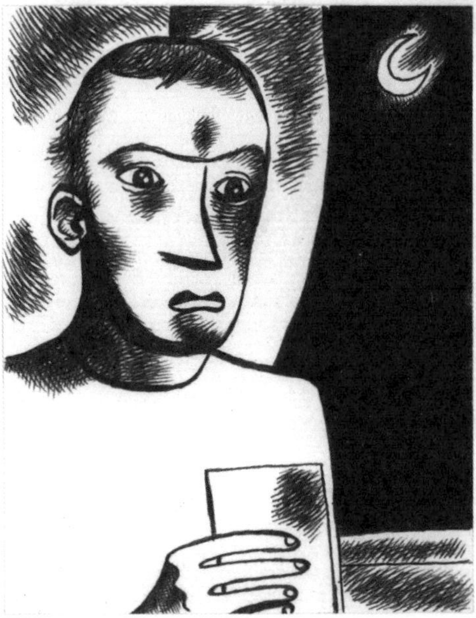

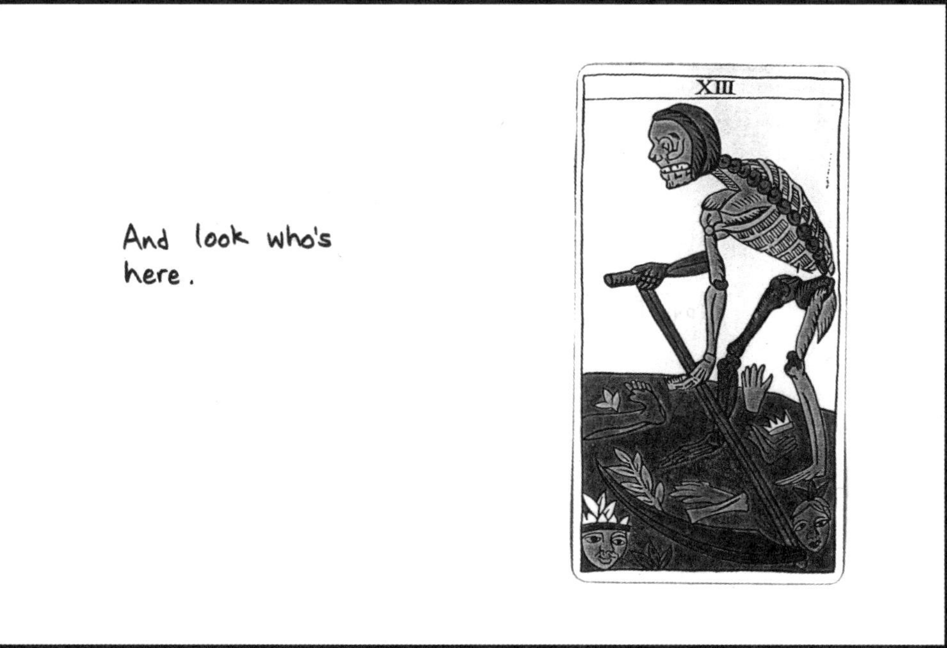
And look who's here.
XIII

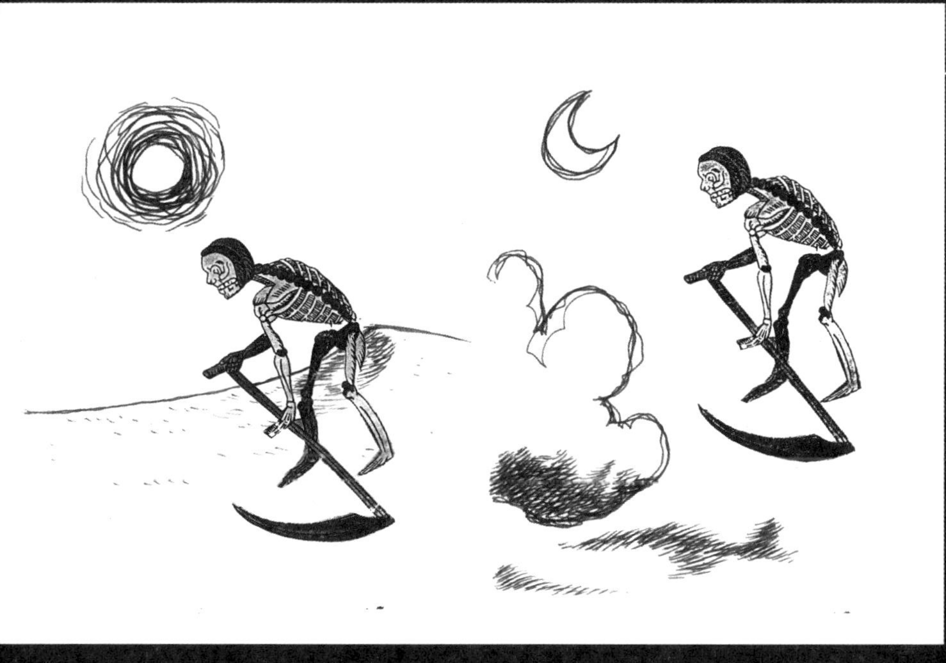

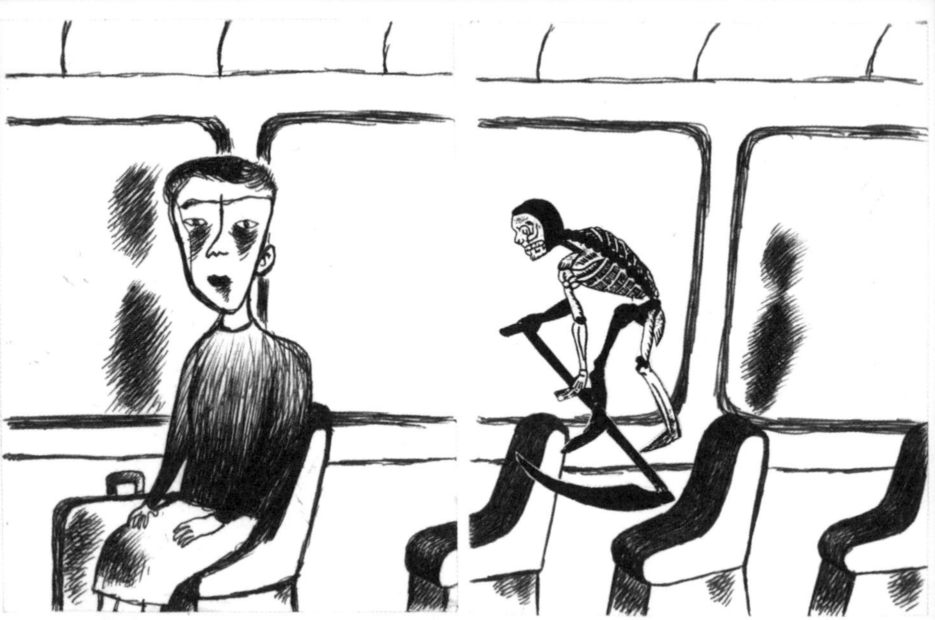

The tea never tastes right, and the doughnuts are always greasy.

The bus is never on time, and the tube is always full.

Now, of course, there might be a bomb on board.

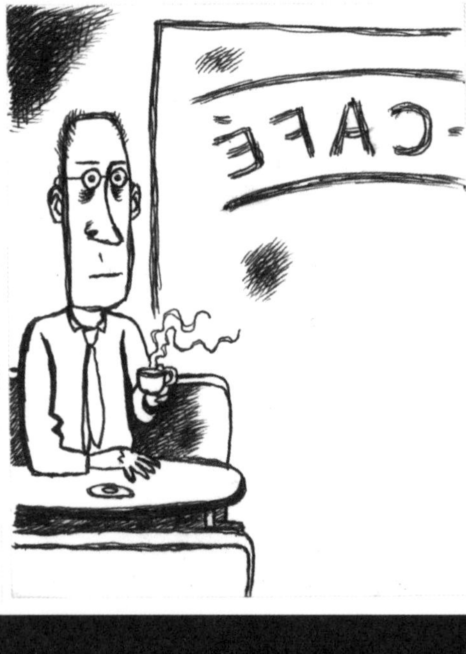

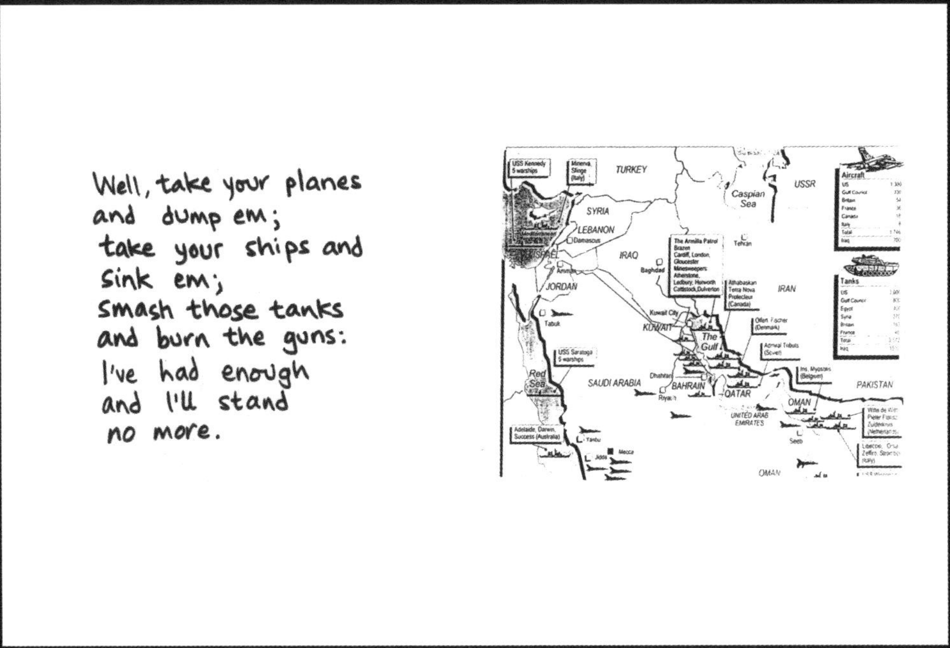
Well, take your planes
and dump em;
take your ships and
sink em;
smash those tanks
and burn the guns:
I've had enough
and I'll stand
no more.
USS Kennedy 5 warships
TURKEY
SYRIA
LEBANON
Damascus
IRAQ
Baghdad
JORDAN
Caspian Sea
USSR
Tehran
IRAN
Aircraft
Tanks
Kuwait City
KUWAIT
The Gulf
Tabuk
USS Saratoga 5 warships
Red Sea
SAUDI ARABIA
Dhahran
Riyadh
BAHRAIN
QATAR
OMAN
PAKISTAN
UNITED ARAB EMIRATES
Yanbu
Mecca
Jidda
Seeb
OMAN

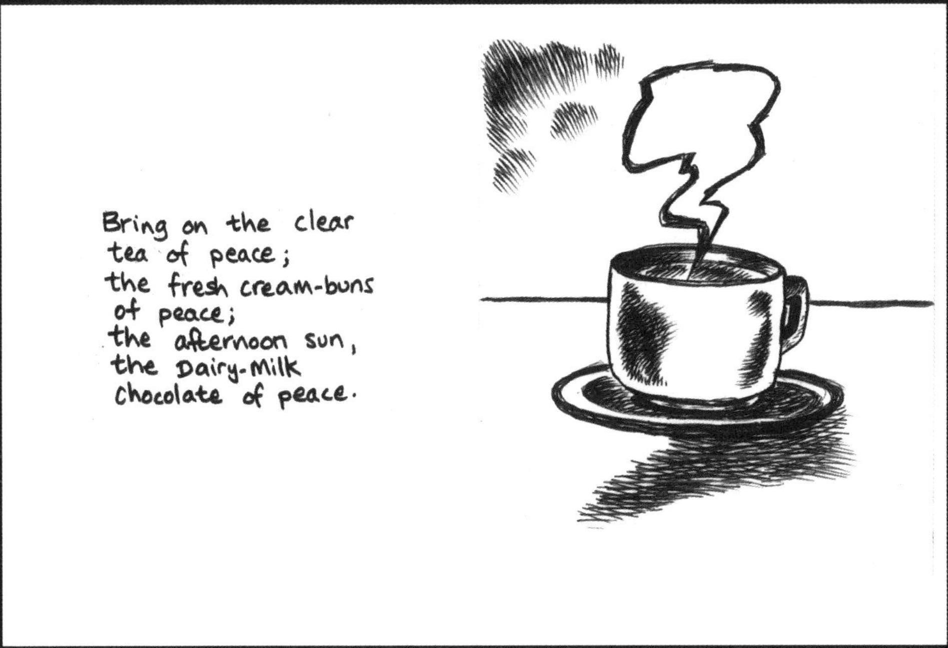
Bring on the clear
tea of peace;
the fresh cream-buns
of peace;
the afternoon sun,
the Dairy-Milk
chocolate of peace.

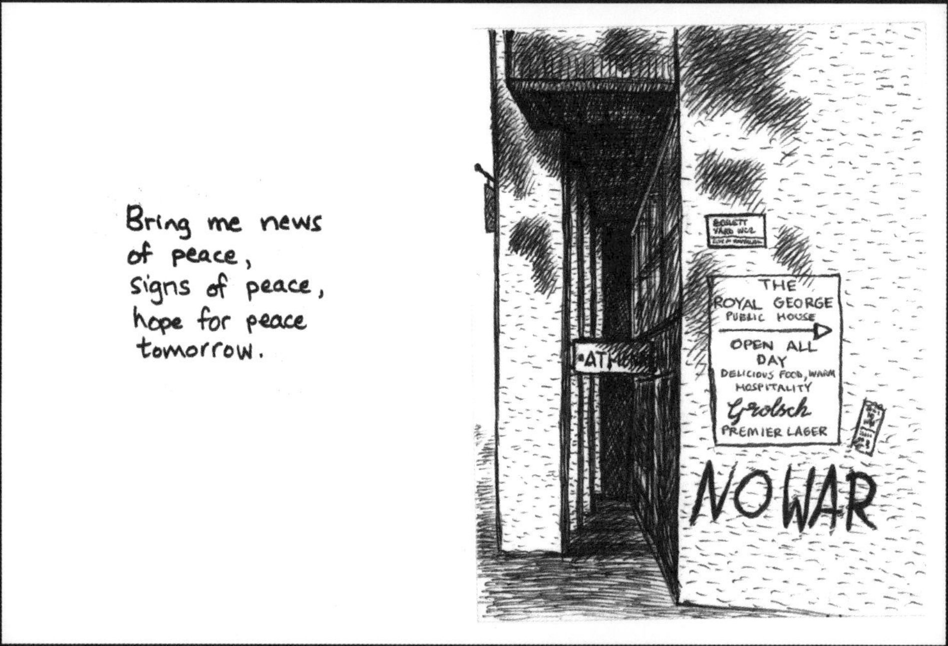
Bring me news of peace, signs of peace, hope for peace tomorrow.
THE ROYAL GEORGE
PUBLIC HOUSE
OPEN ALL DAY
DELICIOUS FOOD, WARM HOSPITALITY
Grolsch
PREMIER LAGER
NO WAR

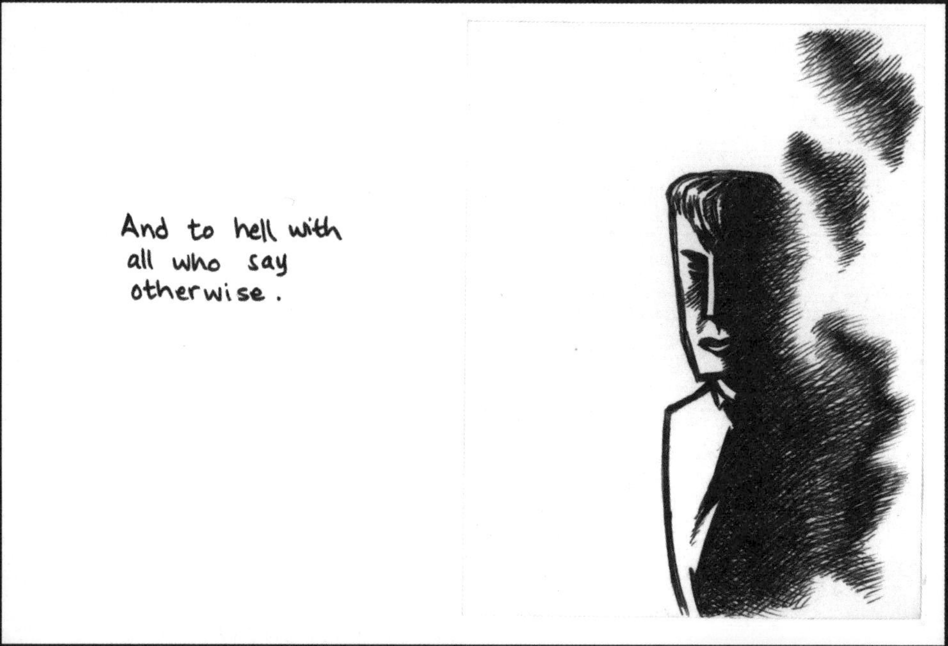
And to hell with all who say otherwise.

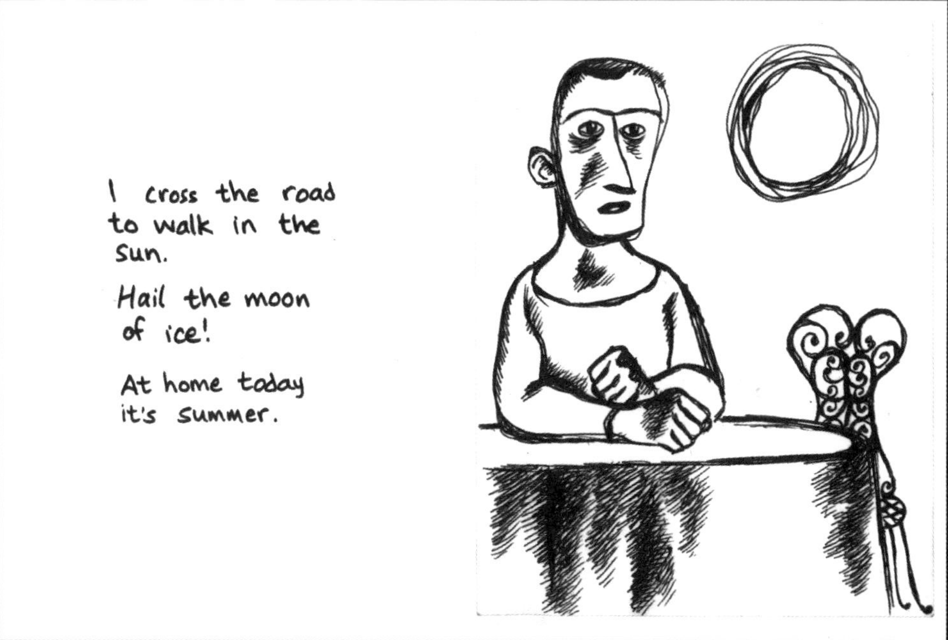
I cross the road to walk in the sun.
Hail the moon of ice!
At home today it's summer.

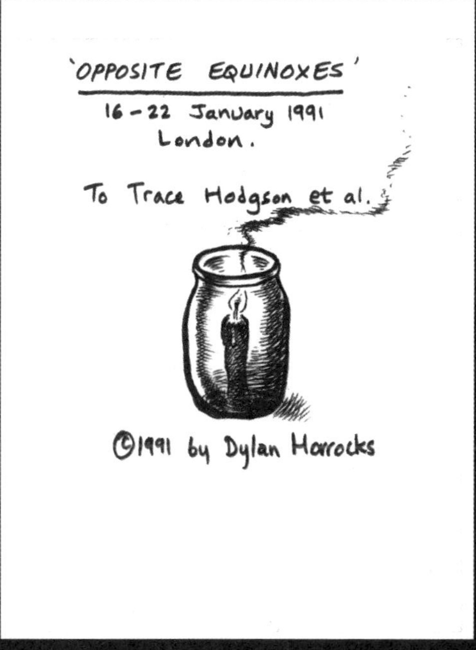
'OPPOSITE EQUINOXES'
16 – 22 January 1991
London.
To Trace Hodgson et al.
©1991 by Dylan Horrocks

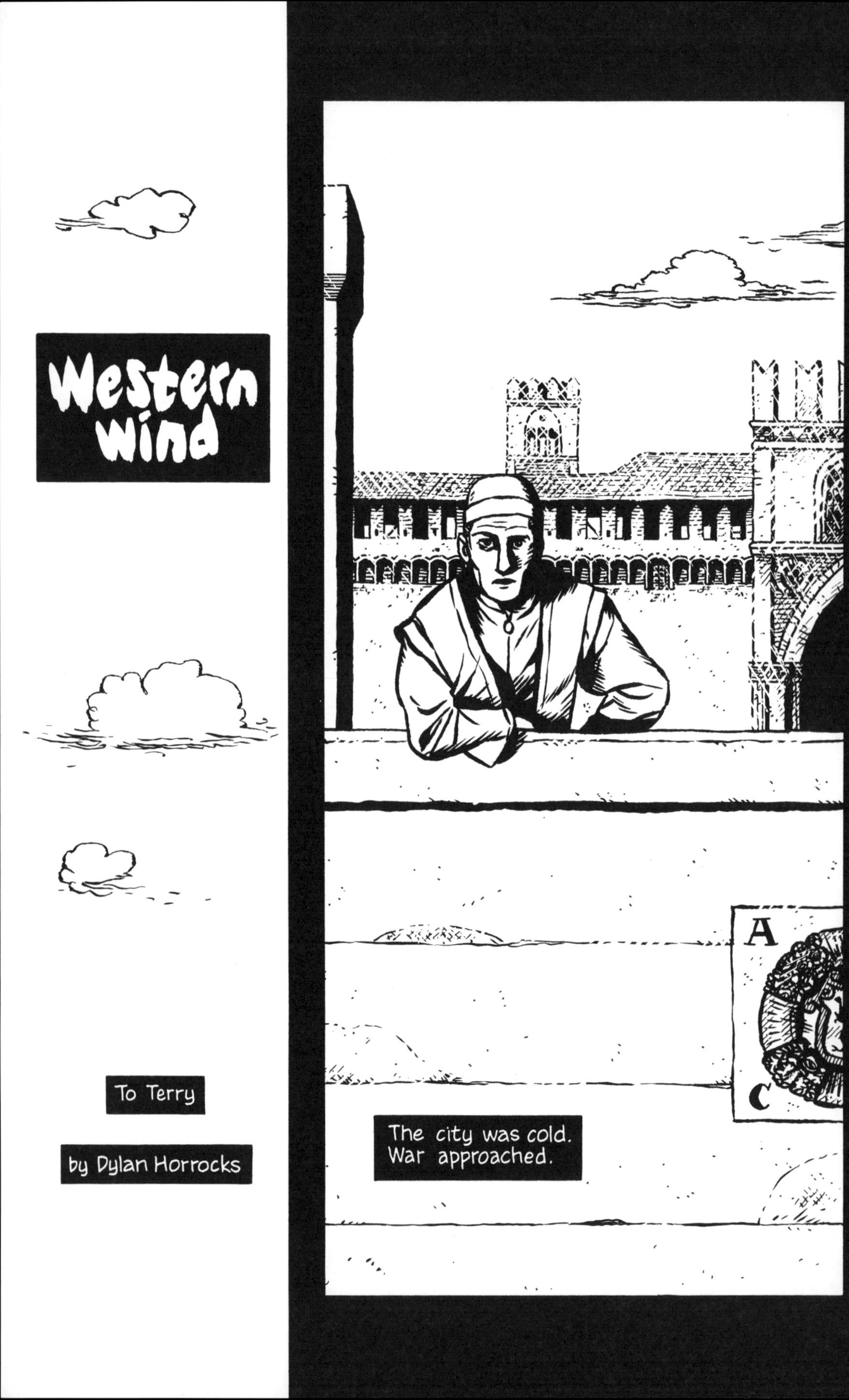
Western Wind
To Terry
by Dylan Horrocks
The city was cold.
War approached.
A
C

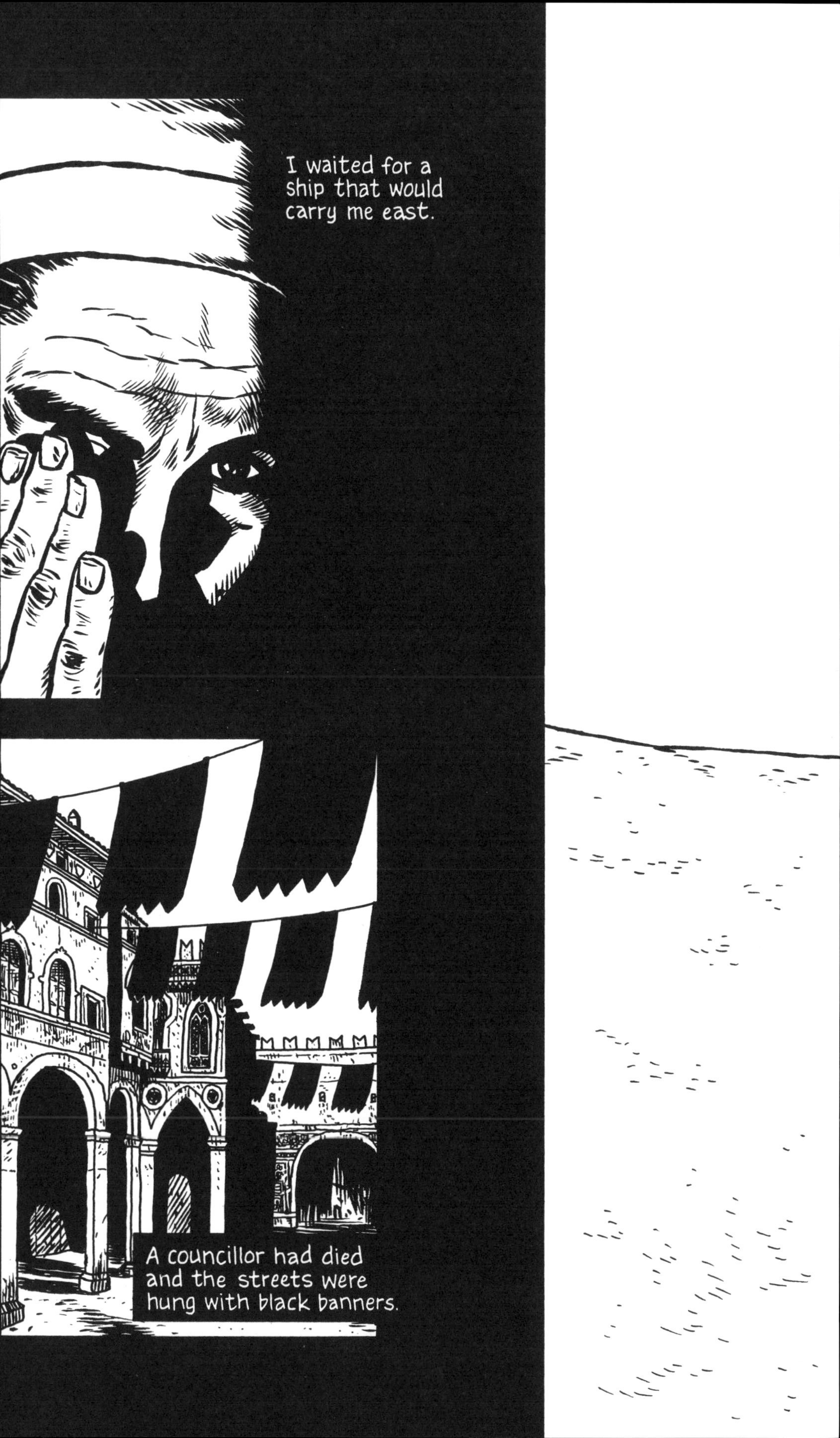
I waited for a ship that would carry me east.
A councillor had died and the streets were hung with black banners.

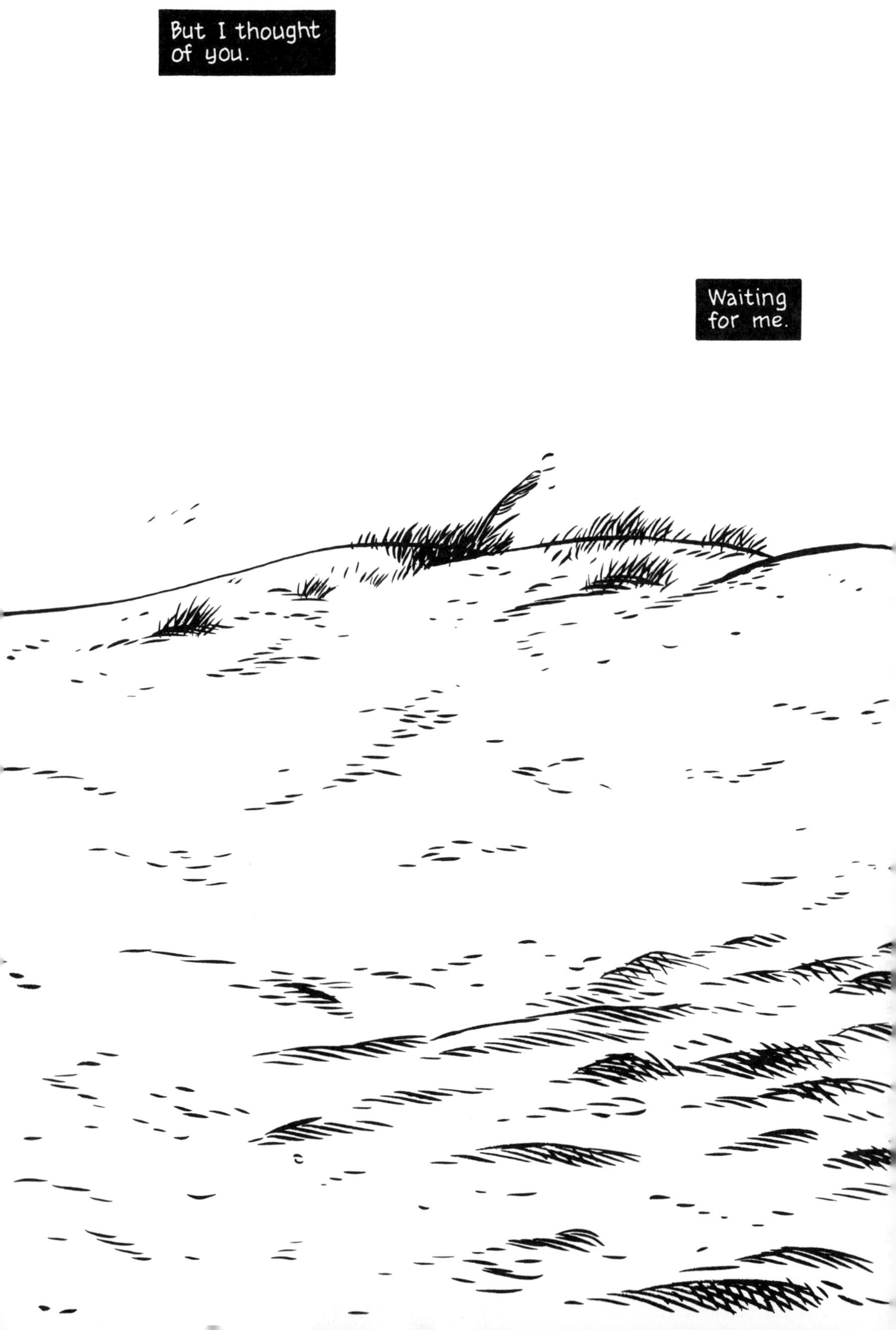
But I thought of you.
Waiting for me.

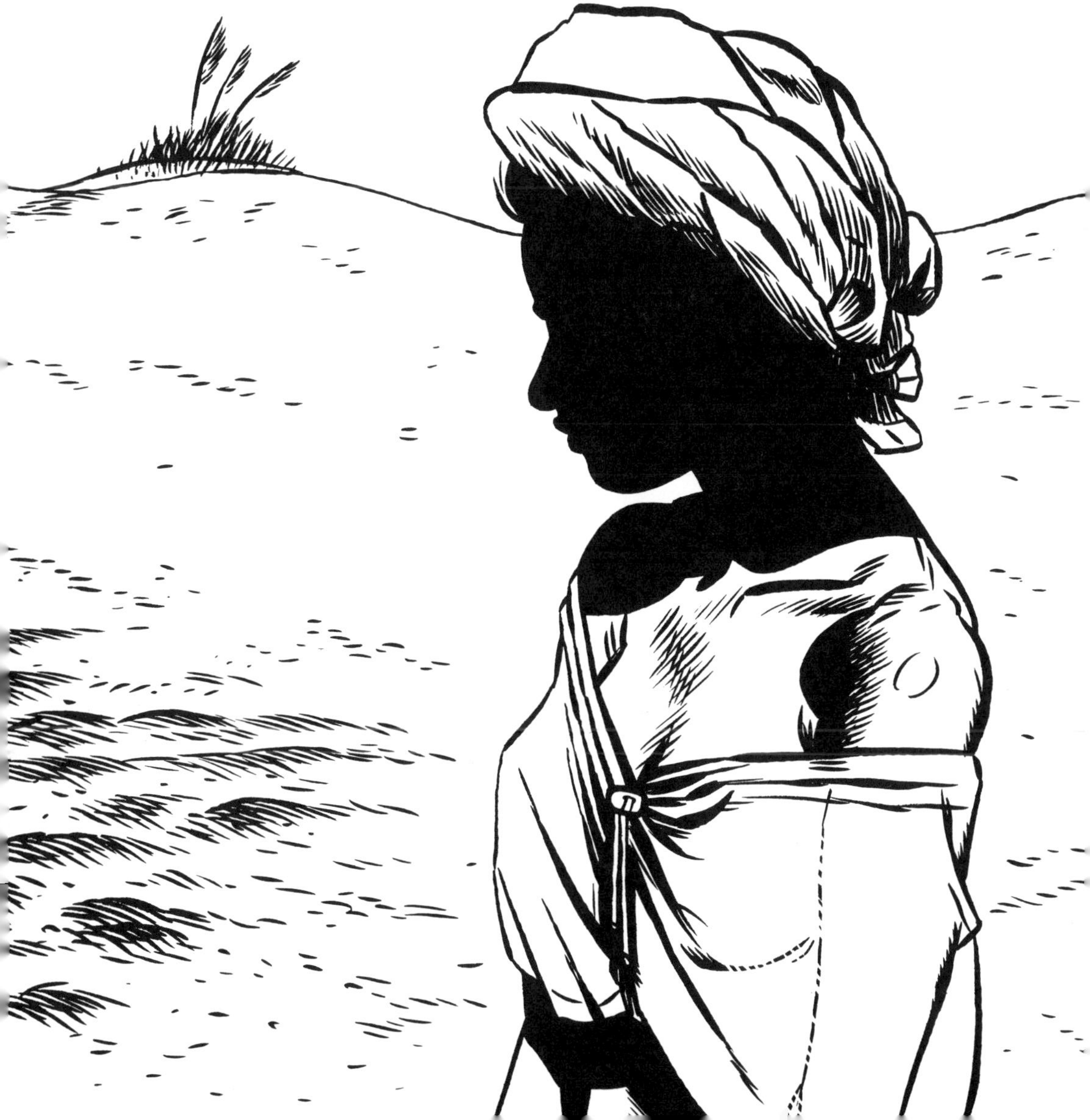

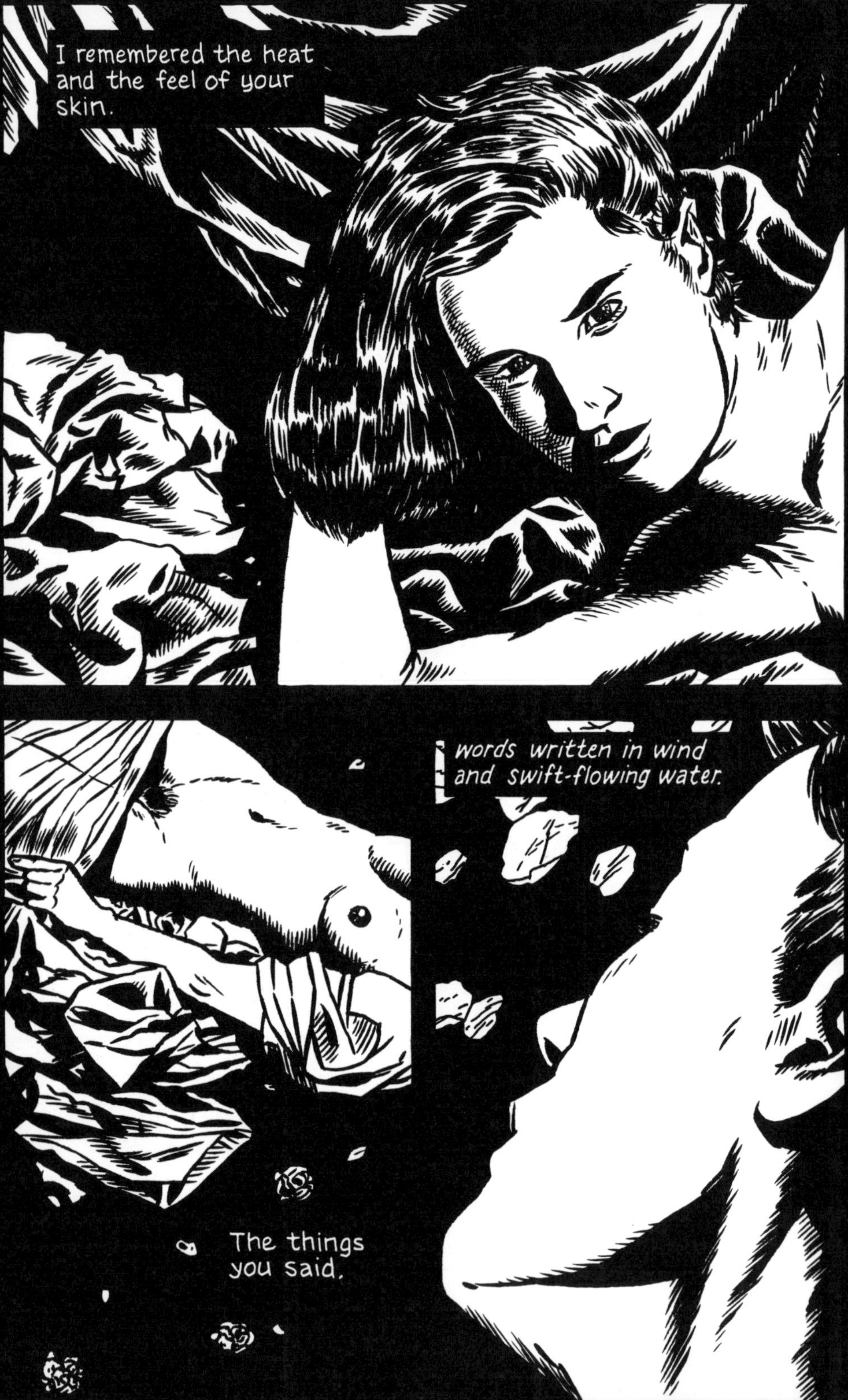
I remembered the heat and the feel of your skin.
The things you said,
words written in wind and swift-flowing water.

(A sailor sang:)

*Western wind, when will thou blow,*
*The small rain down can rain?*
*Christ, if my love were in my arms,*
*And I in my bed again!*

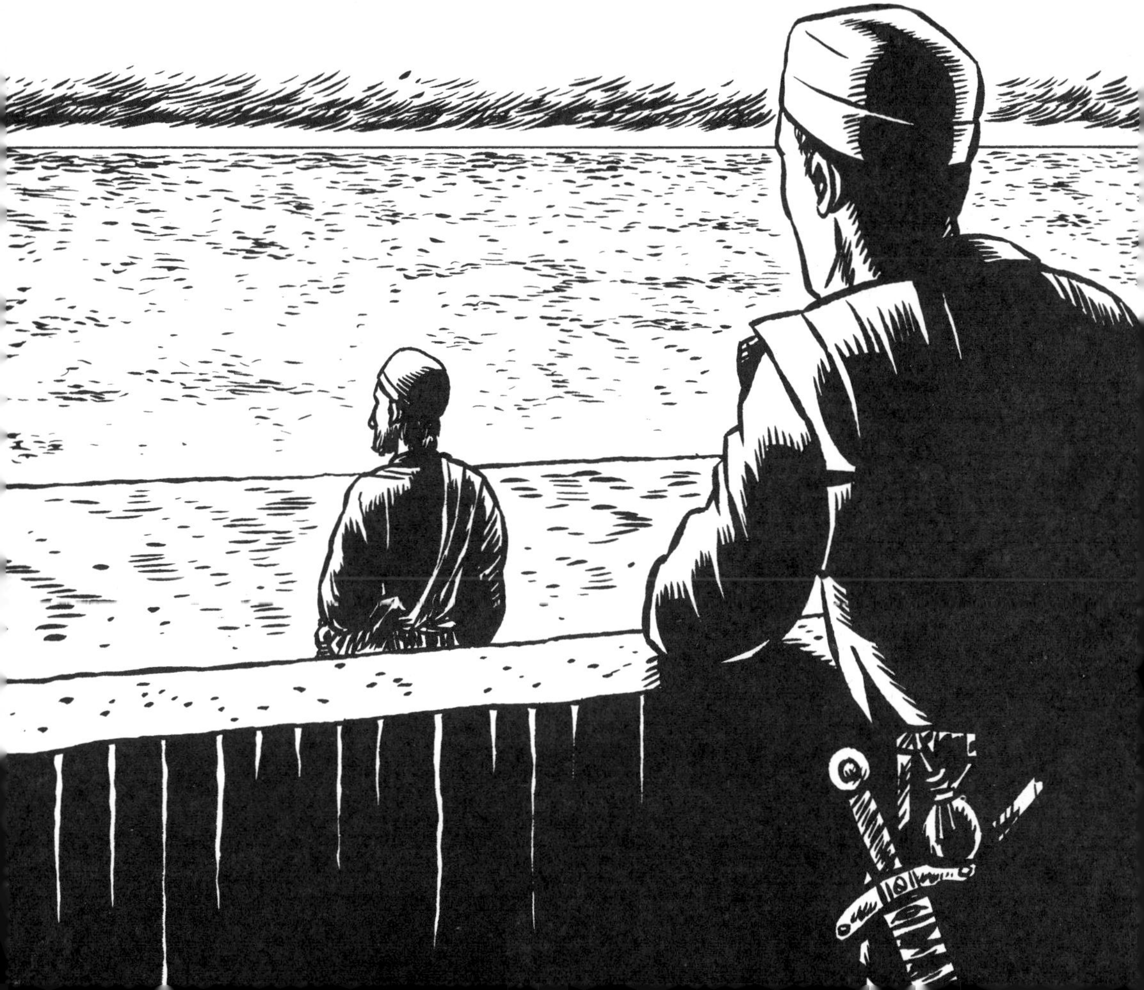

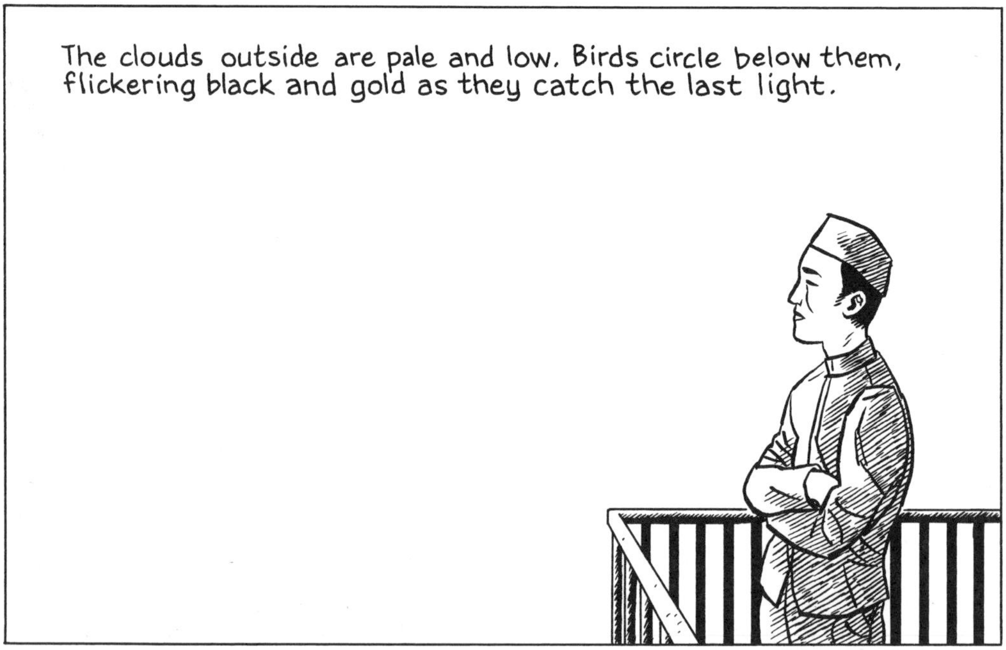
The clouds outside are pale and low. Birds circle below them, flickering black and gold as they catch the last light.

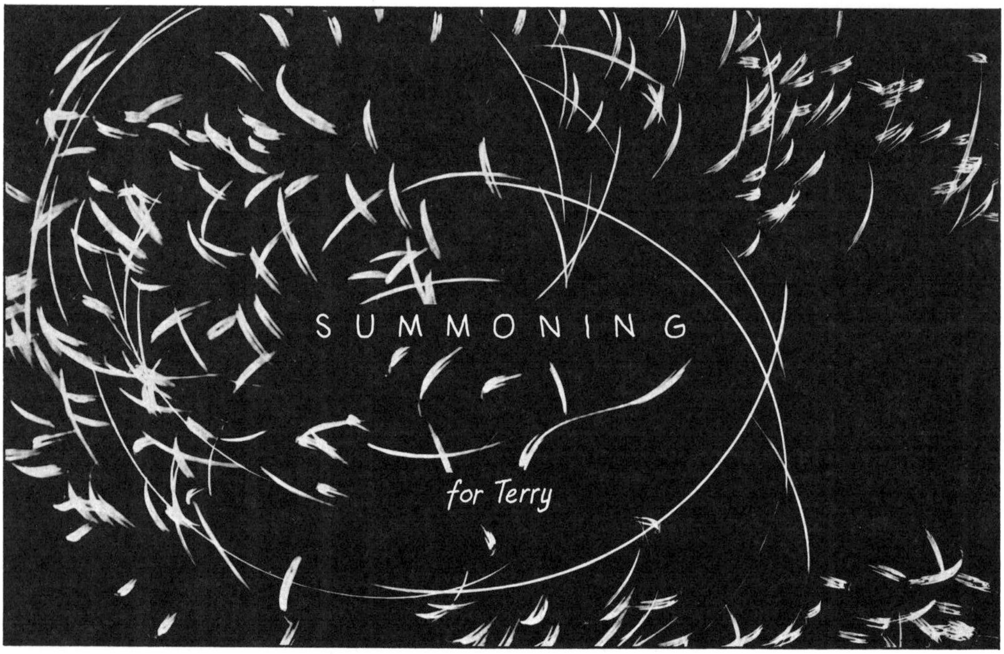
SUMMONING
for Terry

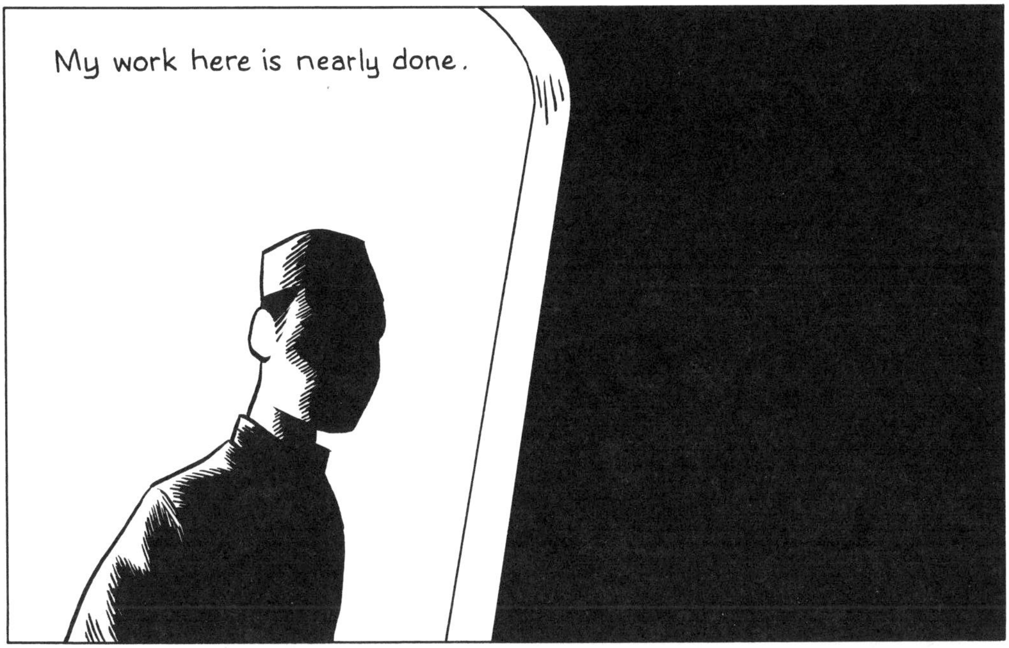
My work here is nearly done.

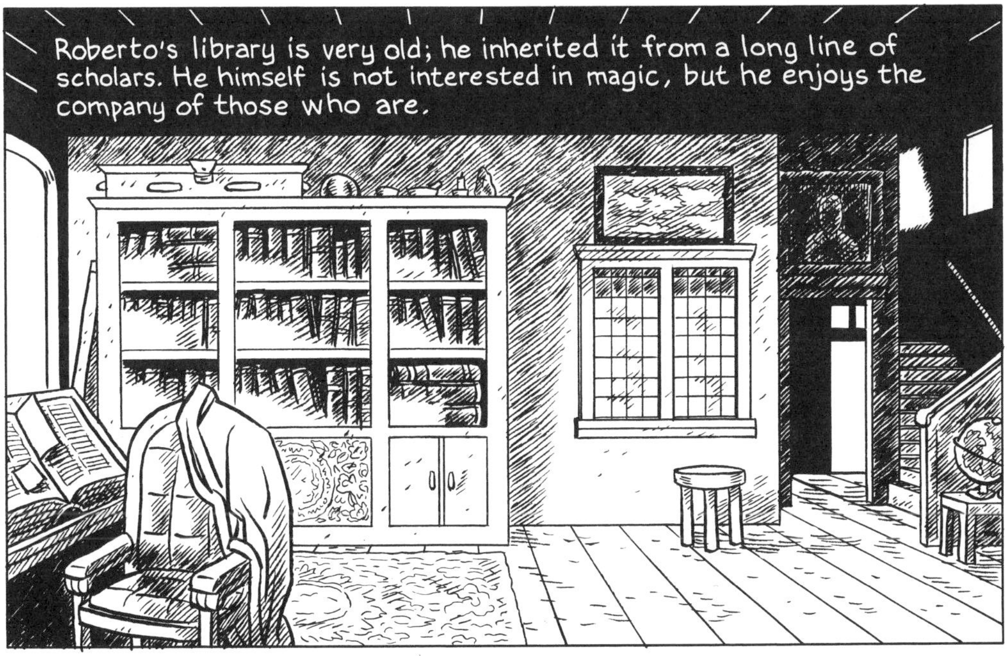
Roberto's library is very old; he inherited it from a long line of scholars. He himself is not interested in magic, but he enjoys the company of those who are.

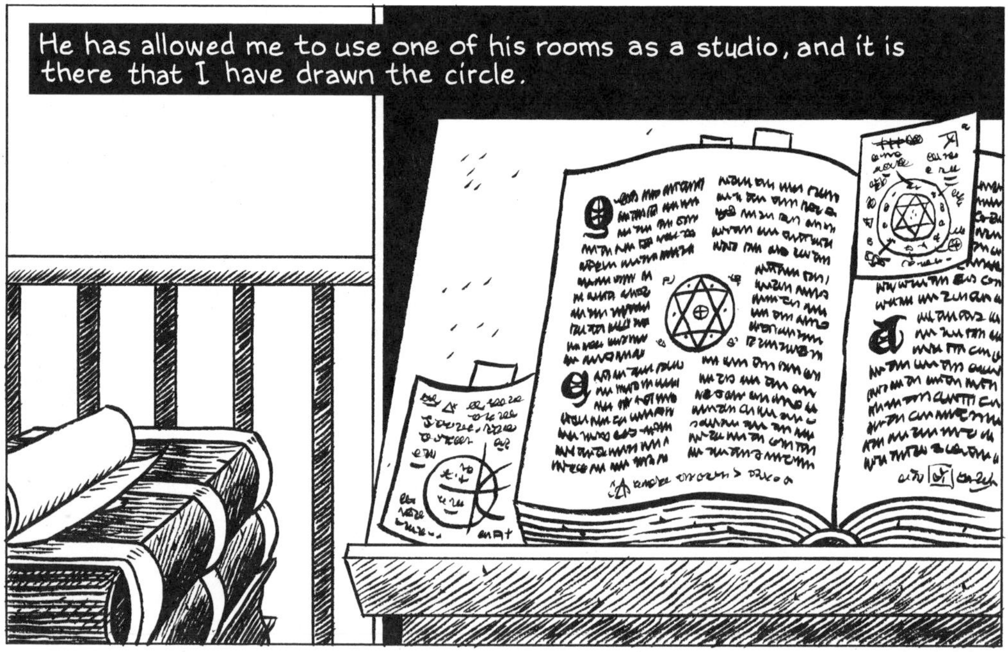
He has allowed me to use one of his rooms as a studio, and it is there that I have drawn the circle.

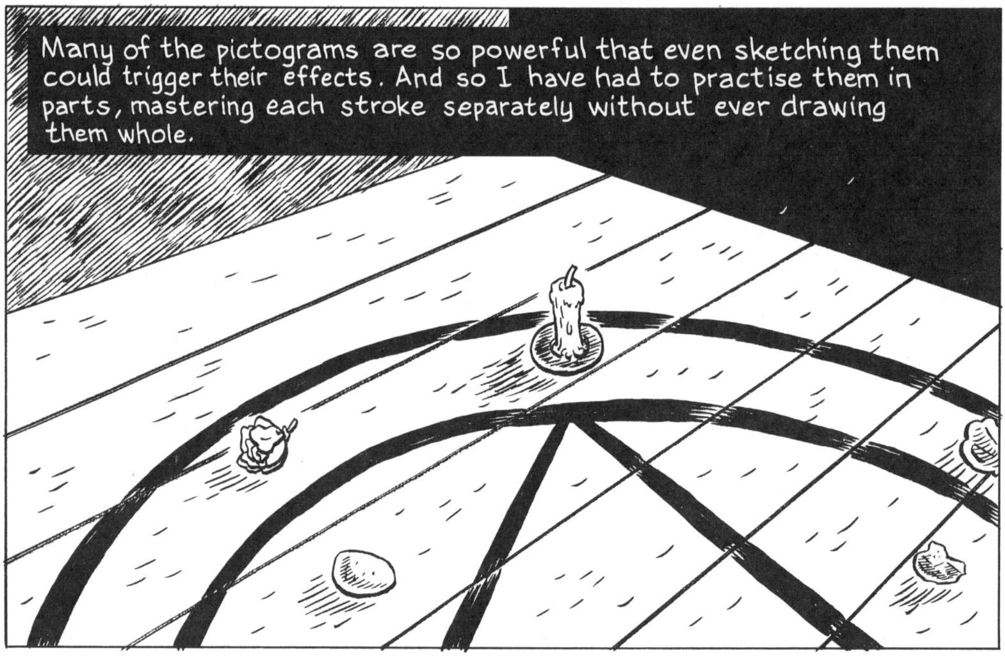
Many of the pictograms are so powerful that even sketching them could trigger their effects. And so I have had to practise them in parts, mastering each stroke separately without ever drawing them whole.

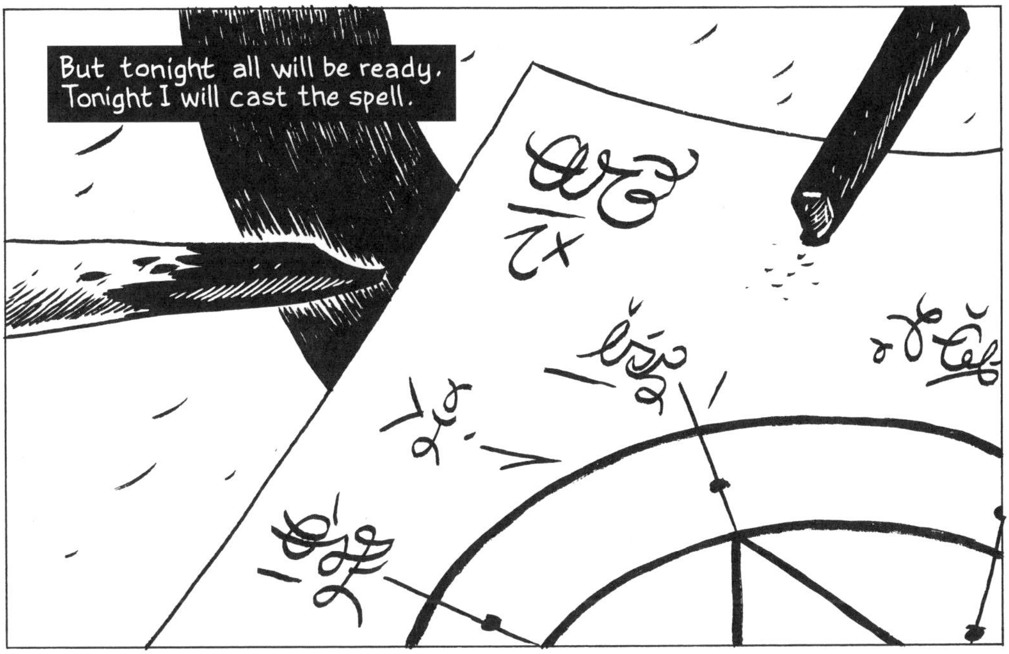
But tonight all will be ready.
Tonight I will cast the spell.

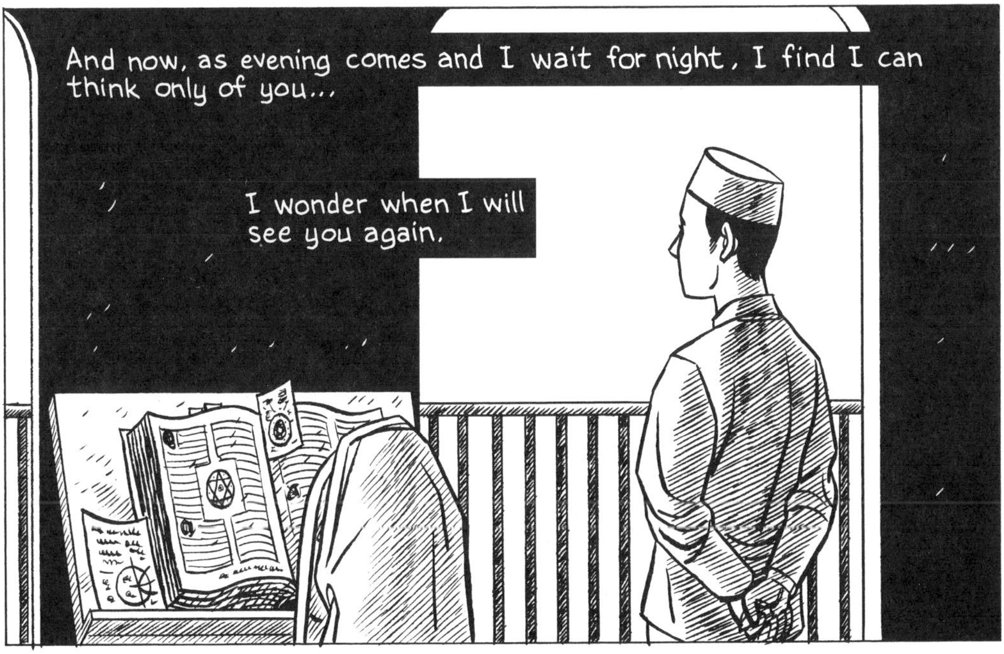
And now, as evening comes and I wait for night, I find I can think only of you...
I wonder when I will see you again.

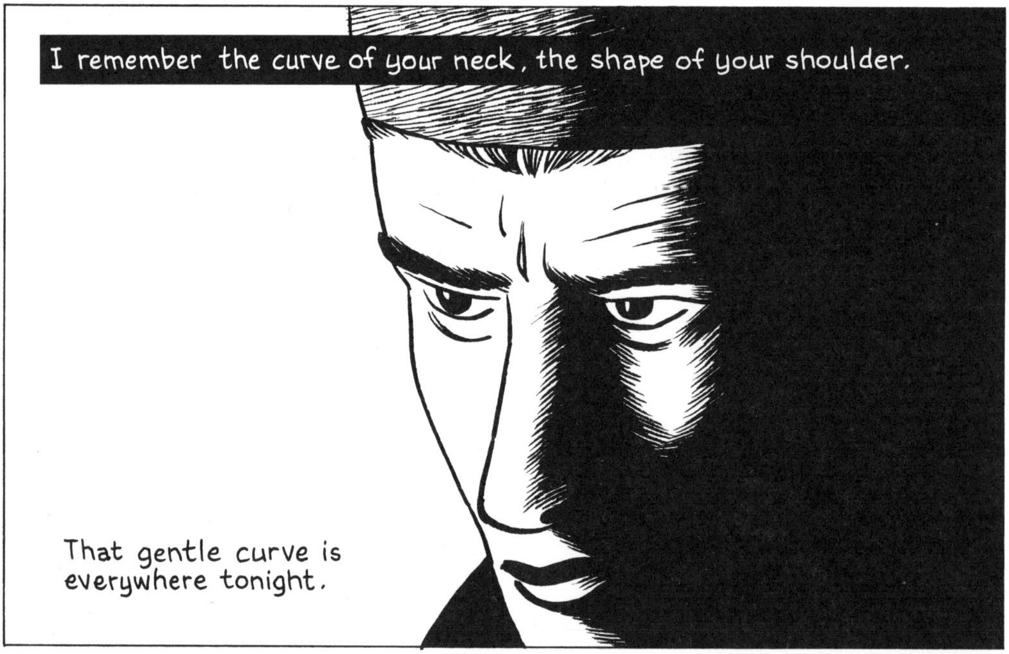
I remember the curve of your neck, the shape of your shoulder.
That gentle curve is everywhere tonight.

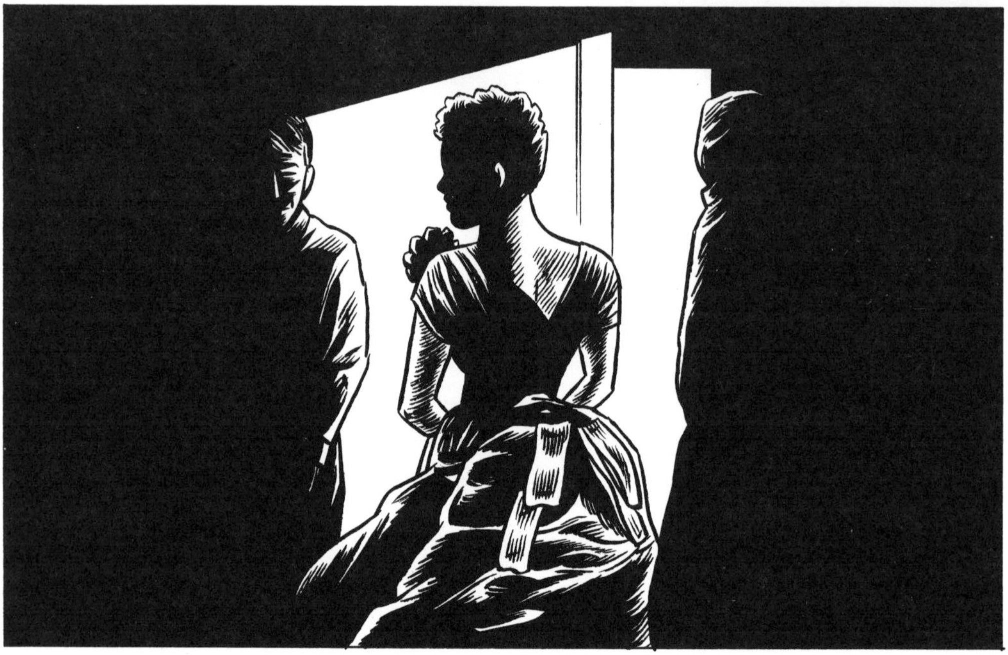

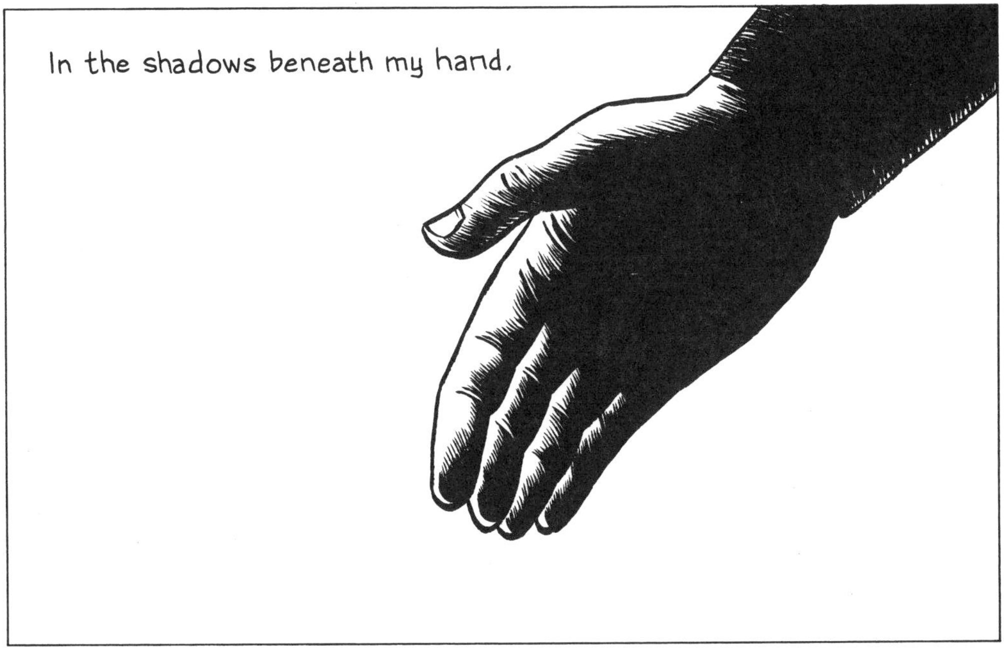
In the shadows beneath my hand,

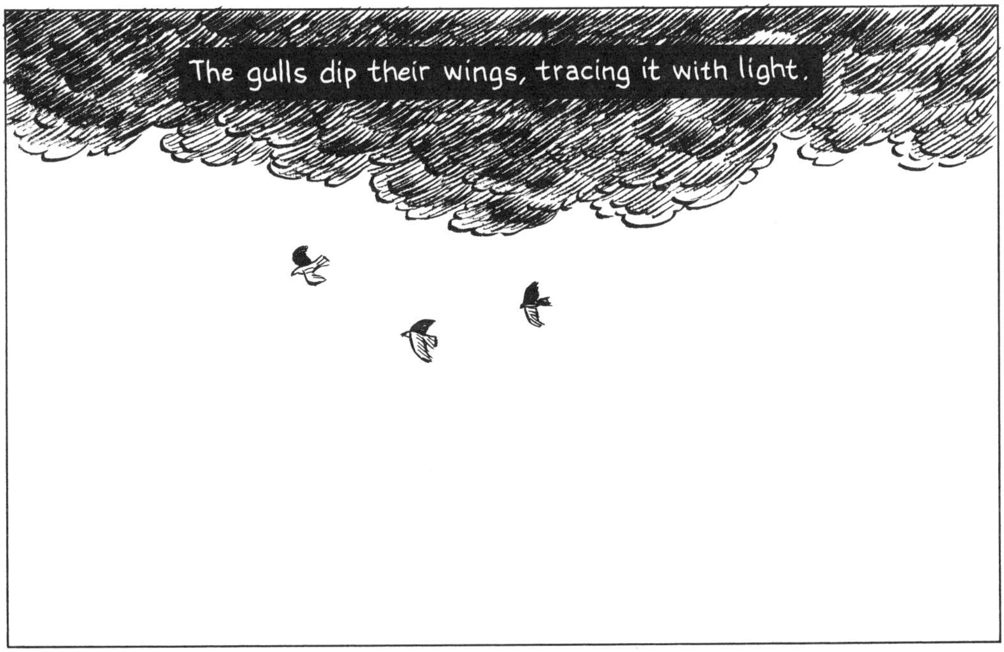
The gulls dip their wings, tracing it with light.

DYLAN HORROCKS 1991, 2011

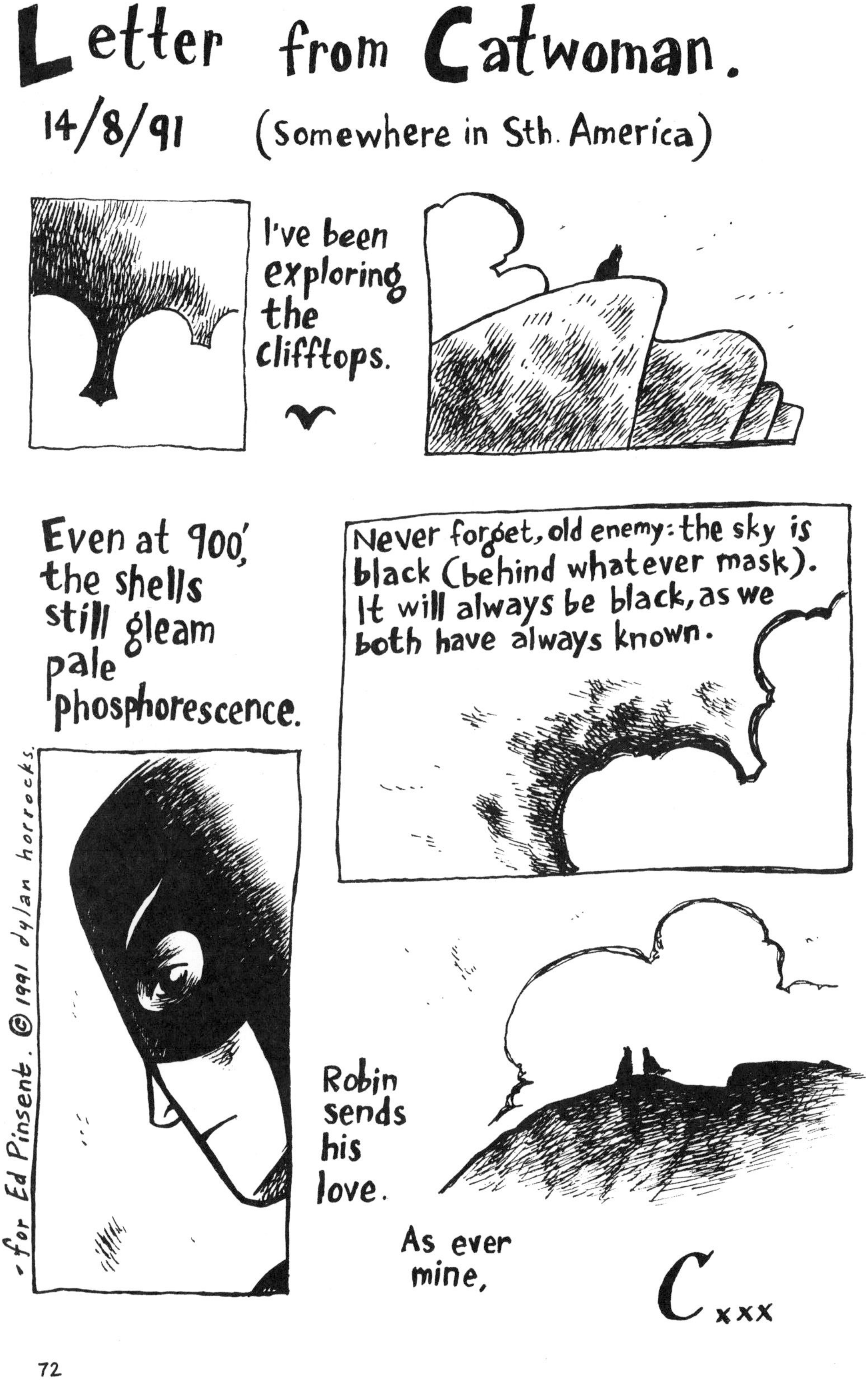

Letter from Catwoman.
14/8/91 (Somewhere in Sth. America)
I've been exploring the clifftops.
Even at 900', the shells still gleam pale phosphorescence.
Never forget, old enemy: the sky is black (behind whatever mask). It will always be black, as we both have always known.
- for Ed Pinsent. © 1991 dylan horrocks.
Robin sends his love.
As ever mine,
C xxx

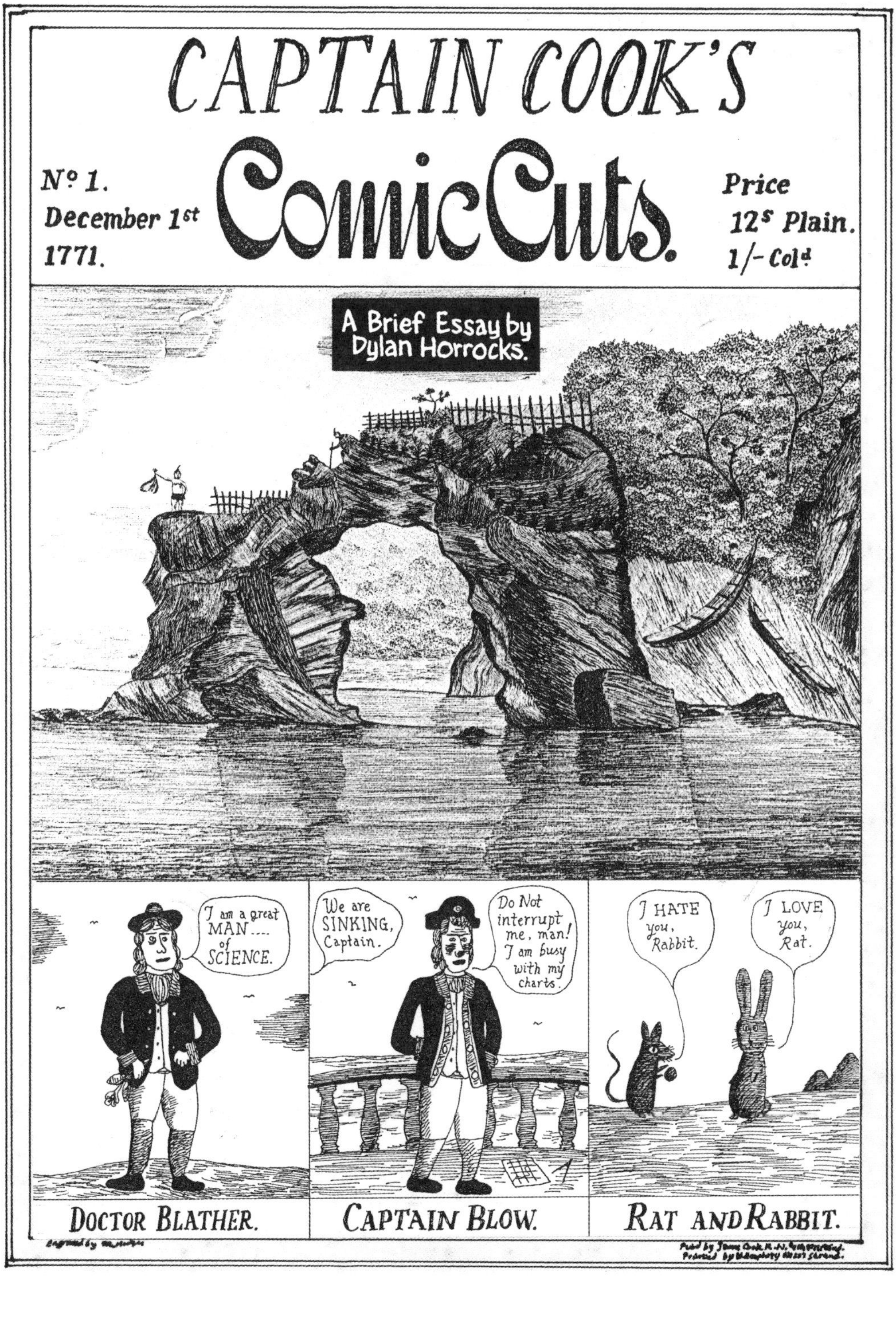

CAPTAIN COOK'S
Nº 1.
December 1st
1771.
Comic Cuts.
Price
12s Plain.
1/- Cold.
A Brief Essay by
Dylan Horrocks.
I am a great MAN.... of SCIENCE.
We are SINKING, Captain.
Do Not interrupt me, man! I am busy with my charts.
I HATE you, Rabbit.
I LOVE you, Rat.
DOCTOR BLATHER.
CAPTAIN BLOW.
RAT AND RABBIT.

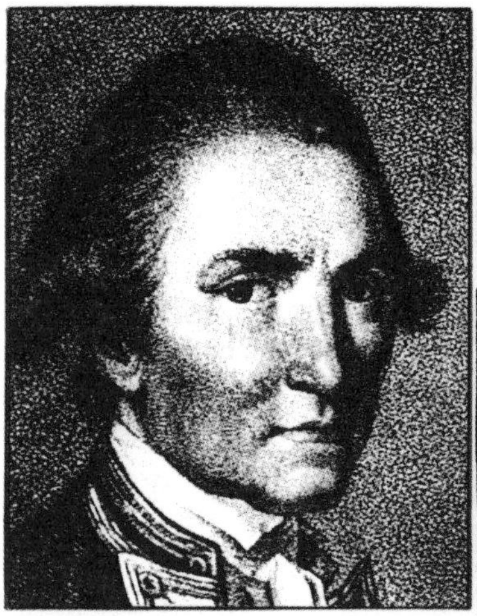

CAPTAIN JAMES COOK, R.N. (1728-1779) is famous for his voyages of discovery in 1768-71, 1772-75, and 1776-80, during which he charted much of the Pacific Ocean - from Alaska to the icy waters of the Antarctic. But few people know of Cook's second - but no less distinguished - career as a cartoonist.

BORN at Marton, Yorkshire, Cook was the son of a Scots-born farm-hand. By the age of 18 Cook was at sea, aboard a Whitby Collier *The Freelove*. At this time he began cartooning, producing a series of caricatures of real and imagined sailing types, later collected and published by Cook's widow in 1782 as *The FREELOVE FUNNIES*.

(*Above*) Cook in 1776, engraved after Webber.

IN 1755 Cook entered the British Navy. After distinguished service in the War with France in Quebec, and later in Newfoundland, he had, by 1767, gained a reputation as the best cartographer in the Navy. He had also begun featuring recurring characters in his cartoons, most notably the blunt and laconic *CAPTAIN BLOW* (a thinly disguised self-parody).

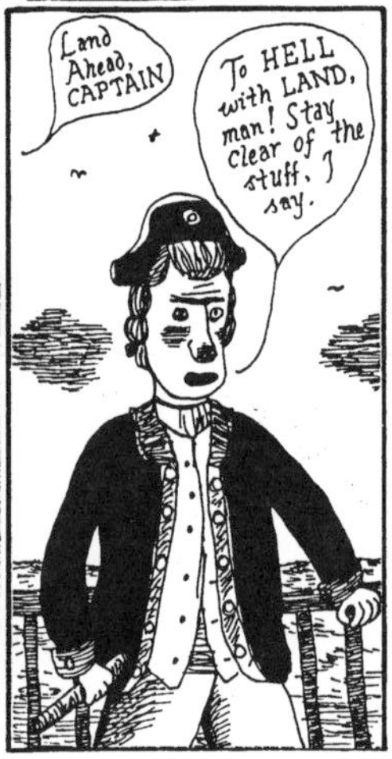
Land Ahead, CAPTAIN
To HELL with LAND, man! Stay clear of the stuff, I say.

(*Left*) A 'Captain Blow' cartoon drawn in 1763 in London soon after the birth of Cook's first son, James.

COOK'S cartoons during this period were published only very rarely - some accompanied his charts in the *NORTH AMERICAN PILOT* - but they proved popular with his crews (though not always with his superiors), a factor which aided him in later years in maintaining discipline during the long exploratory voyages.

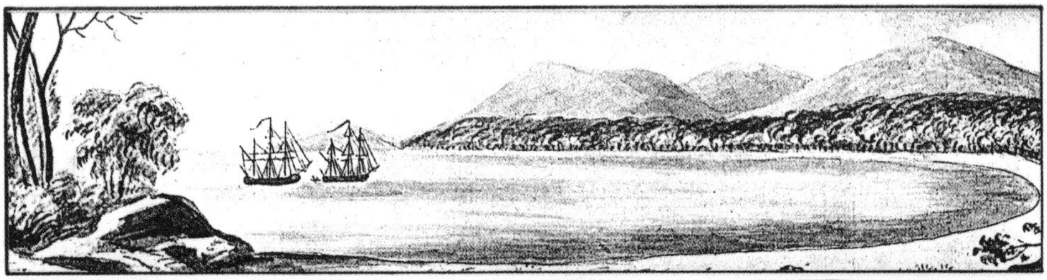

THE first of these voyages left England in 1768, and took Cook to Australia and New Zealand, which he charted with great accuracy, disproving the lingering myth of a huge Southern Continent. Cook fulfilled his mission with such success that the Navy quickly sent him on another; of the final decade of his life, barely two years were spent at home in England. These epic voyages did, however, provide Cook with a wealth of material for his cartoons: exotic landscapes, cultures and species, and - of course - the eccentricities of his ship-mates, particularly the natural historians and scientists who accompanied each voyage. One of these – Joseph Banks – became the unwitting model for the pompous '*DOCTOR BLATHER*', who features in a number of Cook's cartoons after 1768, and who may have partly inspired Thomas Rowlandson's *Doctor Syntax* character. A few of Cook's companions were persuaded by him to try cartooning themselves, notably the Swedish botanist Dr. Daniel Carl Solander, the painter William Hodges ( *Pictured Right* ), and Sydney Parkinson, the natural history draughtsman who died during the return leg of the first voyage, leaving a mere half dozen cartoons by which to judge a potential cruelly cut down by illness.

(*Below*) Dr. Blather, in a typical pose (1772).

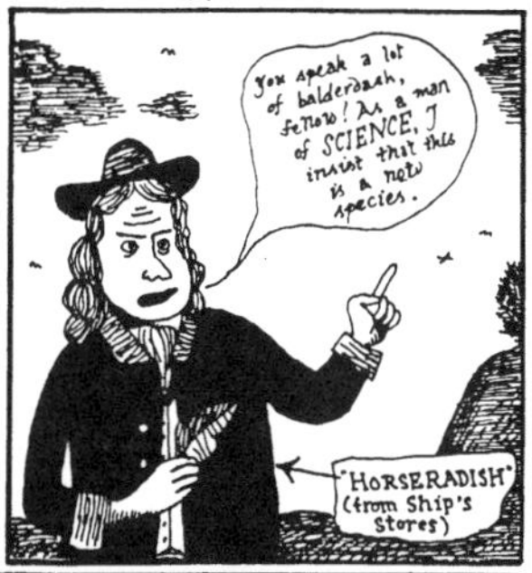
You speak a lot of balderdash, fellow! As a man of SCIENCE, I insist that this is a new species.
"HORSERADISH" (from Ship's Stores)

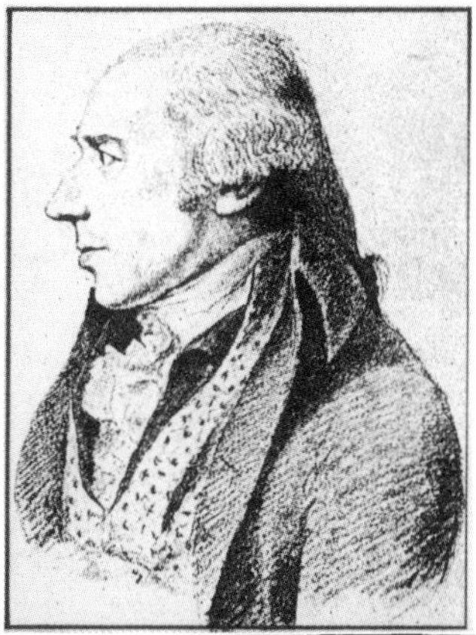

(*Below*) A cartoon by Sydney Parkinson, published in the first edition of *CAPTAIN COOK'S COMIC CUTS*.

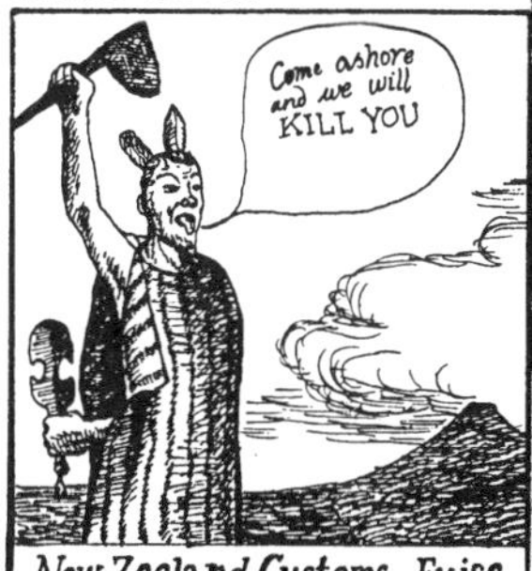
Come ashore and we will KILL YOU

New Zealand Customs Exise.

IT WAS during these long voyages that Cook first began illustrating his journals with long sequences of panels describing humorous events – both real and imaginary. Often these involved his growing cast of characters: *Captain Blow, Dr. Blather*, and two anthropomorphic characters *RABBIT* and *RAT*. By telling his stories with a series of pictures supported only by speech balloons, Cook invented the modern comic strip, decades before Rodolphe Töpffer's picture stories, and more than a century before American newspaper strips.

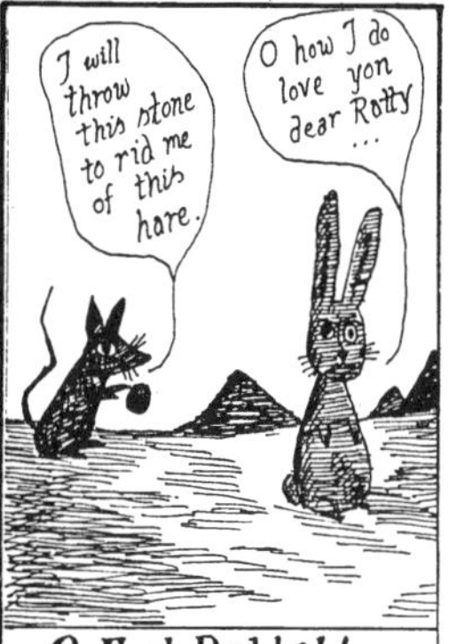
I will throw this stone to rid me of this hare.
O how I do love you dear Rotty ...

O Fool Rabbit!

(*Above*) Rabbit and Rat, circa 1771.

WHEN Cook returned to England after the 1768-1771 voyage, he issued an edition of drawings and maps under the title *CHARTS, PLANS, VIEWS and DRAWINGS* (*Pictured Right*). The 'drawings' included a number of cartoons, which – to Cook's surprise – proved rather popular; sufficiently so that he was persuaded by Banks to publish a further collection, containing only cartoons by Cook and his fellow explorers. And so *CAPTAIN COOK'S COMIC CUTS* was born – an irregular collection of cartoons and strips which never gained the wide readership enjoyed by the satirical sheets of the nineteenth century, but which had an enormous influence on cartoonists of the late eighteenth and early nineteenth centuries, proving to be well ahead of its time, and introducing innovations not popularised until more than a hundred years later.

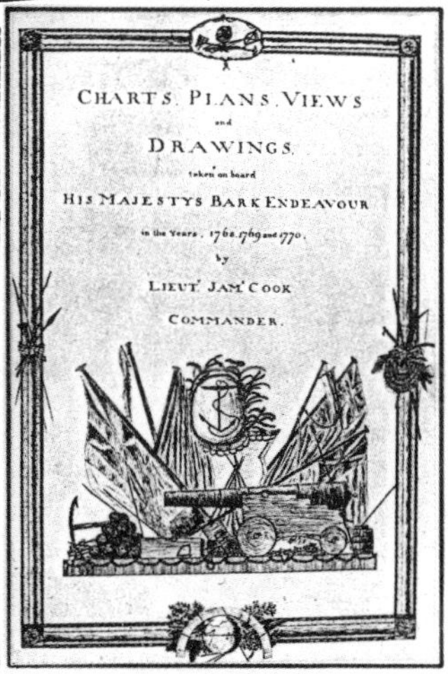
CHARTS, PLANS, VIEWS
and
DRAWINGS,
taken on board
HIS MAJESTYS BARK ENDEAVOUR
in the Years, 1768, 1769 and 1770,
by
LIEUT. JAM. COOK
COMMANDER.

IN all, only six editions of *CAPTAIN COOK'S COMIC CUTS* were published over the following nine years, their erratic schedule determined by Cook's long absences from England. Their unusual format and price (8 to 24-page booklets, sold for between 12 shillings and a guinea plain, and even more coloured) were enough to prohibit a larger audience and subsequently to ensure that few copies have survived to our day. But the inventiveness of their contents had a significant impact on the handful of early cartoonists who saw them, including Thomas Rowlandson (1757-1827) and James Gillray (1757-1815), and helped to inspire the fashion for 'strips' between 1784 and 1794. Cook was never a skilled draughtsman, but throughout the 1770's it was his innovative pamphlets which set the pace.

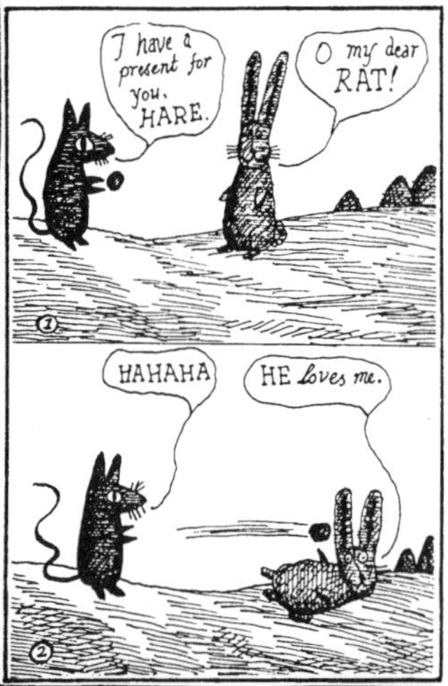
I have a present for you, HARE.
O my dear RAT!
HAHAHA
HE loves me.

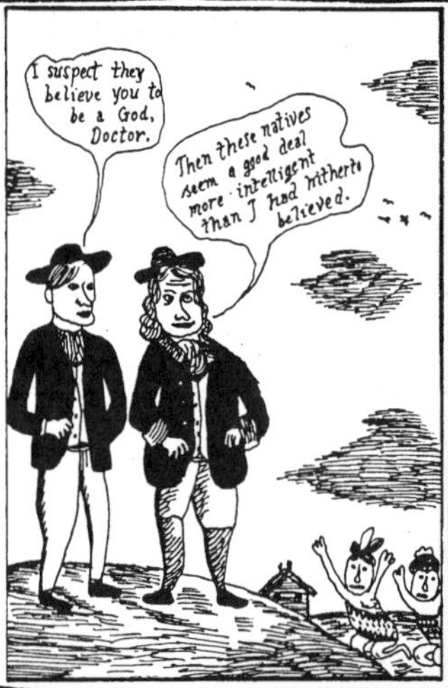
I suspect they believe you to be a God, Doctor.
Then these natives seem a good deal more intelligent than I had hitherto believed.

AFTER Cook was killed in Hawaii in 1779, Hodges prepared a final edition of the *COMIC CUTS*, consisting of work drawn by Cook during his final voyage, and also cartoons and written tributes to the man who had redefined the cartoon by Solander, Banks, Hodges, and the young Thomas Rowlandson, who wrote:

> "Cook was a man unafraid to face the boundaries of our knowledge and then to assault them, with all the fearlessness and invention that the English soul has ever possessed. And in so doing, he was ever charting new territory - whether the richly soil'd lands he explored across the sea, or the richer territory of the mind and of the spirit: the world of that endeavour, that Art, which he made his own."

AND Samuel Johnson (so his faithful biographer records) resolved the two sides of James Cook thus:

> "Garrick here has been saying how curious it seems that the same refined sensibility which produces those scandalously witty Rabbit cartoons could in the next instant order a man flogged for not eating enough sauerkraut. On the contrary, I for one can imagine nothing more in keeping with the sensibility of a satirist. Cook sees quite rightly that there is no use in treading delicately over so grave a matter as sauerkraut."

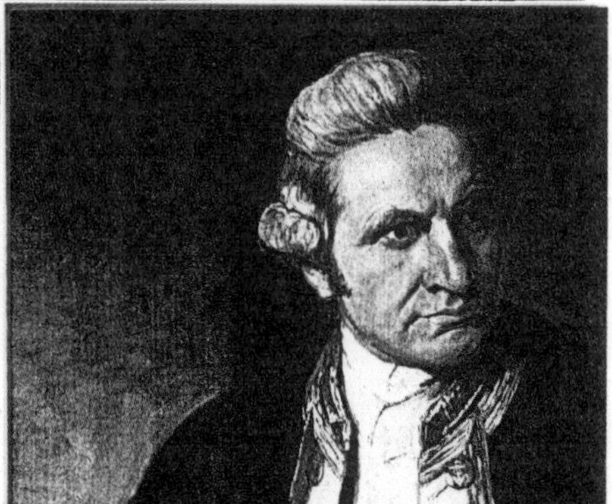

*Dylan Horrocks is currently compiling a collection of work by little-known innovative cartoonists, including Cook, Katherine Mansfield, and Julius Vogel.*

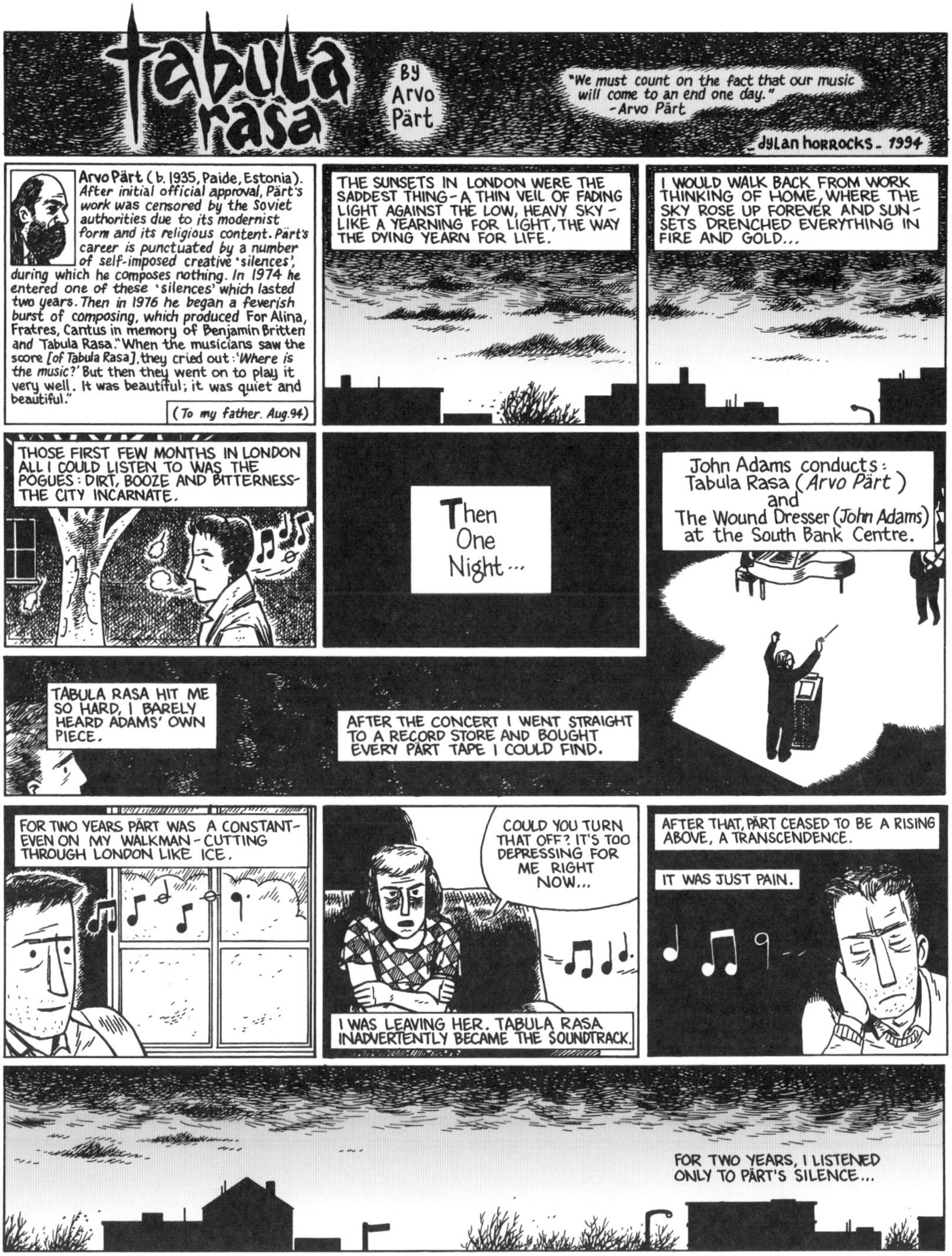

Tabula Rasa
By Arvo Pärt
"We must count on the fact that our music will come to an end one day." -Arvo Pärt
dylan horrocks - 1994
Arvo Pärt (b. 1935, Paide, Estonia). After initial official approval, Pärt's work was censored by the Soviet authorities due to its modernist form and its religious content. Pärt's career is punctuated by a number of self-imposed creative 'silences', during which he composes nothing. In 1974 he entered one of these 'silences' which lasted two years. Then in 1976 he began a feverish burst of composing, which produced For Alina, Fratres, Cantus in memory of Benjamin Britten and Tabula Rasa." When the musicians saw the score [of Tabula Rasa], they cried out: 'Where is the music?' But then they went on to play it very well. It was beautiful; it was quiet and beautiful."
(To my father. Aug.94)
THE SUNSETS IN LONDON WERE THE SADDEST THING - A THIN VEIL OF FADING LIGHT AGAINST THE LOW, HEAVY SKY - LIKE A YEARNING FOR LIGHT, THE WAY THE DYING YEARN FOR LIFE.
I WOULD WALK BACK FROM WORK THINKING OF HOME, WHERE THE SKY ROSE UP FOREVER AND SUNSETS DRENCHED EVERYTHING IN FIRE AND GOLD...
THOSE FIRST FEW MONTHS IN LONDON ALL I COULD LISTEN TO WAS THE POGUES: DIRT, BOOZE AND BITTERNESS - THE CITY INCARNATE.
Then One Night...
John Adams conducts: Tabula Rasa (Arvo Pärt) and The Wound Dresser (John Adams) at the South Bank Centre.
TABULA RASA HIT ME SO HARD, I BARELY HEARD ADAMS' OWN PIECE.
AFTER THE CONCERT I WENT STRAIGHT TO A RECORD STORE AND BOUGHT EVERY PÄRT TAPE I COULD FIND.
FOR TWO YEARS PÄRT WAS A CONSTANT - EVEN ON MY WALKMAN - CUTTING THROUGH LONDON LIKE ICE.
COULD YOU TURN THAT OFF? IT'S TOO DEPRESSING FOR ME RIGHT NOW...
I WAS LEAVING HER. TABULA RASA INADVERTENTLY BECAME THE SOUNDTRACK.
AFTER THAT, PÄRT CEASED TO BE A RISING ABOVE, A TRANSCENDENCE.
IT WAS JUST PAIN.
FOR TWO YEARS, I LISTENED ONLY TO PÄRT'S SILENCE...

# the State of THINGS – with Snowy And Soo!

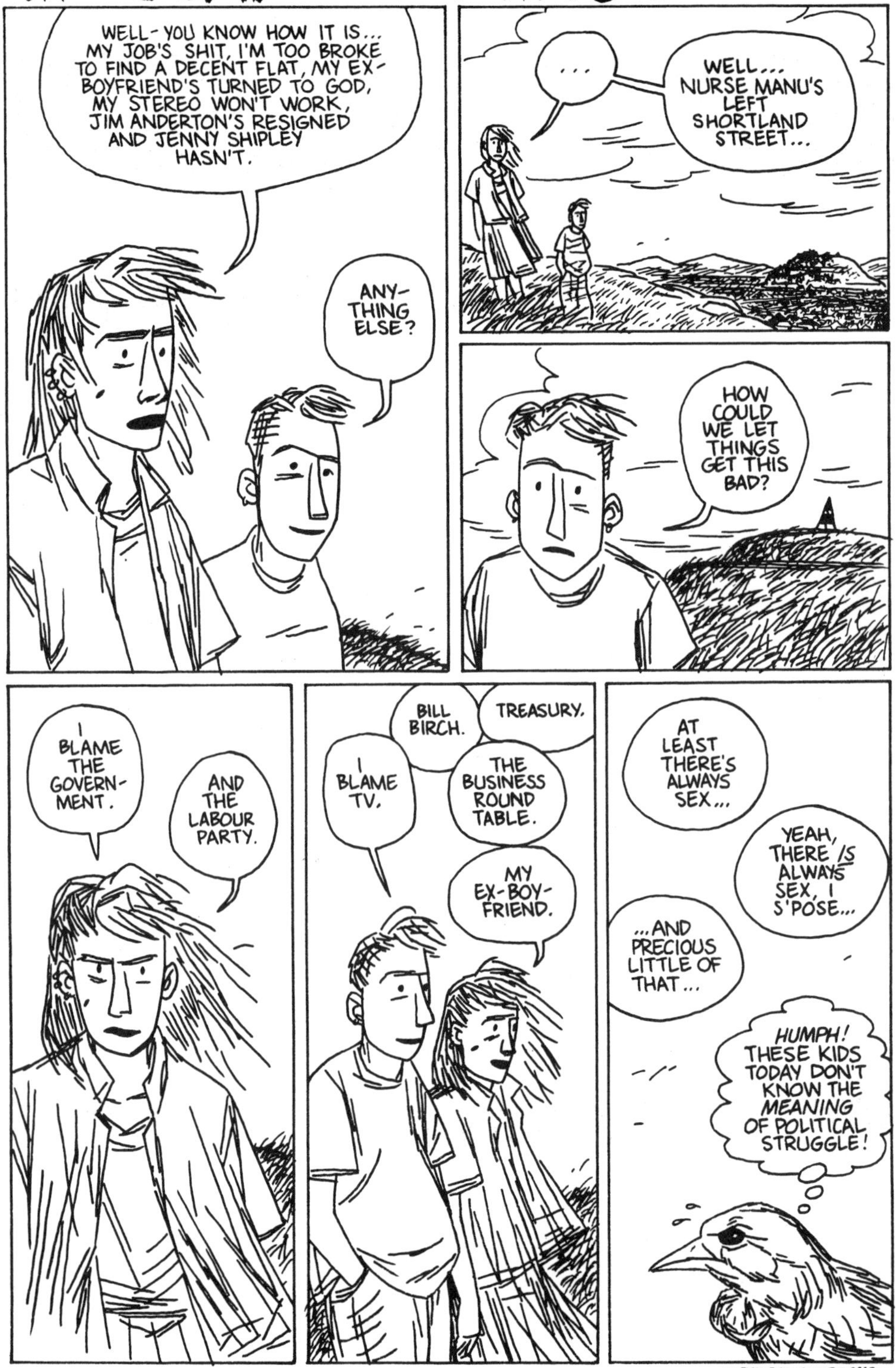

WELL- YOU KNOW HOW IT IS... MY JOB'S SHIT, I'M TOO BROKE TO FIND A DECENT FLAT, MY EX-BOYFRIEND'S TURNED TO GOD, MY STEREO WON'T WORK, JIM ANDERTON'S RESIGNED AND JENNY SHIPLEY HASN'T.
ANY-THING ELSE?
...
WELL... NURSE MANU'S LEFT SHORTLAND STREET...
HOW COULD WE LET THINGS GET THIS BAD?
I BLAME THE GOVERN-MENT.
AND THE LABOUR PARTY.
I BLAME TV.
BILL BIRCH.
TREASURY.
THE BUSINESS ROUND TABLE.
MY EX-BOY-FRIEND.
AT LEAST THERE'S ALWAYS SEX...
YEAH, THERE IS ALWAYS SEX, I S'POSE...
...AND PRECIOUS LITTLE OF THAT...
HUMPH! THESE KIDS TODAY DON'T KNOW THE MEANING OF POLITICAL STRUGGLE!


~DYLAN HORROCKS~

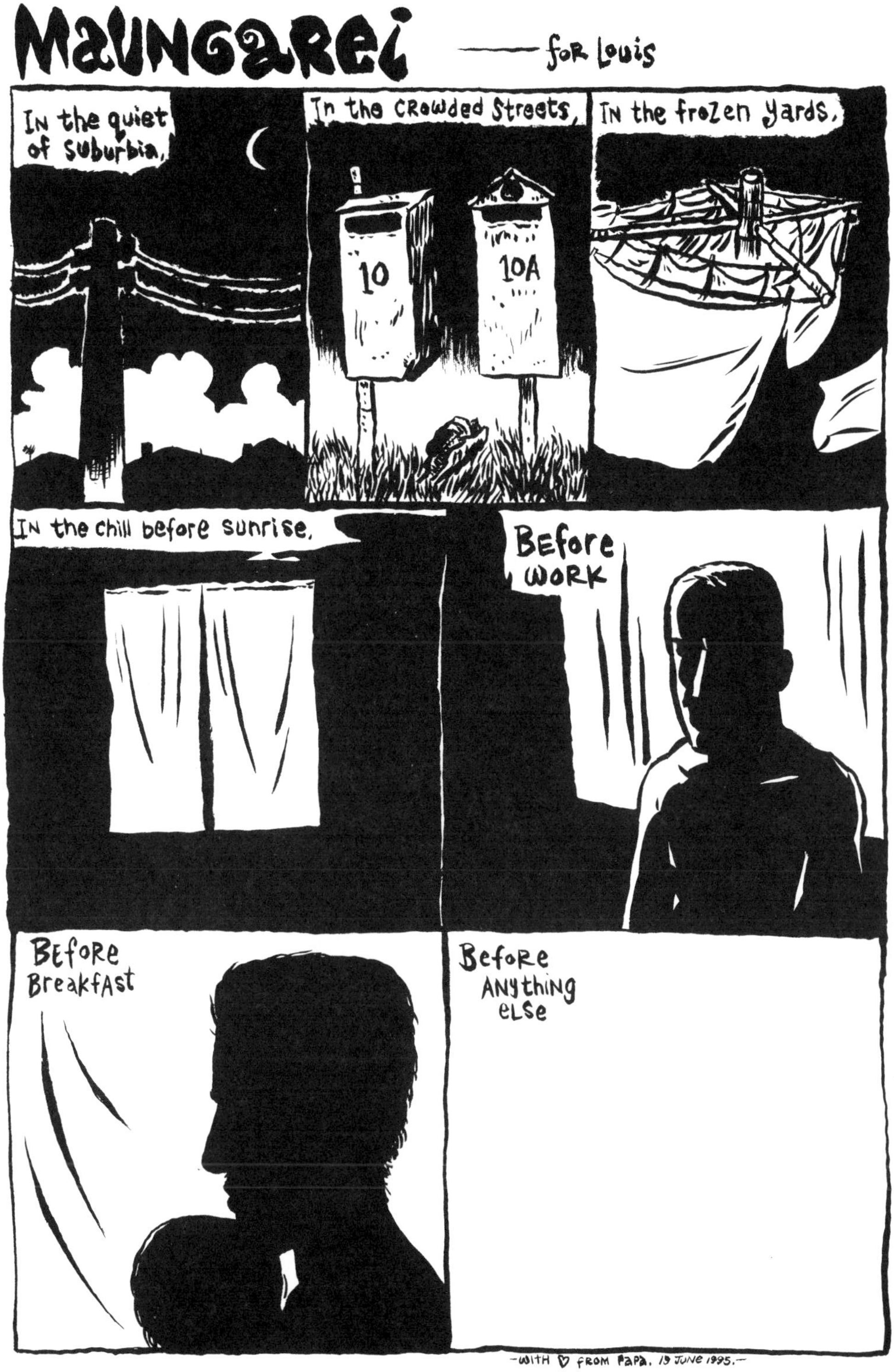
Maungarei
—— for Louis
In the quiet of suburbia,
In the crowded streets,
10
10A
In the frozen yards,
In the chill before sunrise,
Before work
Before Breakfast
Before anything else
—with ♡ from Papa. 19 June 1995.—

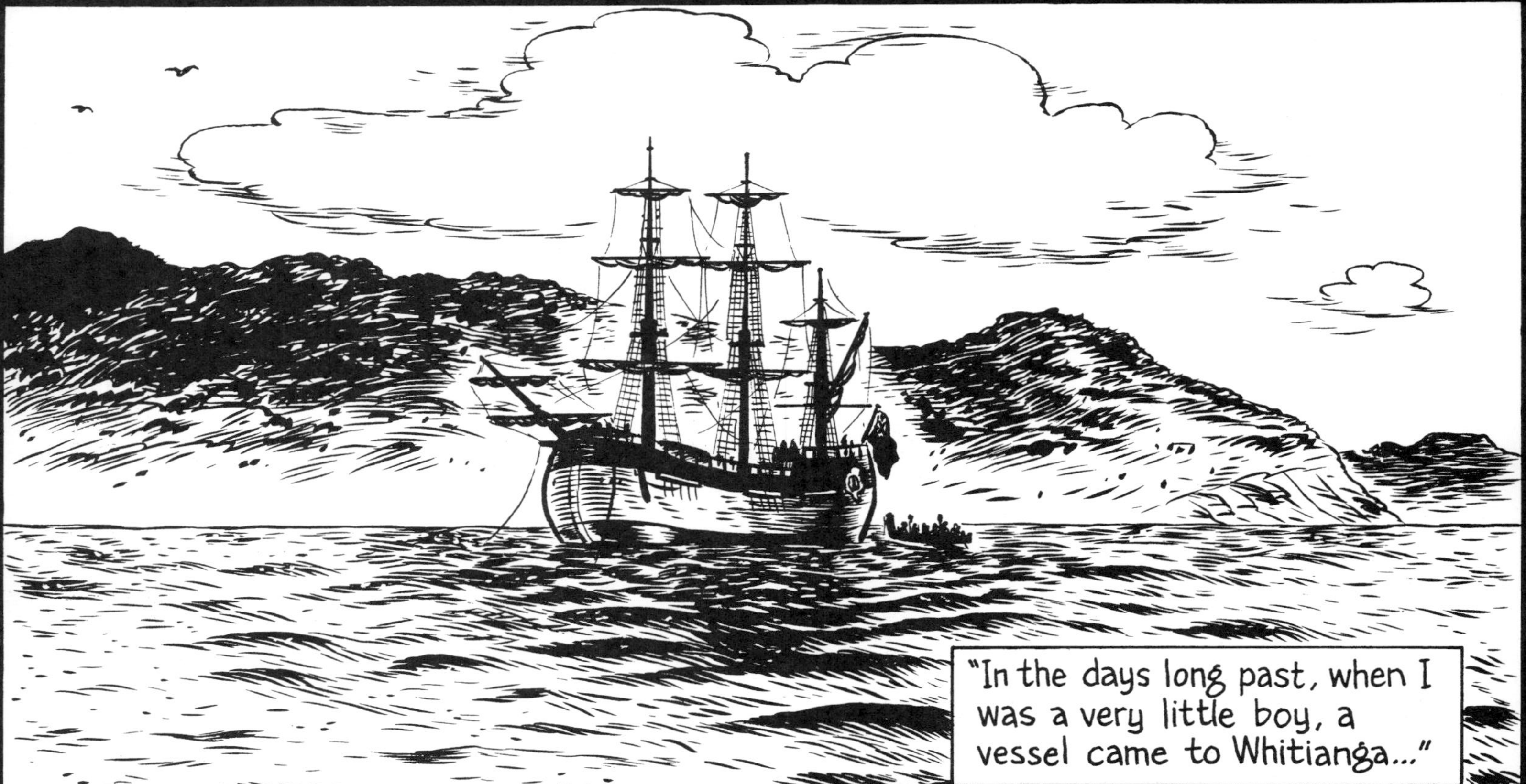
"In the days long past, when I was a very little boy, a vessel came to Whitianga..."

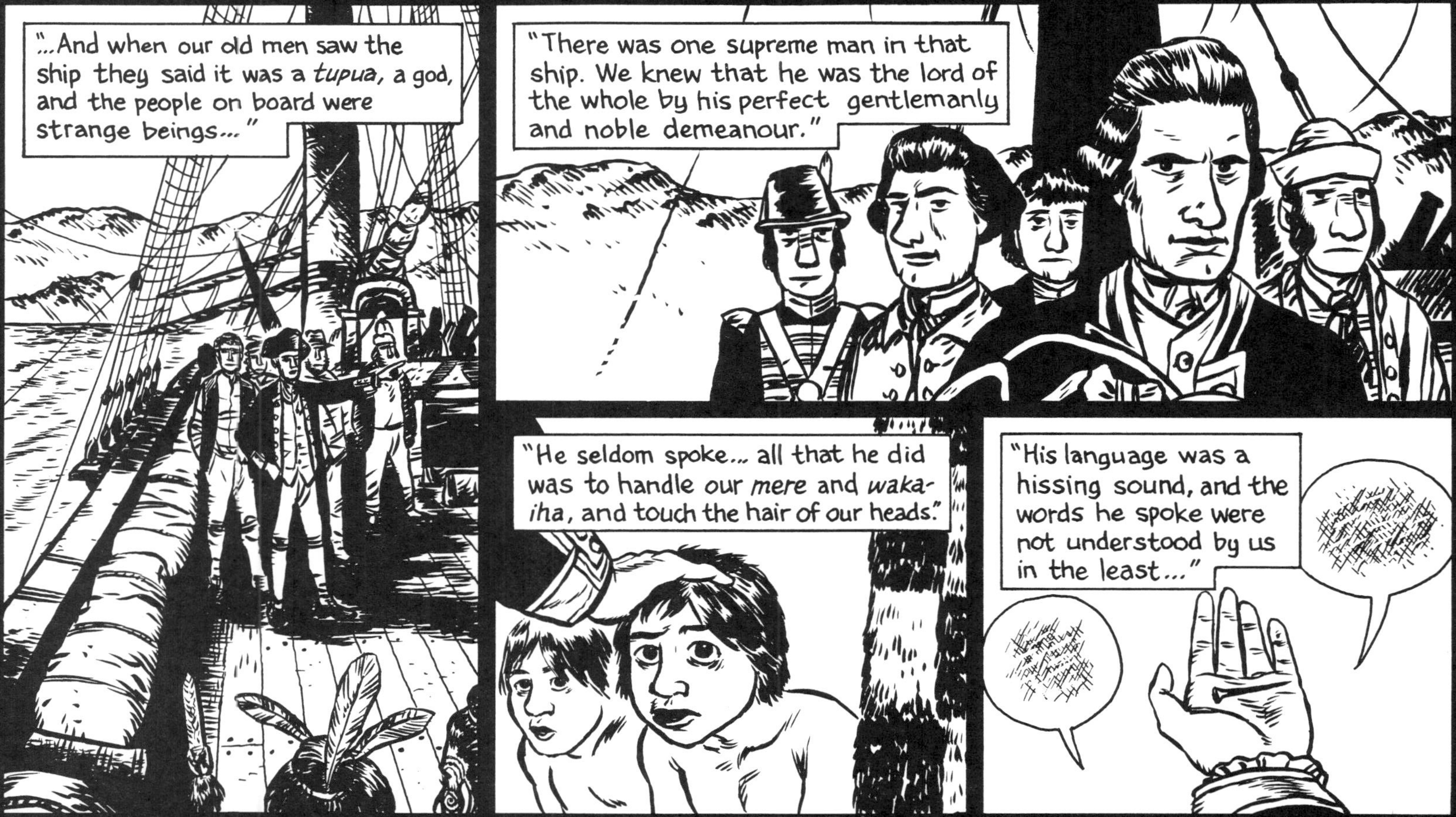
"...And when our old men saw the ship they said it was a *tupua*, a god, and the people on board were strange beings..."
"There was one supreme man in that ship. We knew that he was the lord of the whole by his perfect gentlemanly and noble demeanour."
"He seldom spoke... all that he did was to handle our *mere* and *waka-iha*, and touch the hair of our heads."
"His language was a hissing sound, and the words he spoke were not understood by us in the least..."

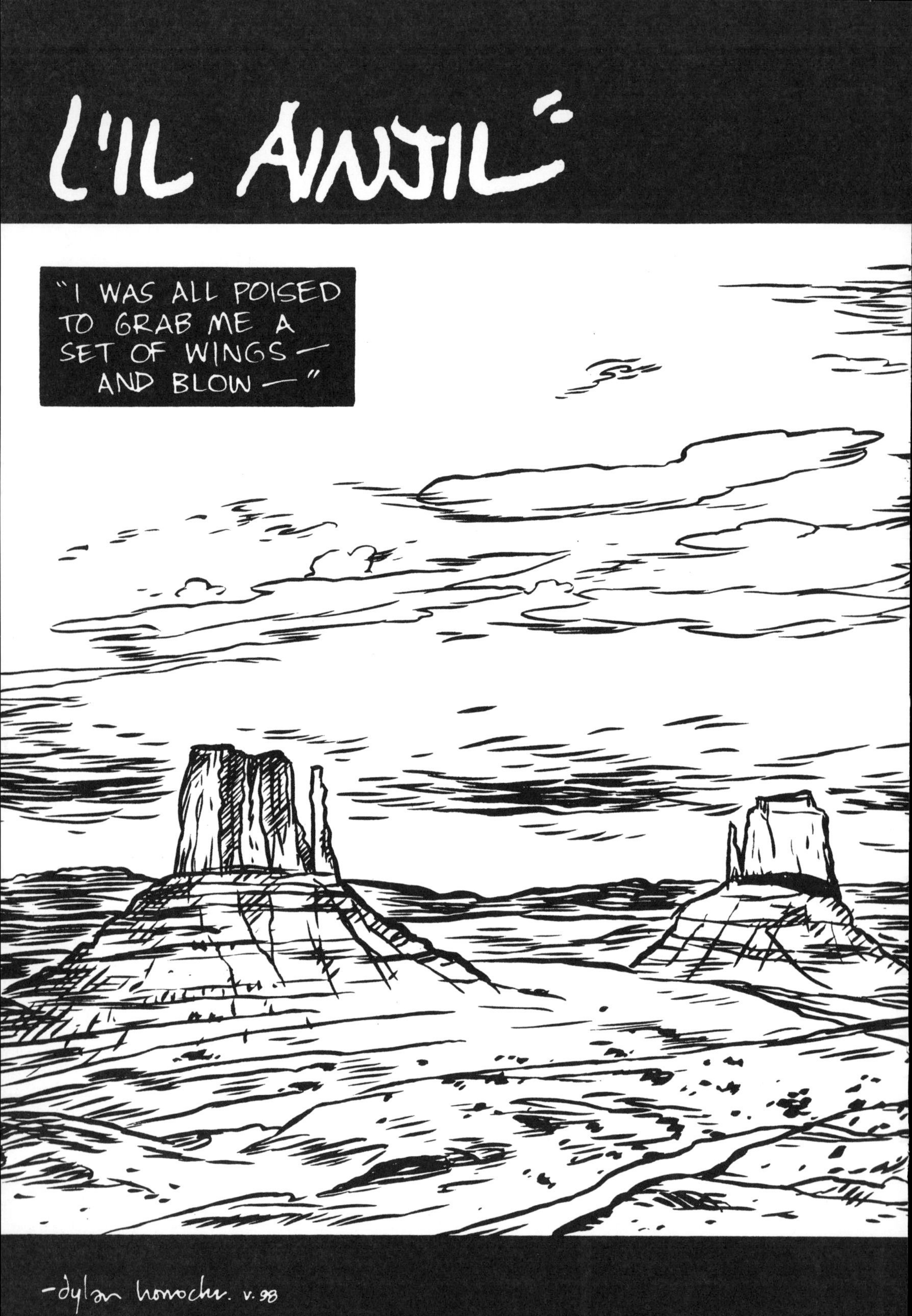

L'IL ANJIL
"I WAS ALL POISED TO GRAB ME A SET OF WINGS — AND BLOW —"
-dylan horrocks. v.98

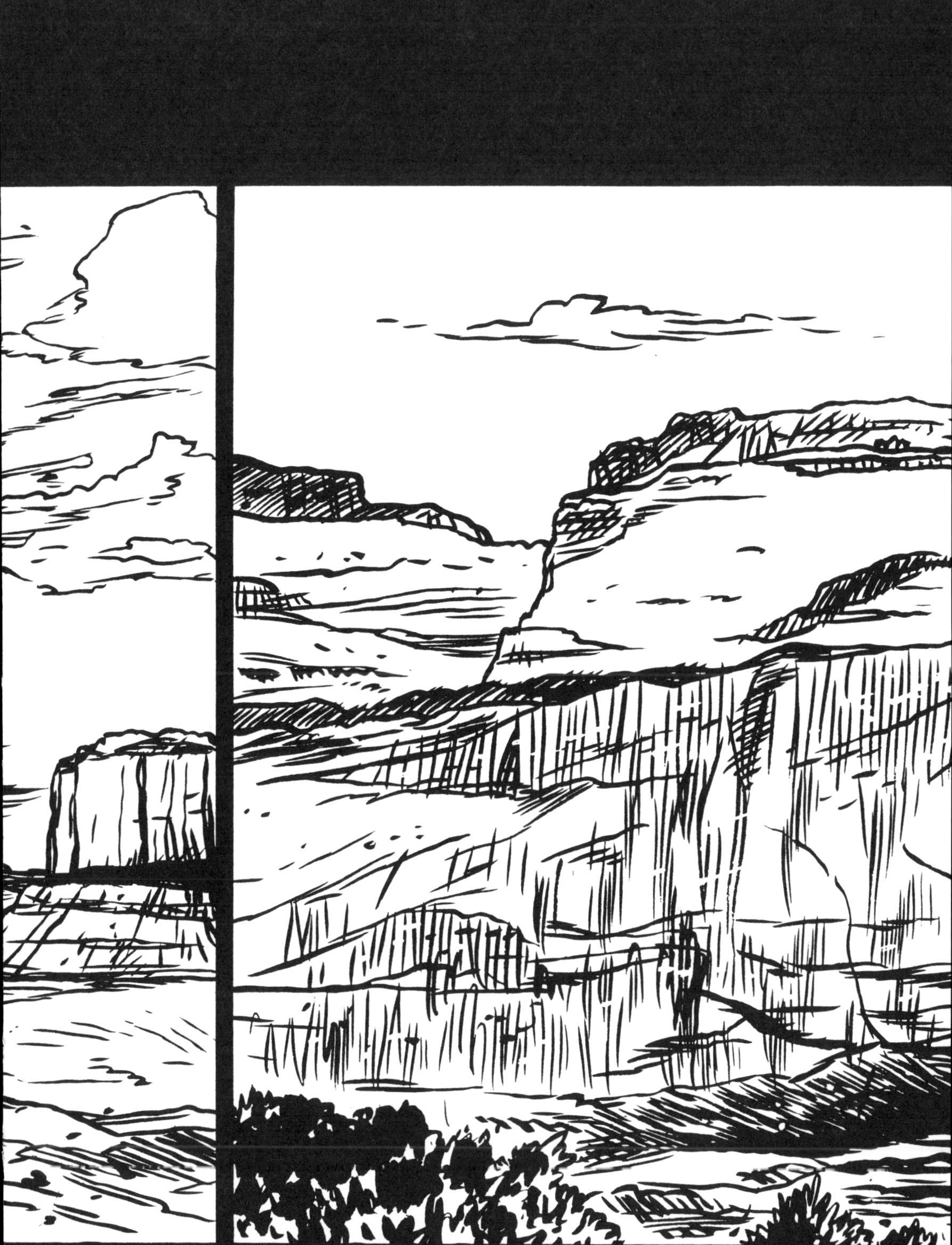

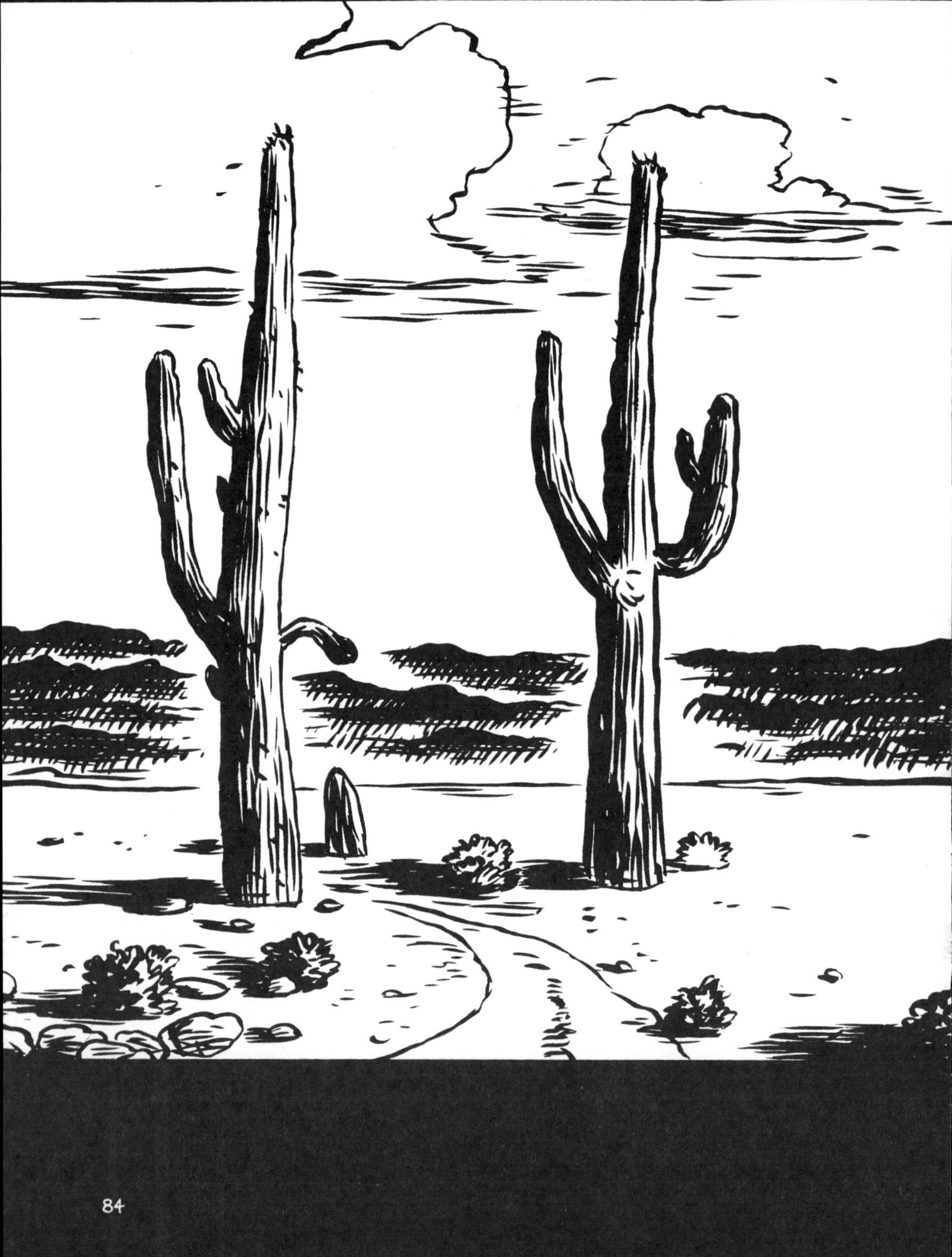

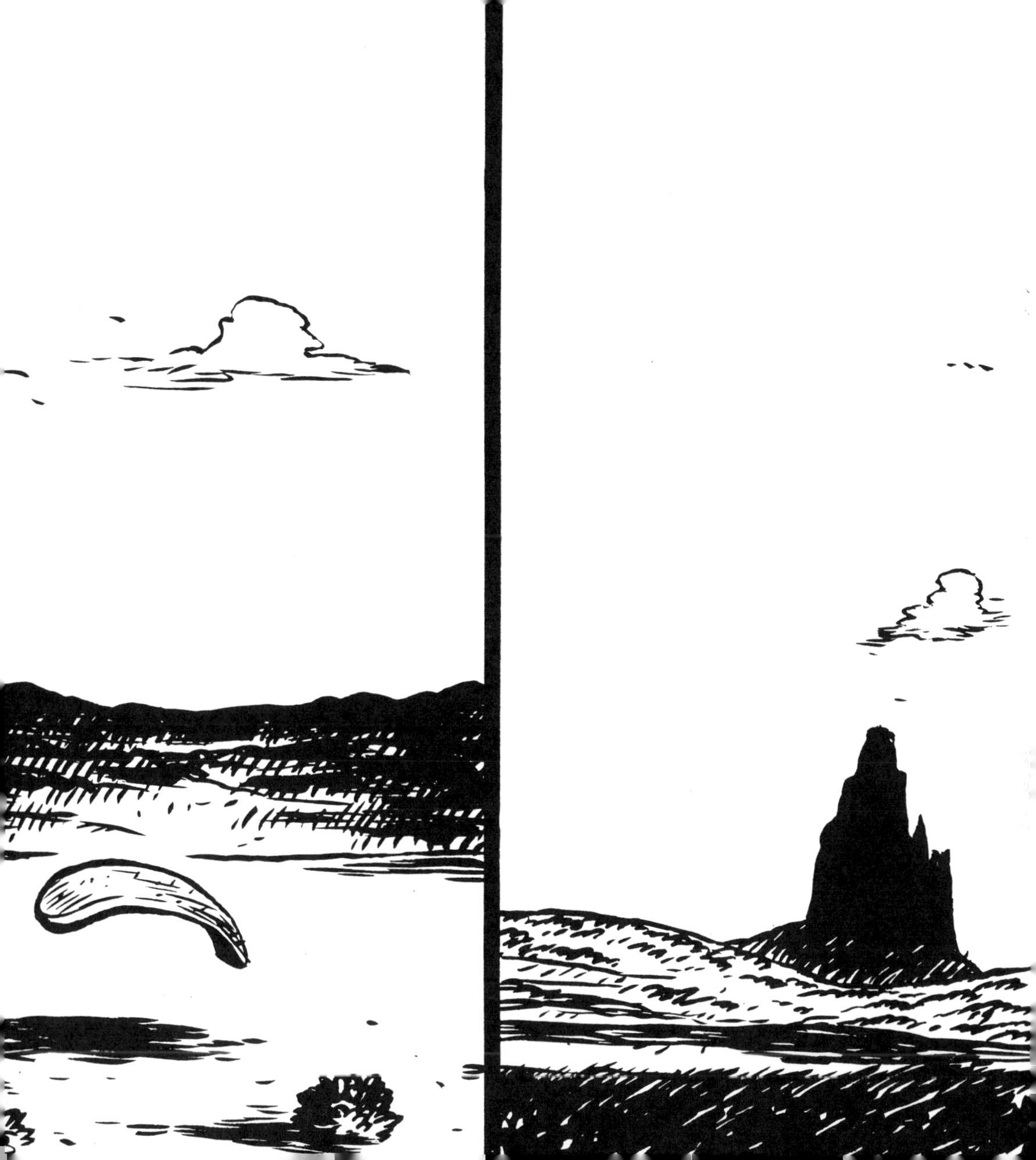

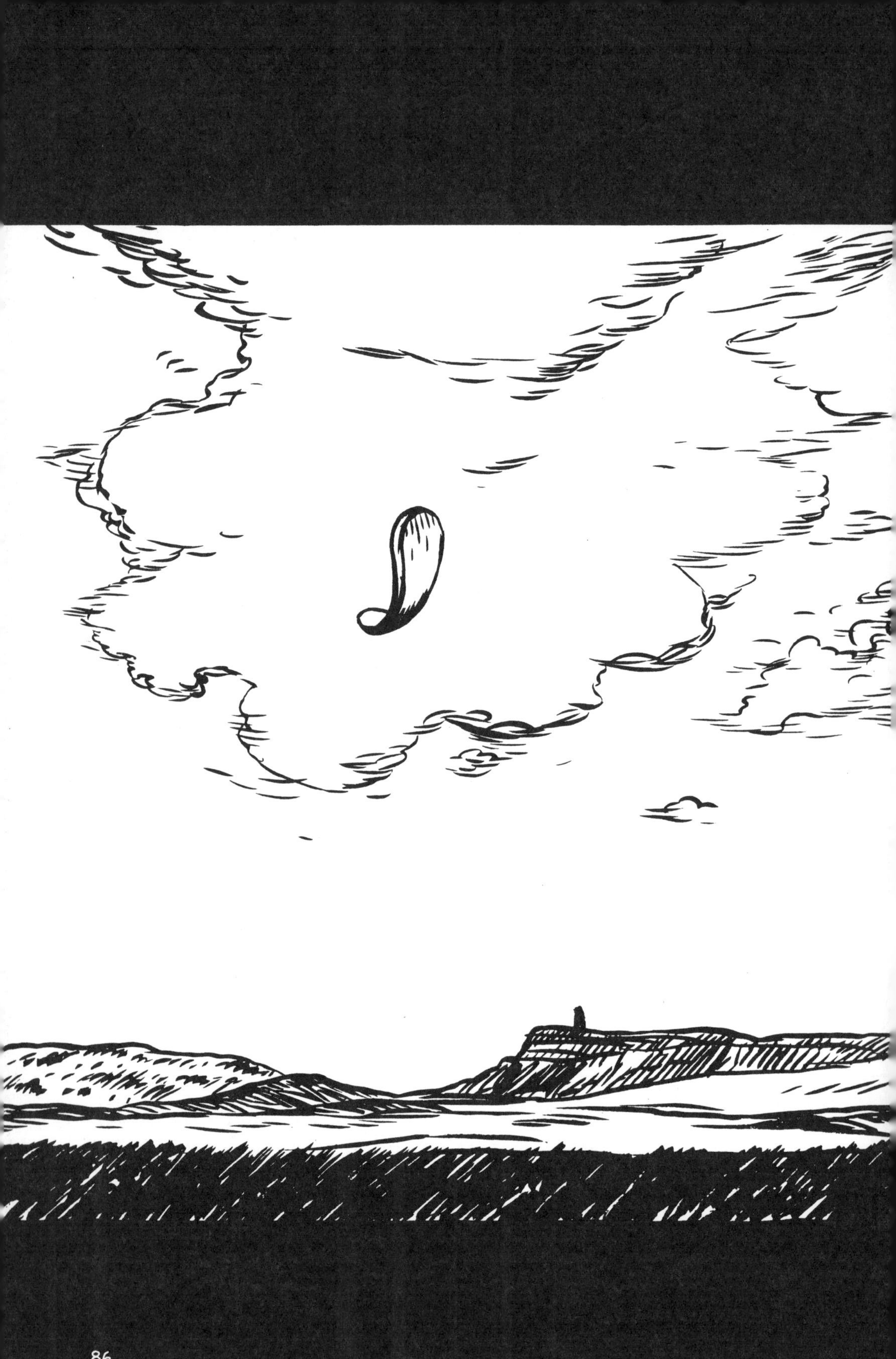

'Gilbert Seldes recalled that Herriman wanted to end his life in Monument Valley, "lying down on a cactus leaf until he was shrivelled up and blown away by the wind ....",'

**Pickle Comics** #1, c.1945 (artist unkown; probably Dylan Horrocks). *Courtesy of the Tim Bollinger collection.*

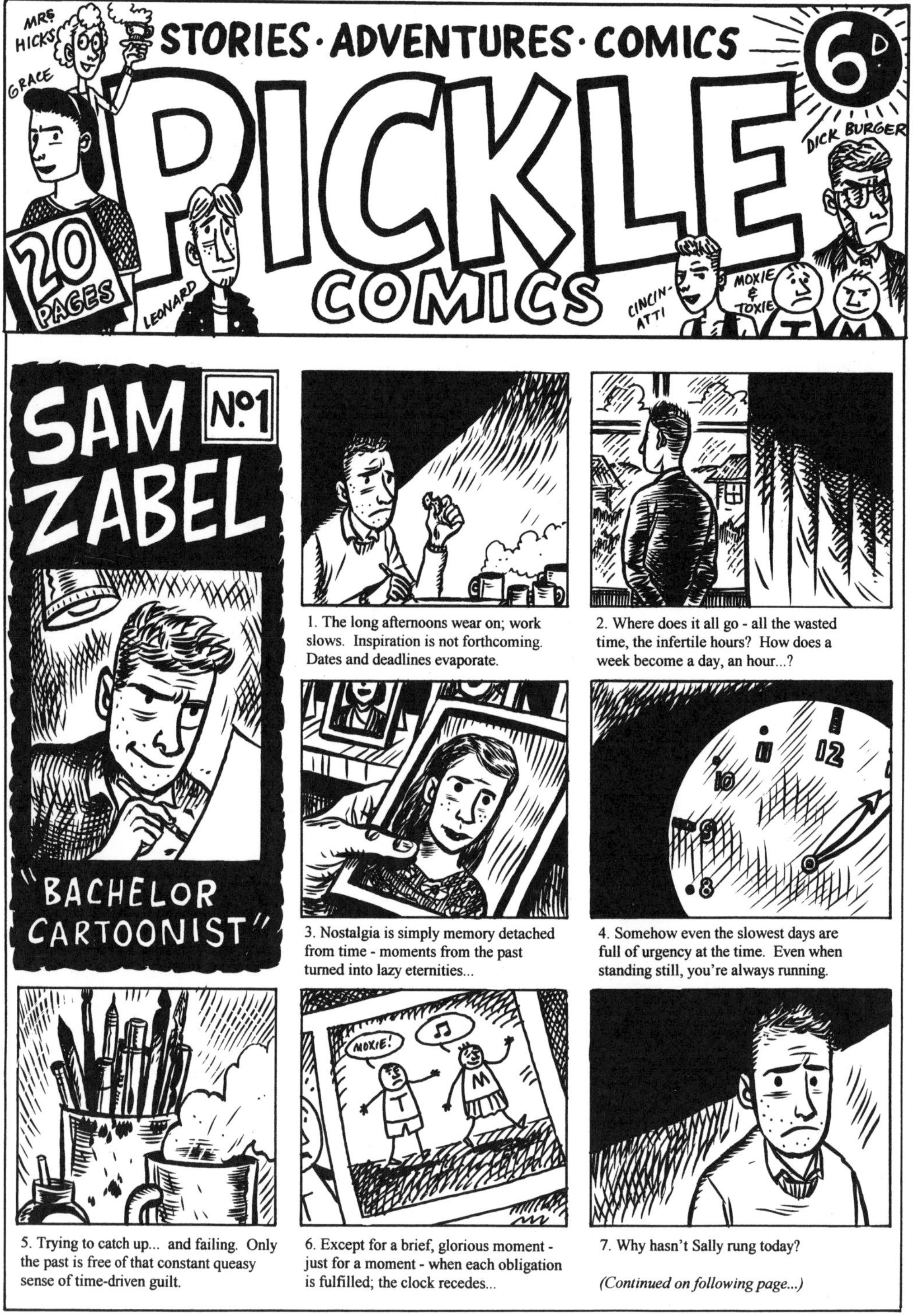
STORIES · ADVENTURES · COMICS
6D
PICKLE
COMICS
MRS HICKS
GRACE
20 PAGES
LEONARD
DICK BURGER
CINCIN-ATTI
MOXIE & TOXIE
SAM ZABEL
No. 1
"BACHELOR CARTOONIST"
1. The long afternoons wear on; work slows. Inspiration is not forthcoming. Dates and deadlines evaporate.
2. Where does it all go - all the wasted time, the infertile hours? How does a week become a day, an hour...?
3. Nostalgia is simply memory detached from time - moments from the past turned into lazy eternities...
4. Somehow even the slowest days are full of urgency at the time. Even when standing still, you're always running.
5. Trying to catch up... and failing. Only the past is free of that constant queasy sense of time-driven guilt.
MOXIE!
6. Except for a brief, glorious moment - just for a moment - when each obligation is fulfilled; the clock recedes...
7. Why hasn't Sally rung today?
(Continued on following page...)

# If I Were a POP STAR

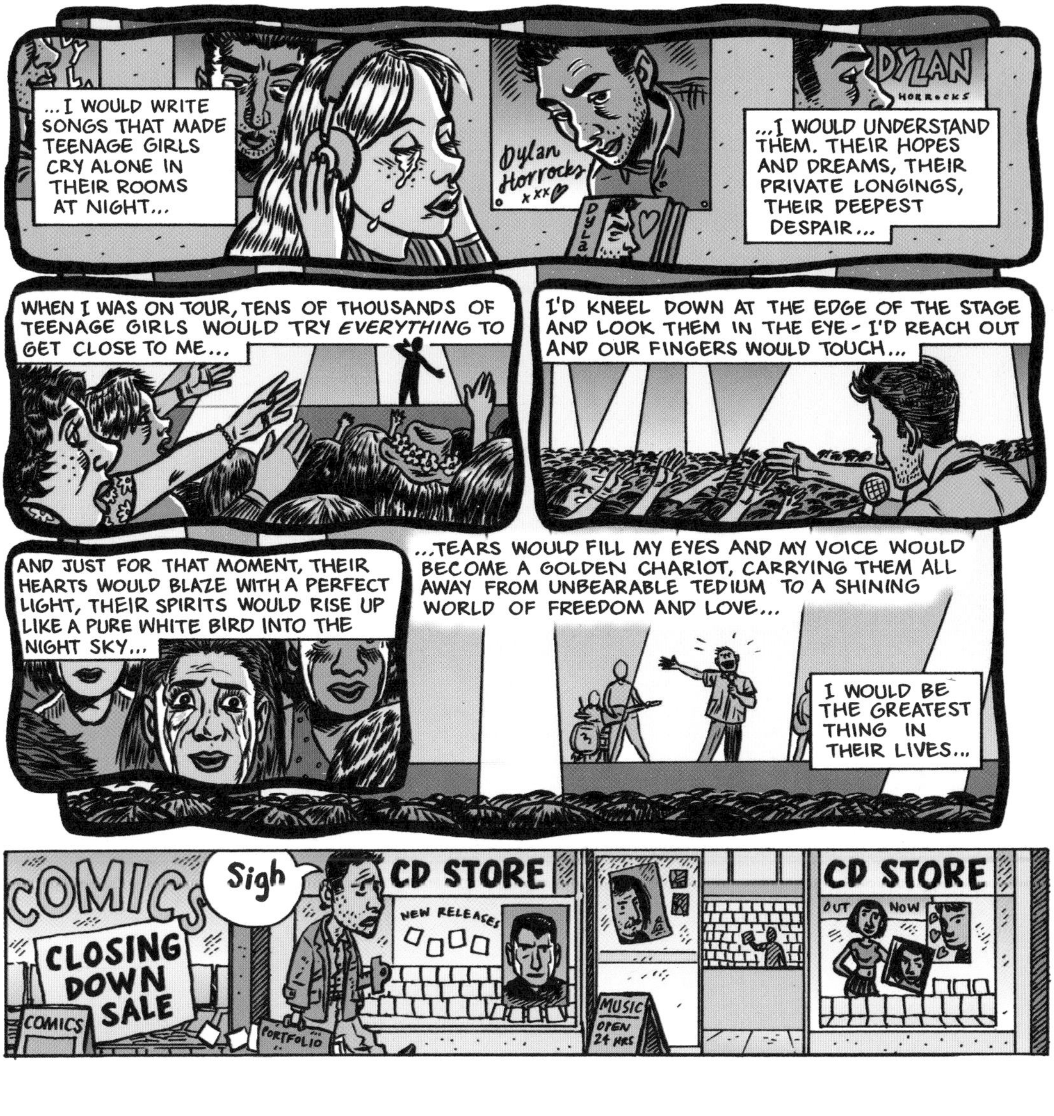

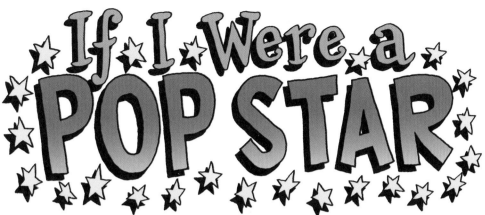

DYLAN
HORROCKS
...I WOULD WRITE SONGS THAT MADE TEENAGE GIRLS CRY ALONE IN THEIR ROOMS AT NIGHT...
Dylan Horrocks xxx
...I WOULD UNDERSTAND THEM. THEIR HOPES AND DREAMS, THEIR PRIVATE LONGINGS, THEIR DEEPEST DESPAIR...
WHEN I WAS ON TOUR, TENS OF THOUSANDS OF TEENAGE GIRLS WOULD TRY *EVERYTHING* TO GET CLOSE TO ME...
I'D KNEEL DOWN AT THE EDGE OF THE STAGE AND LOOK THEM IN THE EYE - I'D REACH OUT AND OUR FINGERS WOULD TOUCH...
AND JUST FOR THAT MOMENT, THEIR HEARTS WOULD BLAZE WITH A PERFECT LIGHT, THEIR SPIRITS WOULD RISE UP LIKE A PURE WHITE BIRD INTO THE NIGHT SKY...
...TEARS WOULD FILL MY EYES AND MY VOICE WOULD BECOME A GOLDEN CHARIOT, CARRYING THEM ALL AWAY FROM UNBEARABLE TEDIUM TO A SHINING WORLD OF FREEDOM AND LOVE...
I WOULD BE THE GREATEST THING IN THEIR LIVES...
COMICS
Sigh
CLOSING DOWN SALE
COMICS
PORTFOLIO
CD STORE
NEW RELEASES
MUSIC
OPEN 24 HRS
CD STORE
OUT NOW

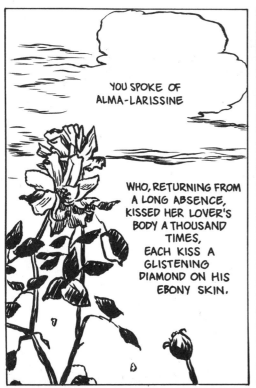

YOU SPOKE OF
ALMA-LARISSINE

WHO, RETURNING FROM
A LONG ABSENCE,
KISSED HER LOVER'S
BODY A THOUSAND
TIMES,
EACH KISS A
GLISTENING
DIAMOND ON HIS
EBONY SKIN.

YOU SPOKE OF ERIANU
WHO SHOWERED HIS LOVE WITH PETALS
WHICH, WHEN CRUSHED BETWEEN THEIR
    BODIES          AND THE BED,
GAVE OFF A SCENT NOW CALLED
'THE LOVE OF ERIANU'.

IT FILLS THE AIR
  ROUND TIERA
JUST BEFORE DAWN,

LOVERS GATHER THE DEW
  IN TINY BOTTLES.

IT IS OFTEN GIVEN
  NEVER SOLD.

THEN YOU SPOKE OF NOTHING

*NOTHING OF WORDS*
*NOTHING OF SOUND*

To MATTHEW & SHELLEY
13 MAY 1997
LOVE

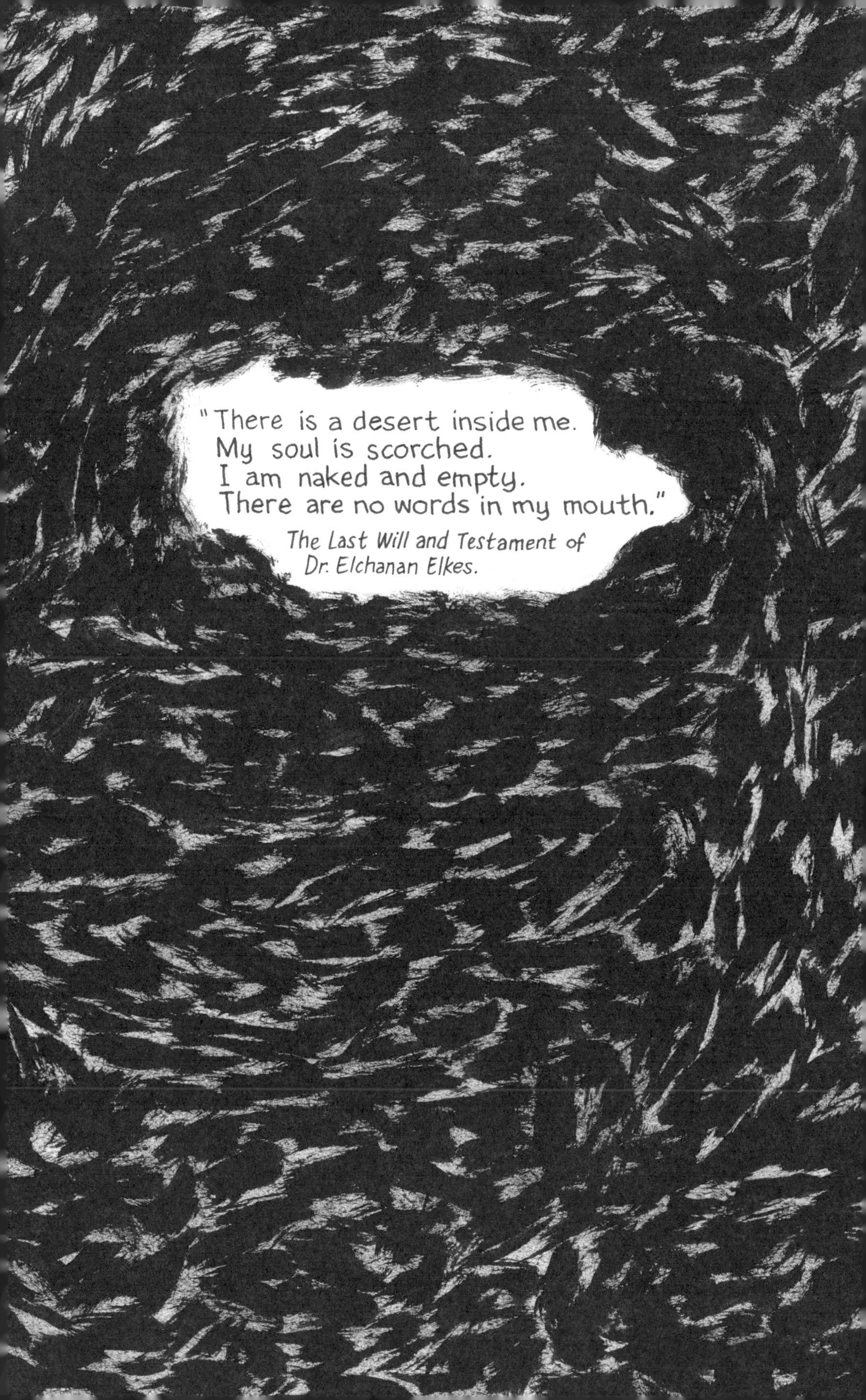
"There is a desert inside me.
My soul is scorched.
I am naked and empty.
There are no words in my mouth."
The Last Will and Testament of
Dr. Elchanan Elkes.

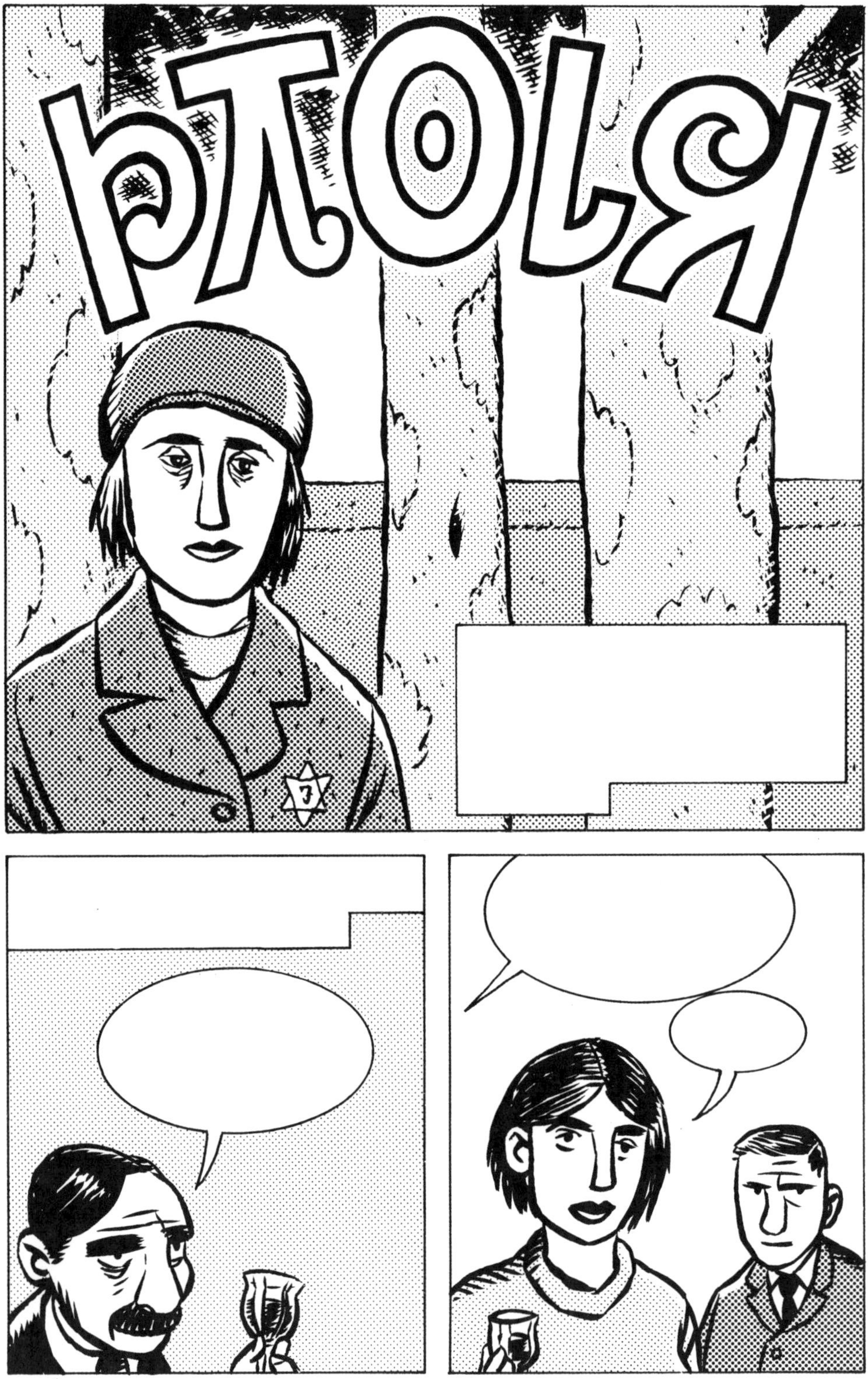

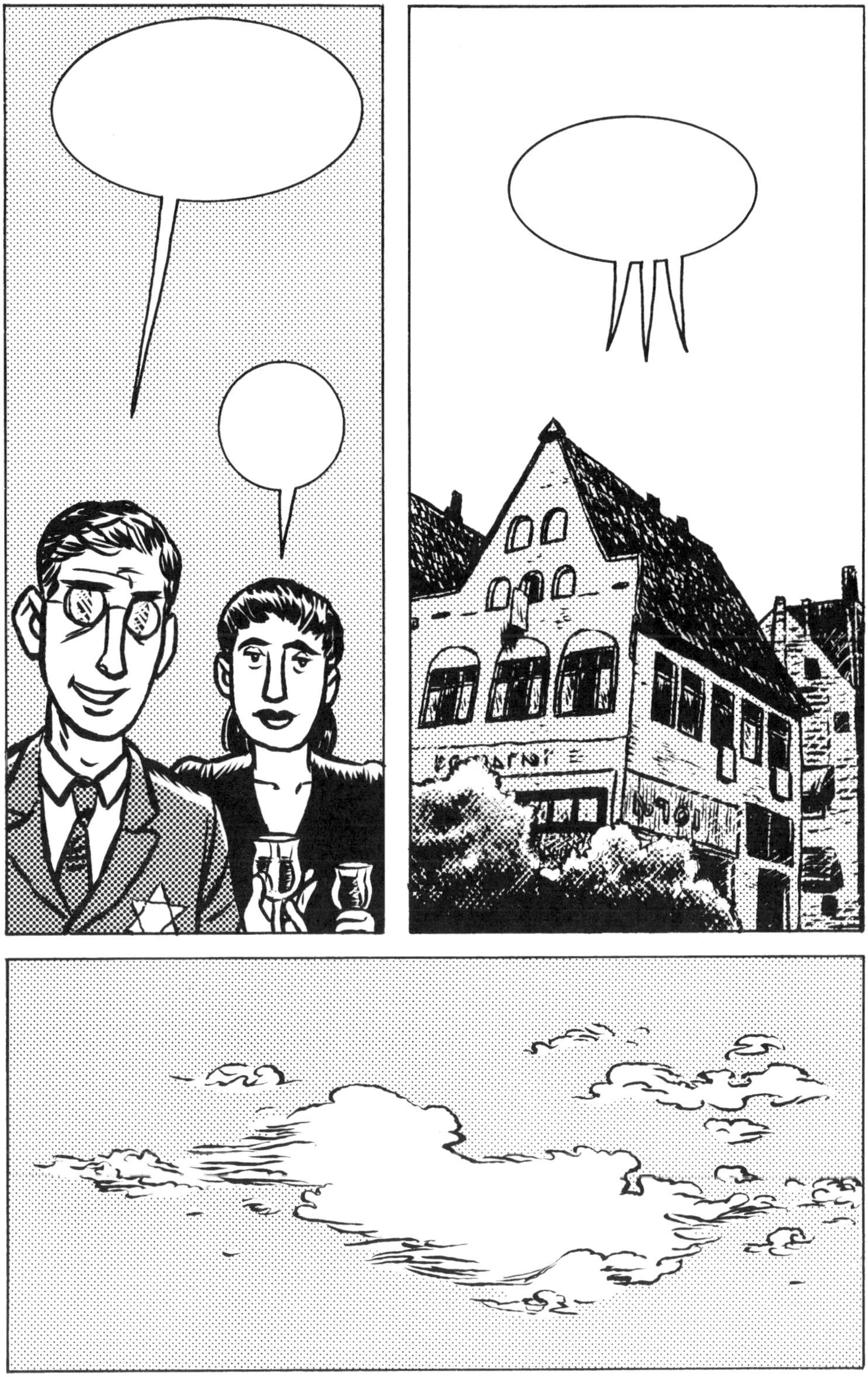

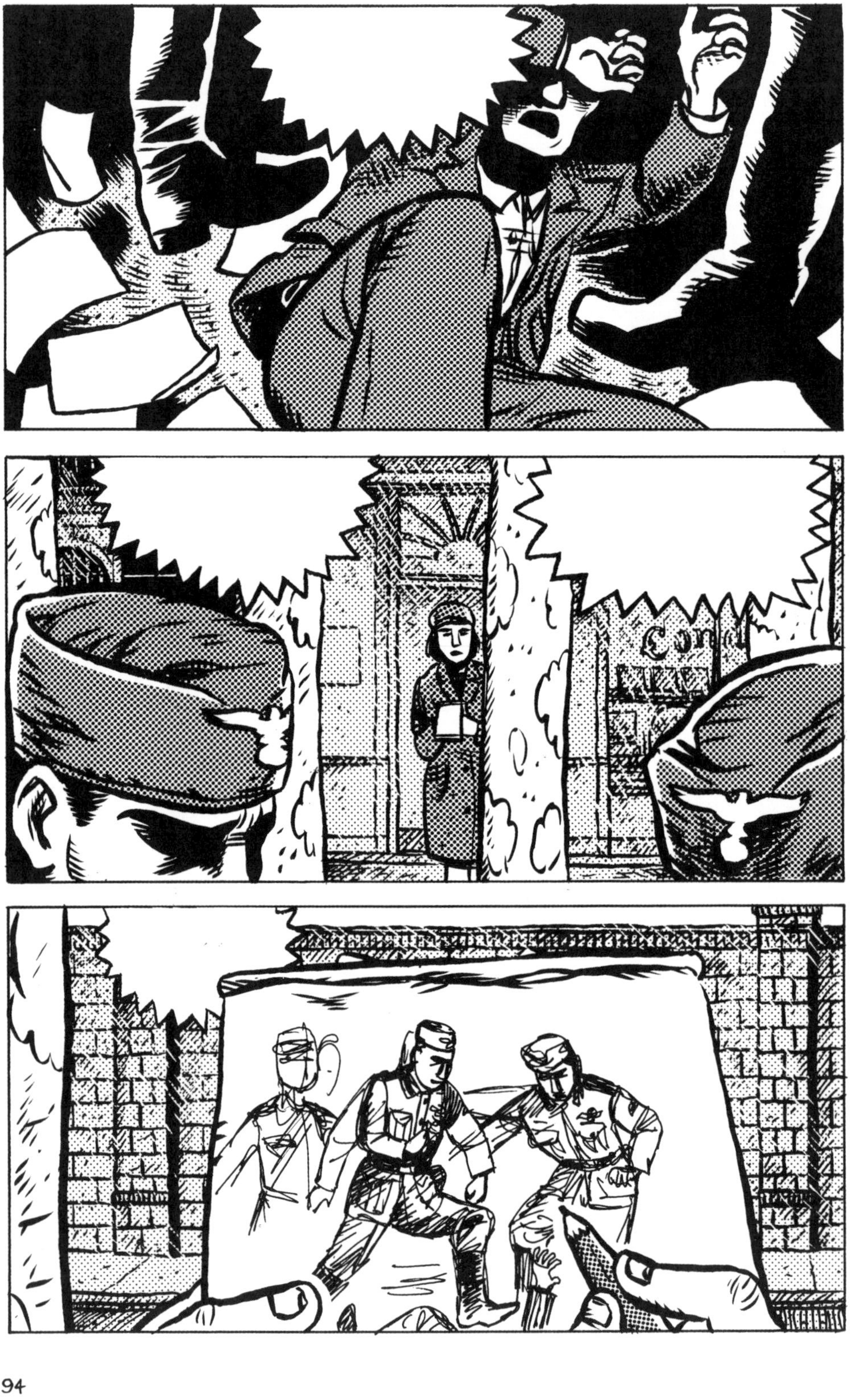

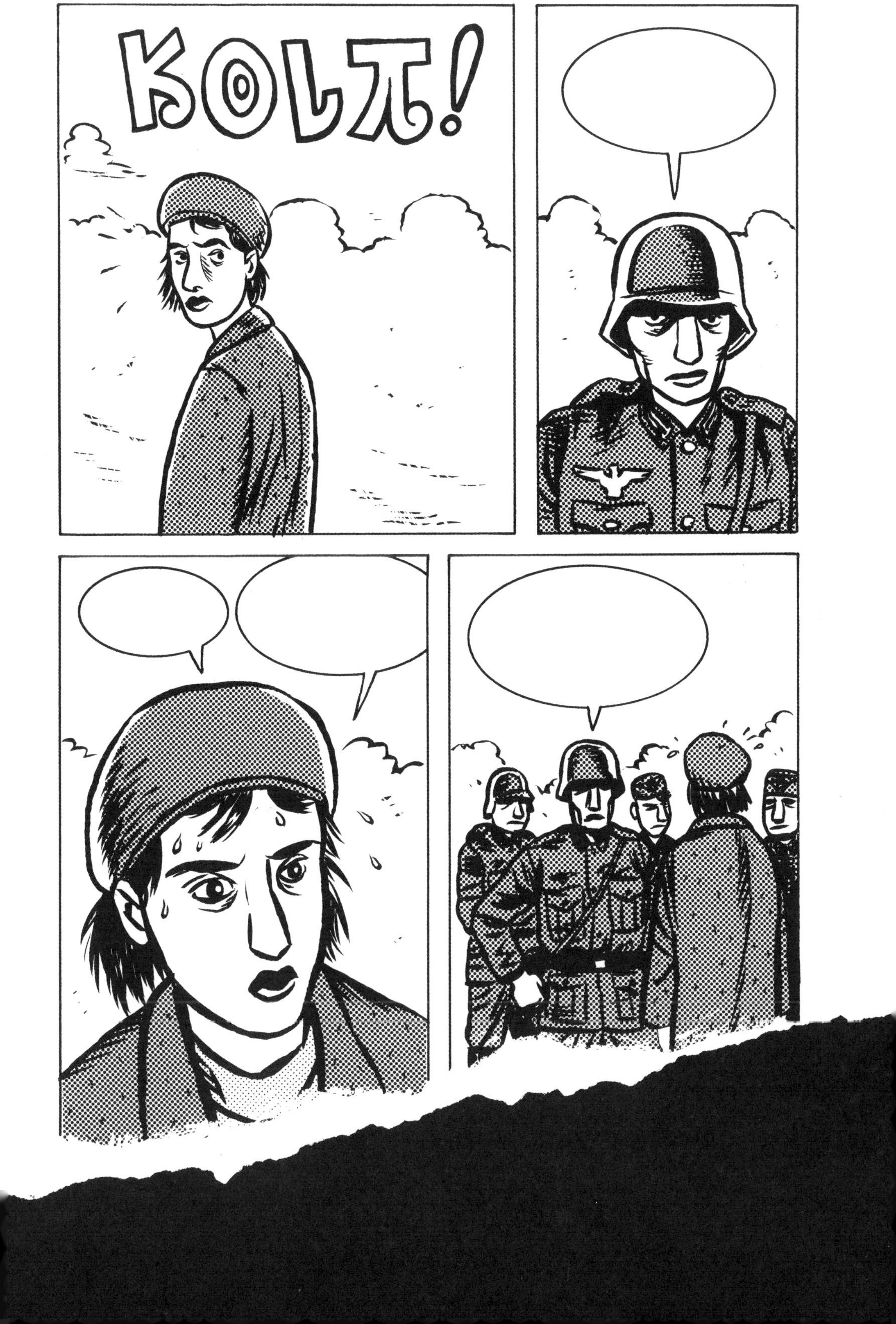
KOLT!

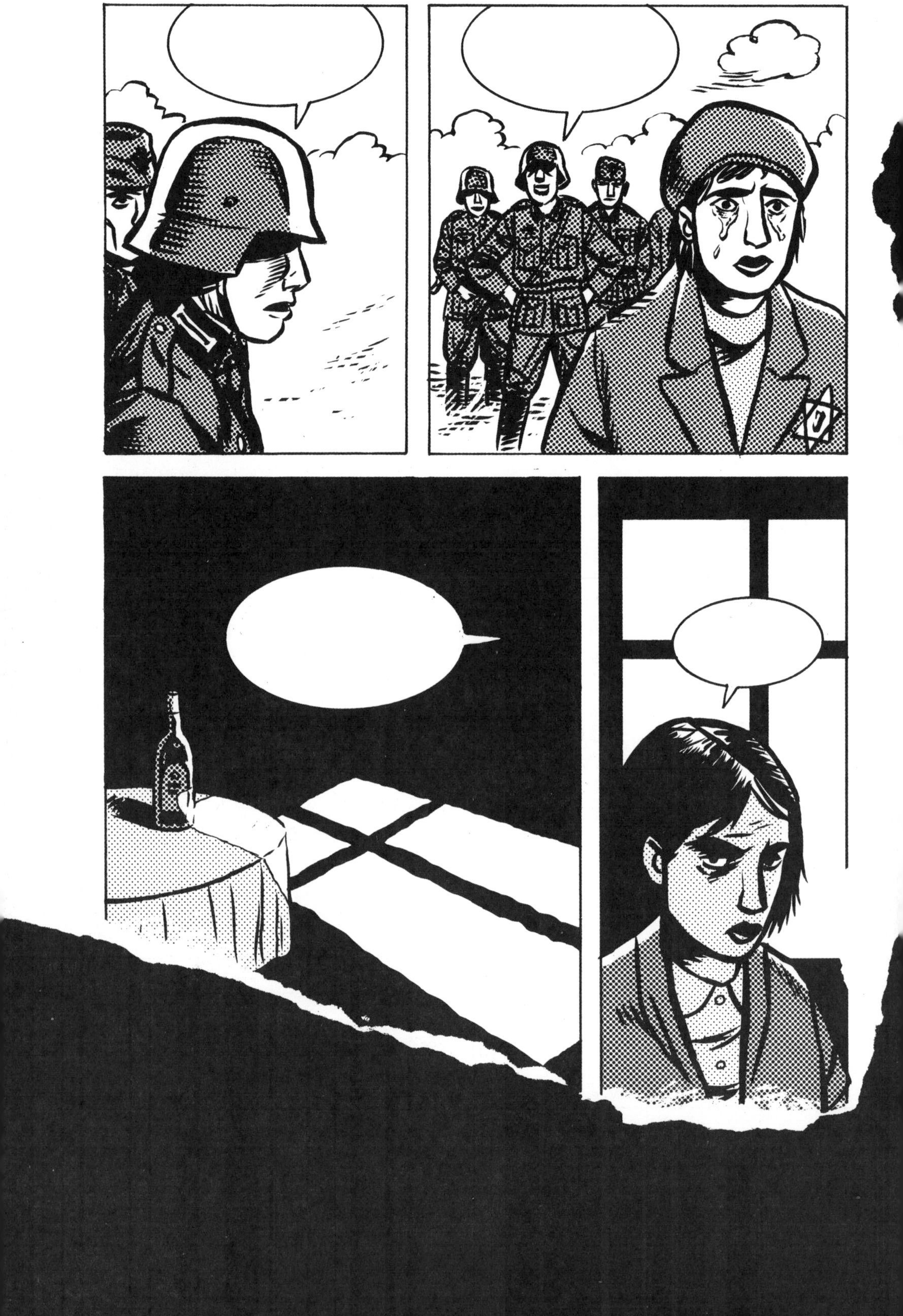

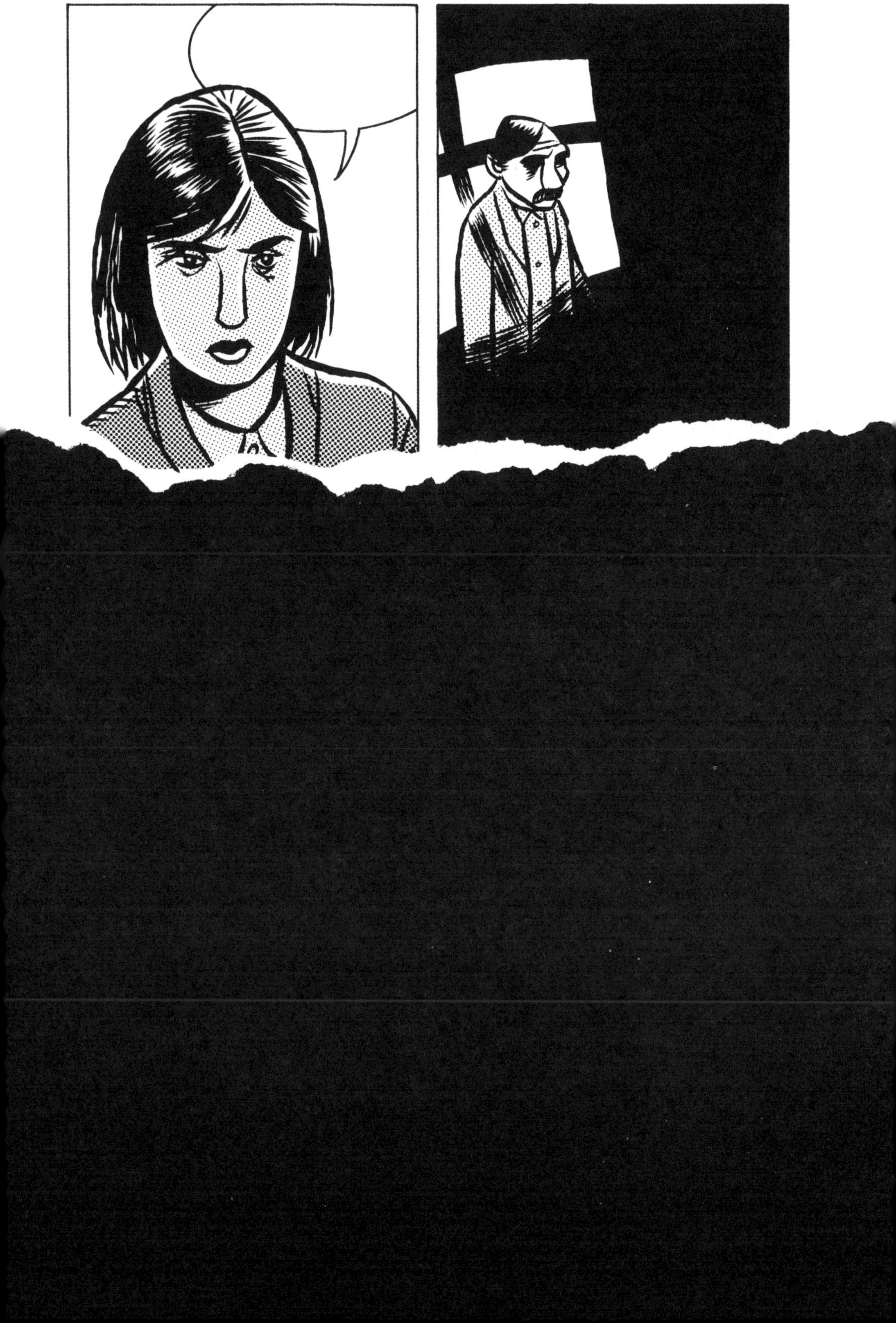

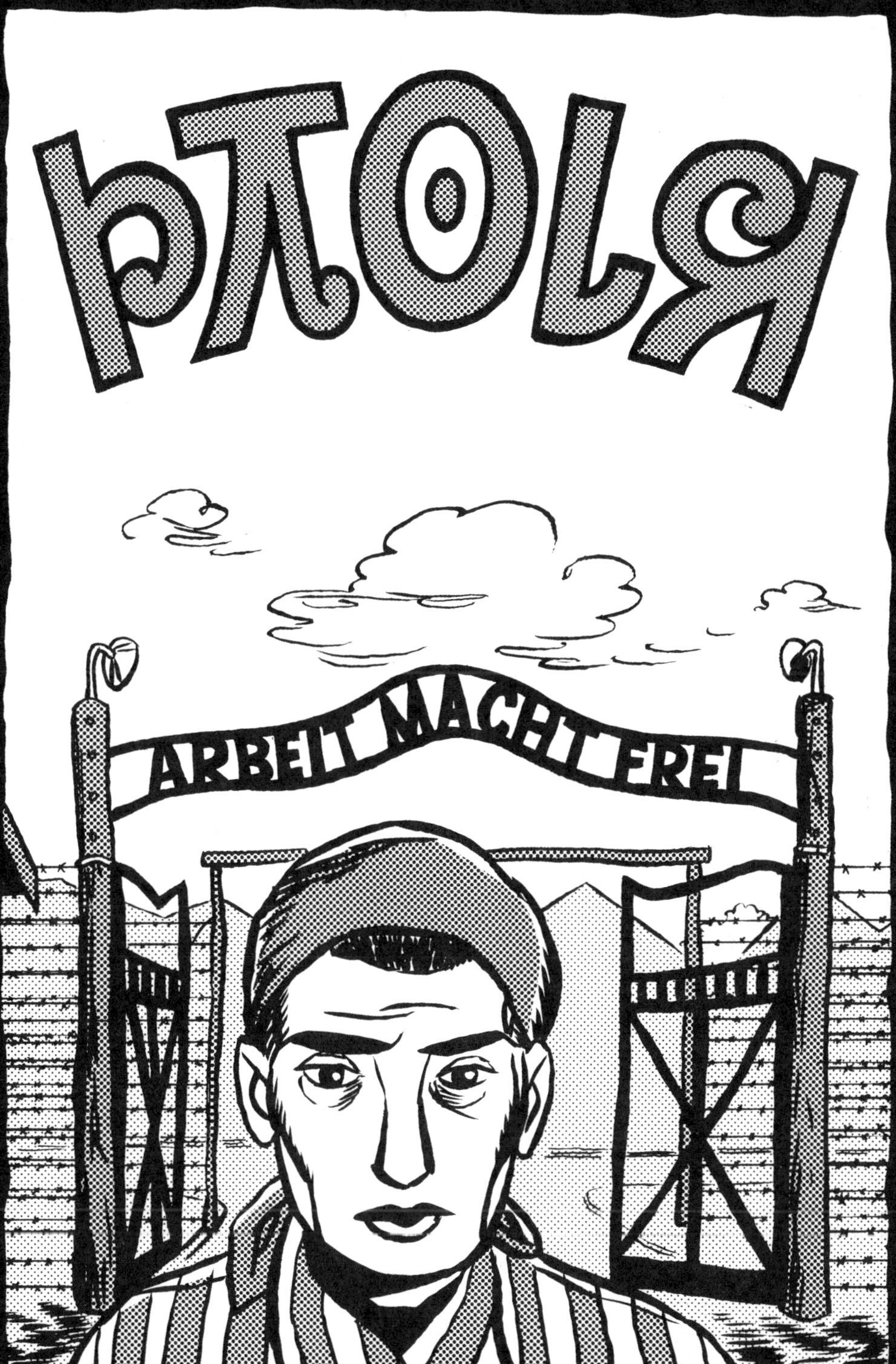
ARBEIT MACHT FREI

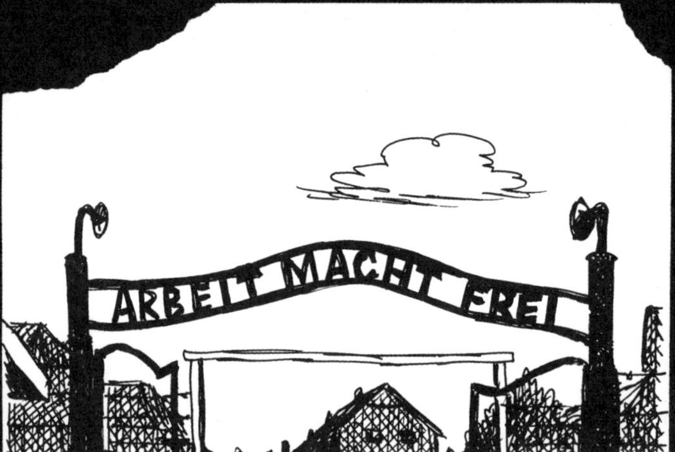
ARBEIT MACHT FREI

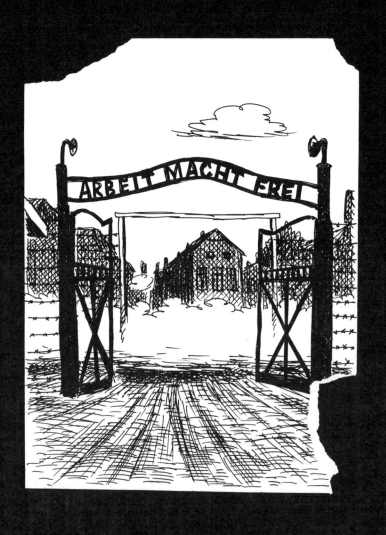

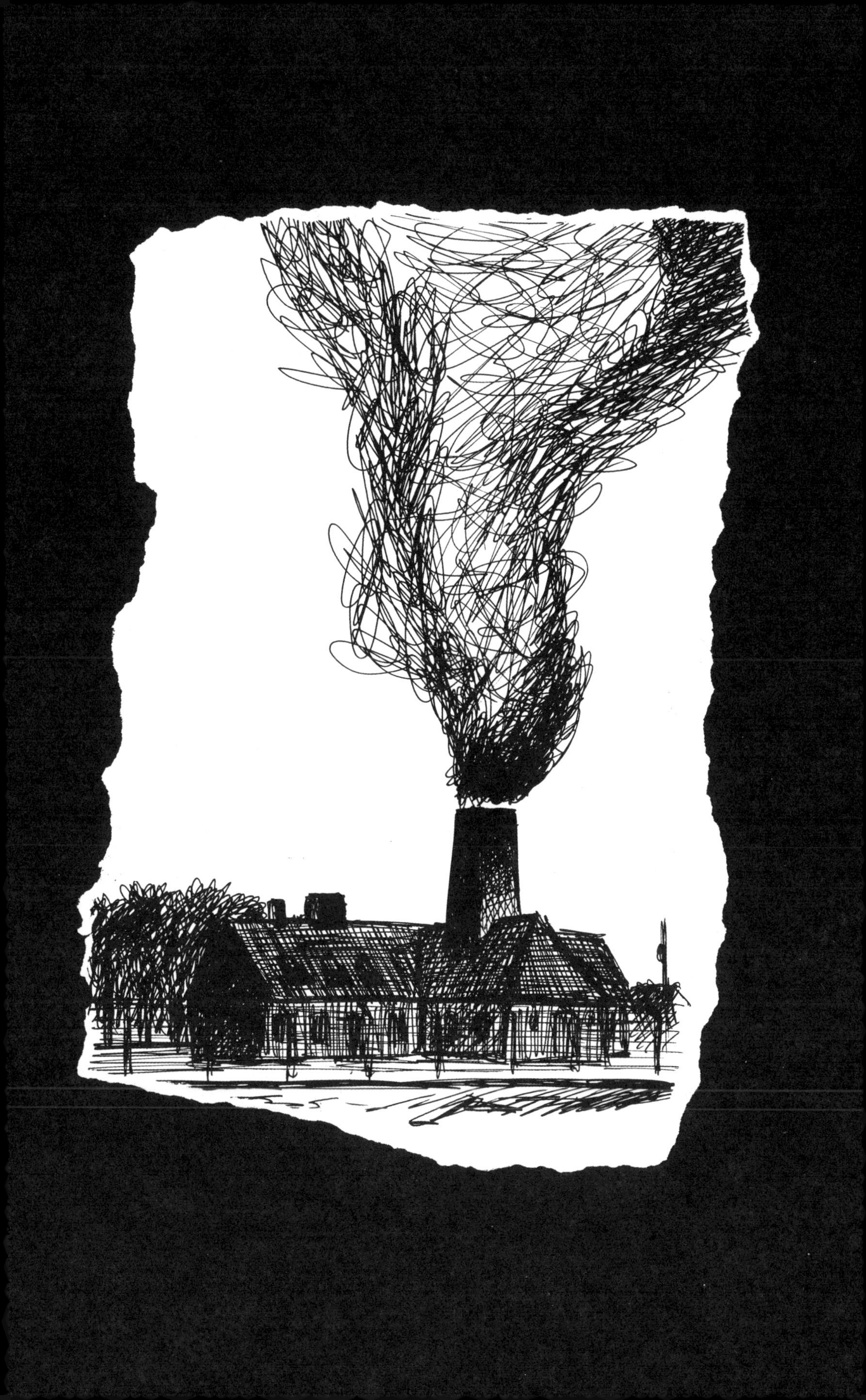

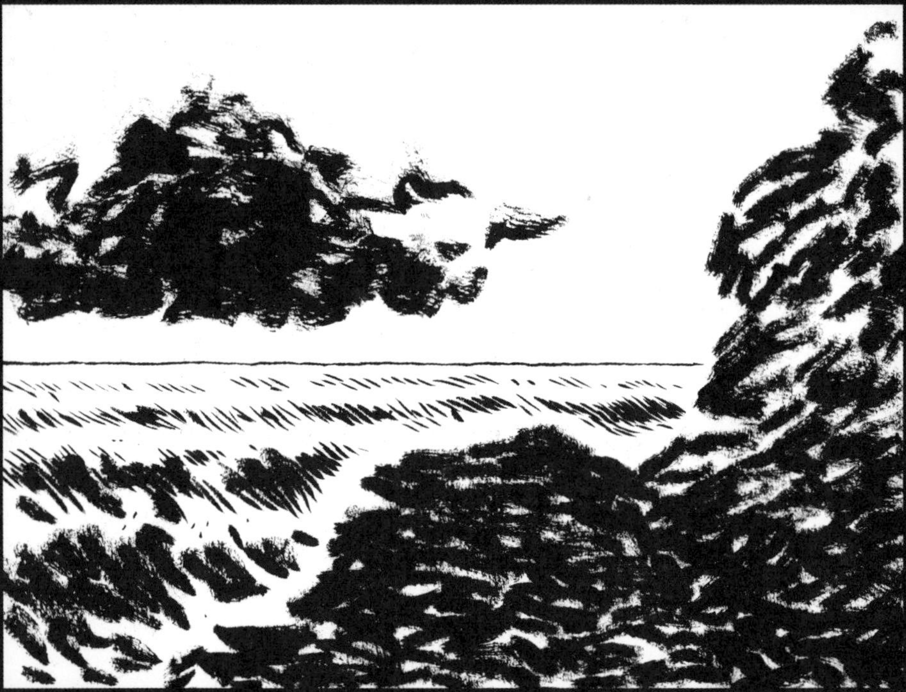

I'm climbing around the rocks as the tide comes in.

Somewhere up ahead are my wife and child. She's a better climber than I am, but our son is only six and these rocks are getting pretty steep.

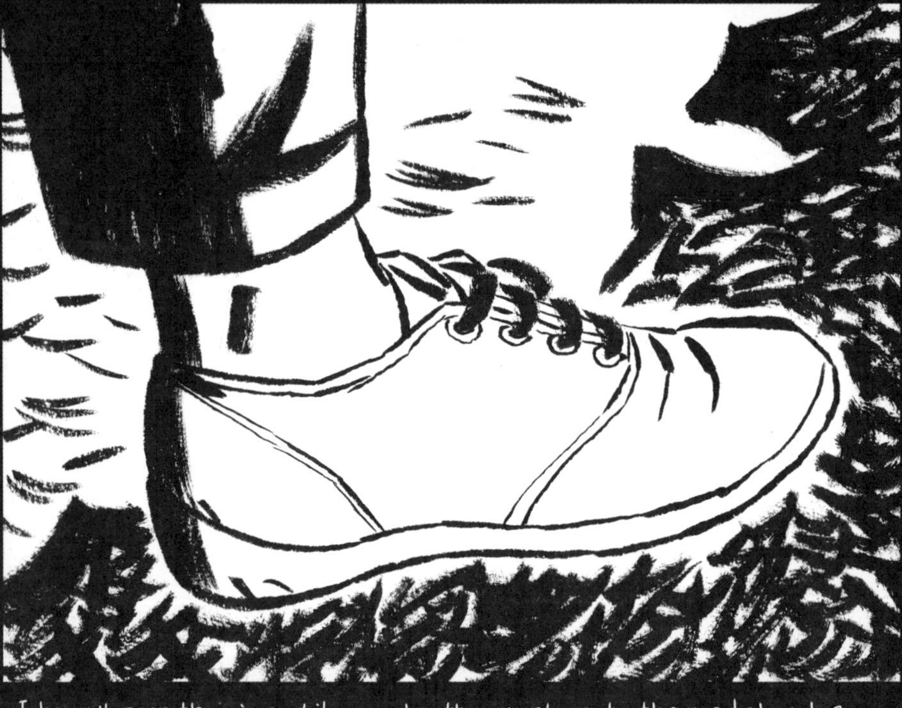

I haven't seen them in a while – maybe they went up to the road already? Or maybe they're around the next corner, playing in a sheltered bay...

The sea covers my shoes, tugs at my legs. Rocks scrape the skin on my hands.

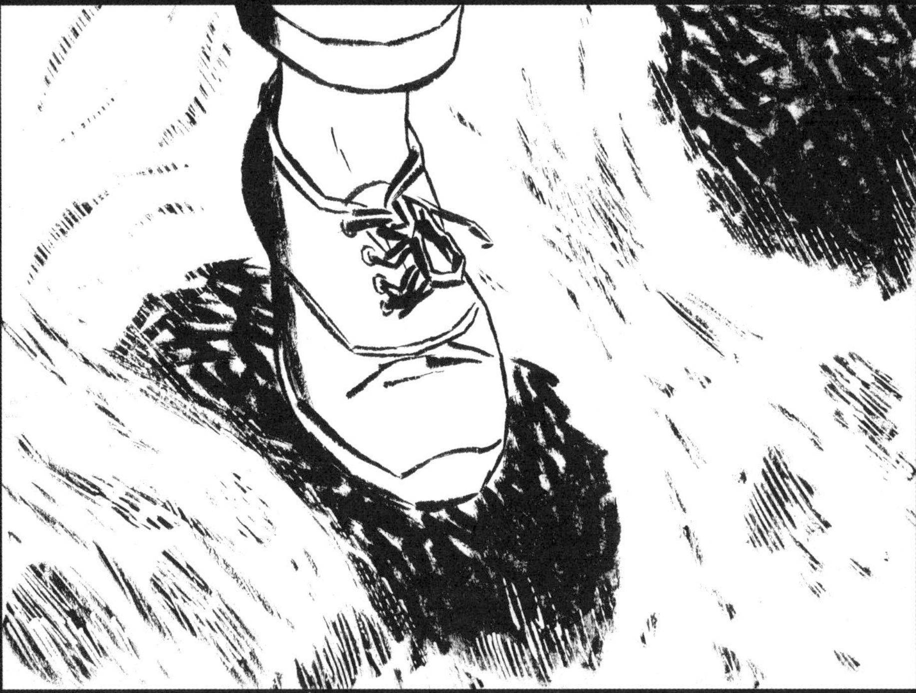

The tide is coming in.

And I keep climbing

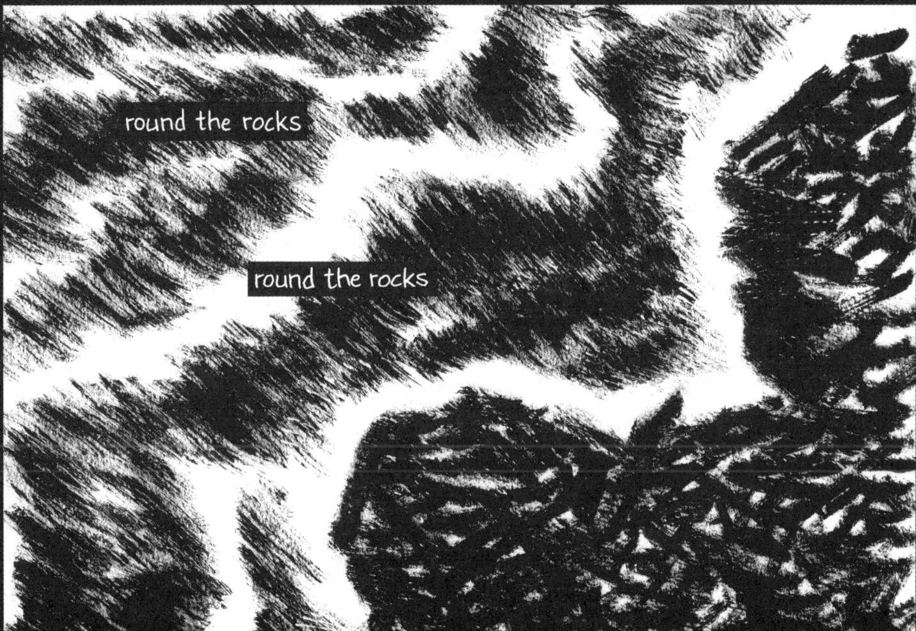
round the rocks
round the rocks

Dylan Horrocks. 10-7-01

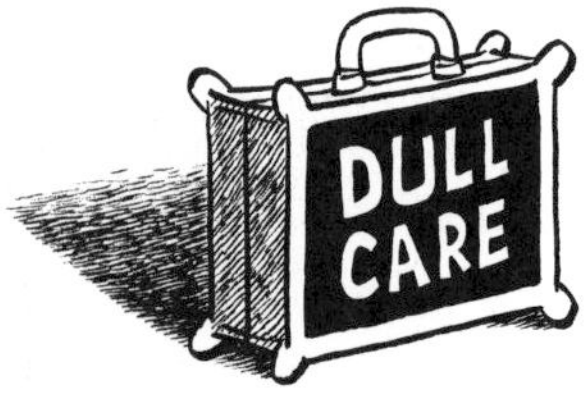
DULL
CARE

DYLAN
HORROCKS
'05

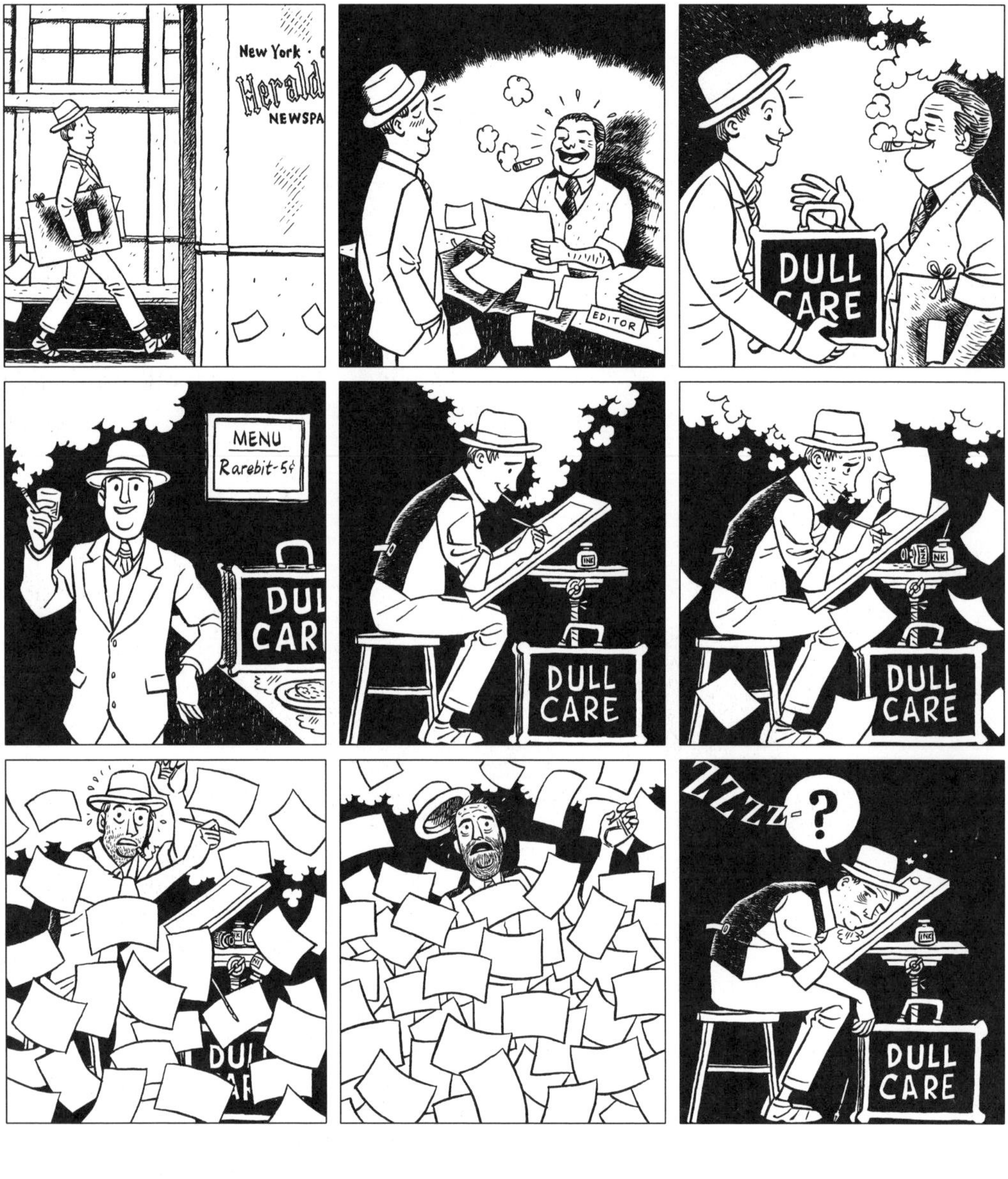
New York ·
NEWSPA
EDITOR
DULL
CARE
MENU
Rarebit-5¢
INK
DULL
CARE
DULL
CARE
ZZzz-?
INK
DULL
CARE

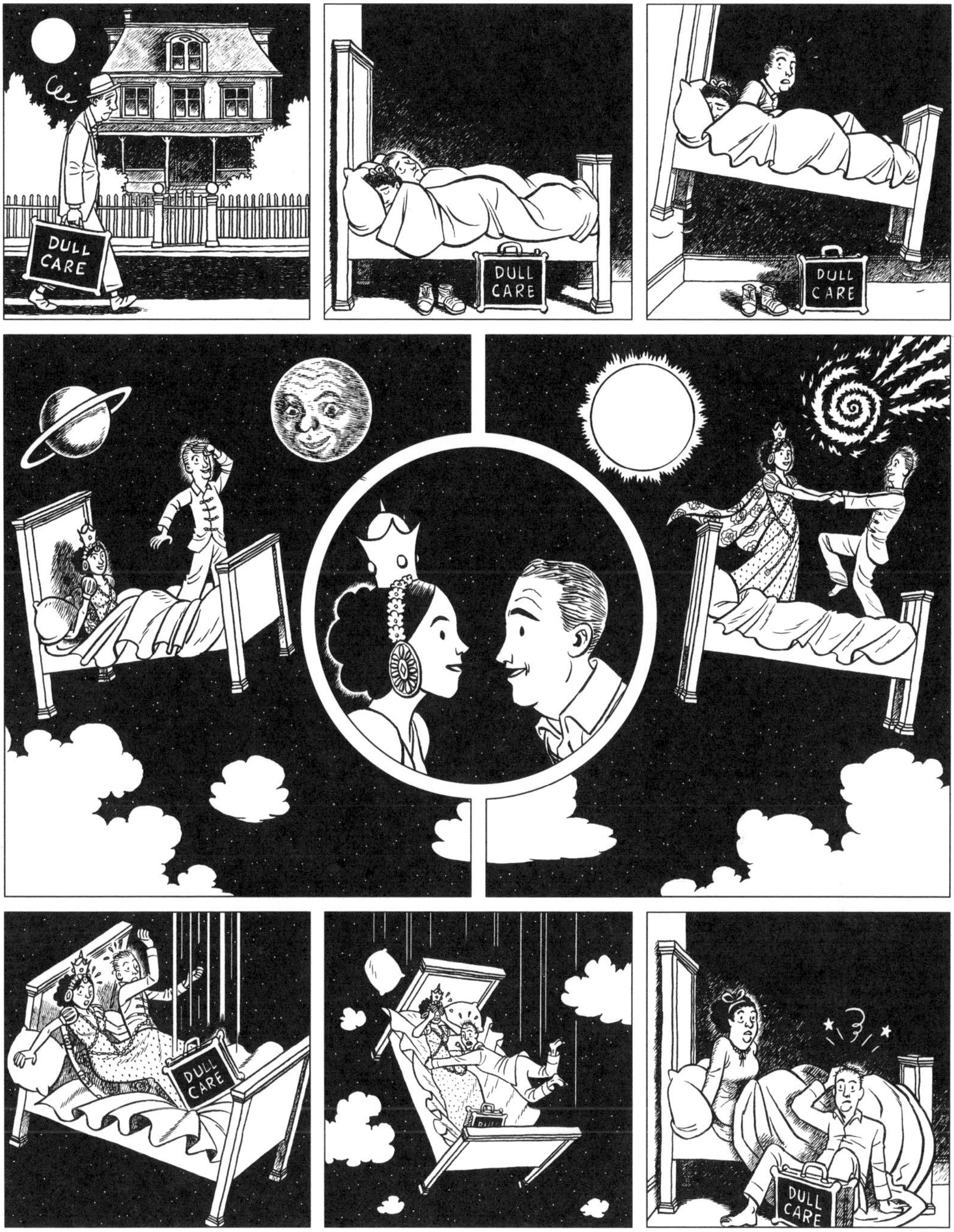
DULL CARE
DULL CARE
DULL CARE
DULL CARE
DULL CARE

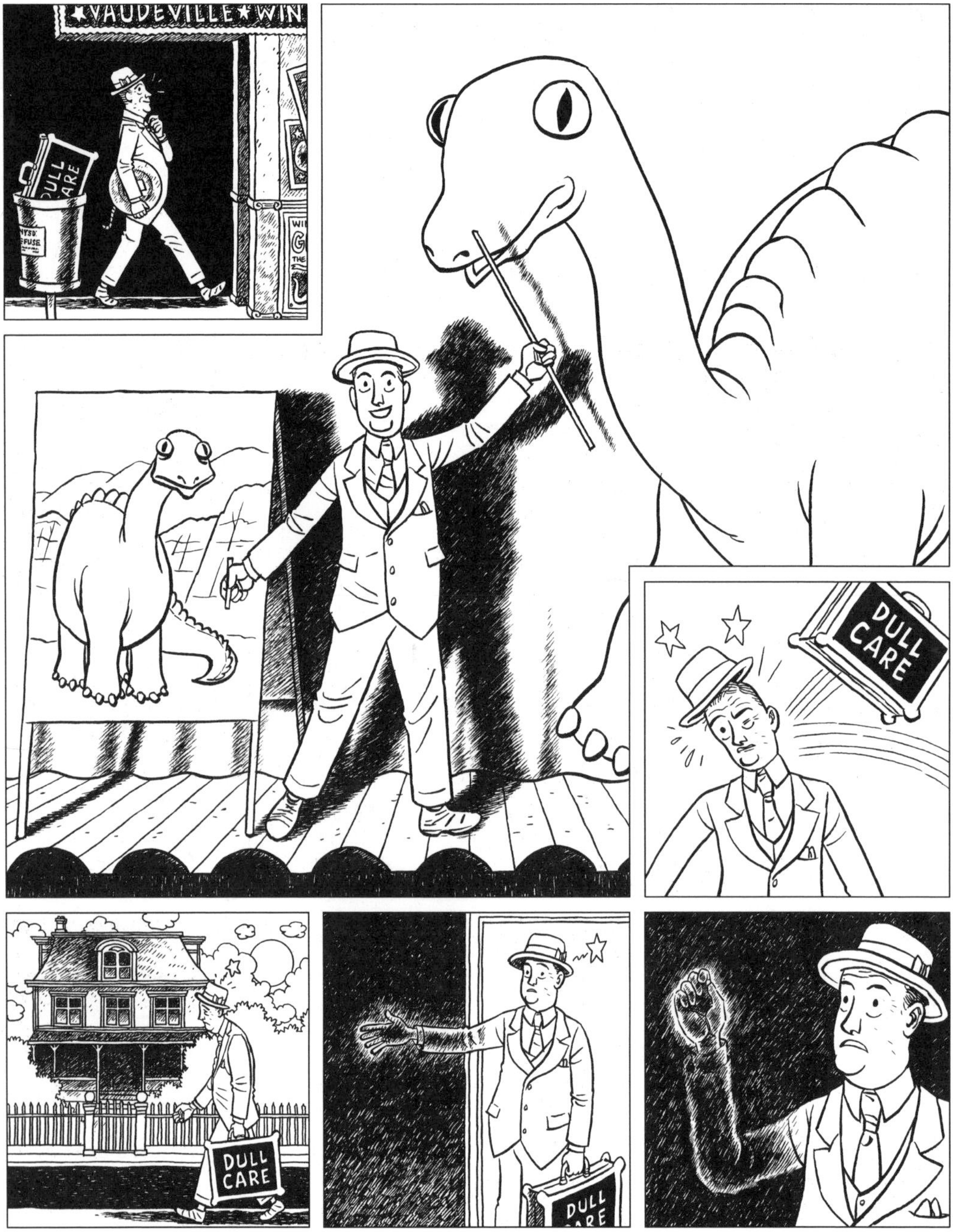
VAUDEVILLE
DULL CARE
DULL CARE
DULL CARE

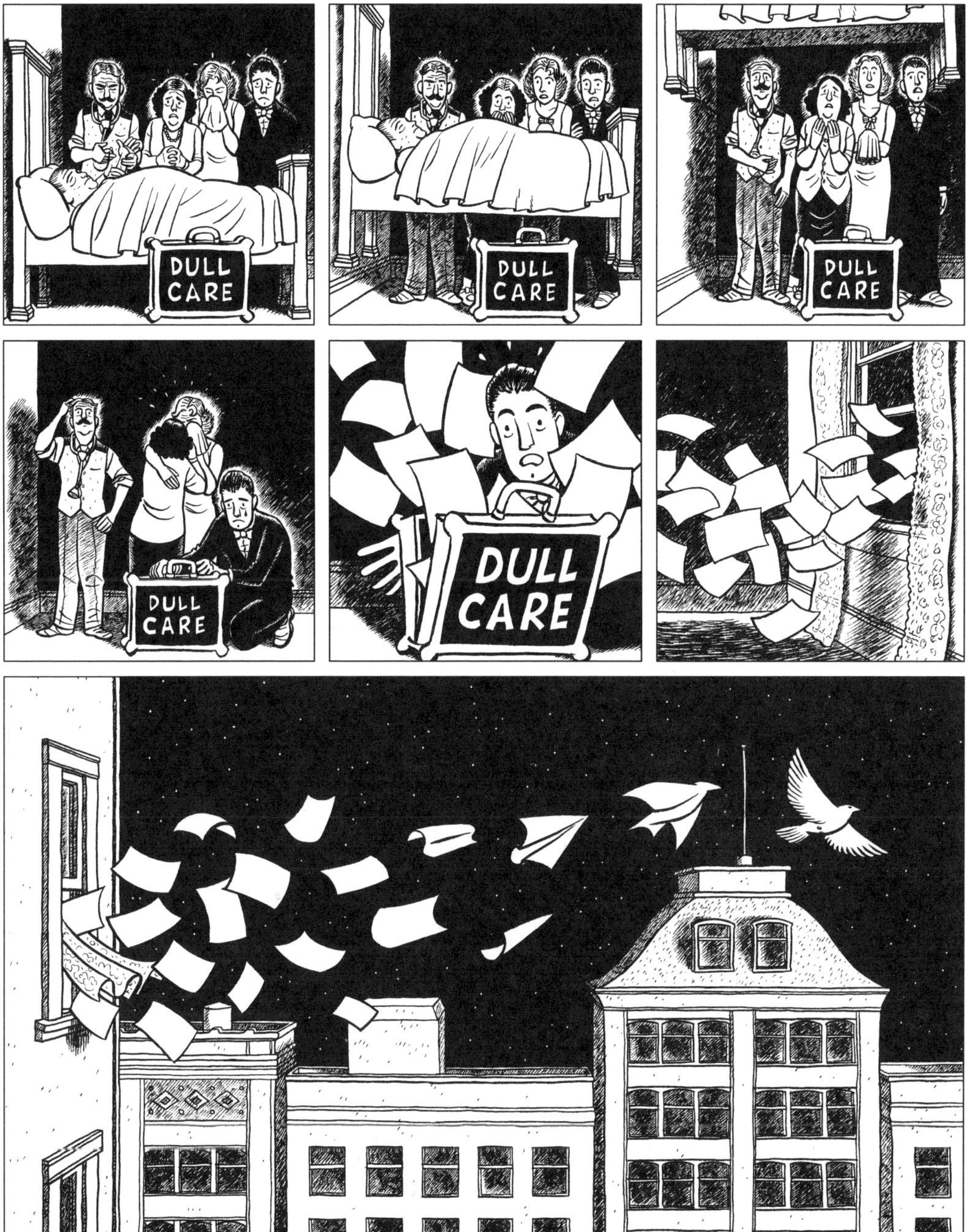
DULL CARE
DULL CARE
DULL CARE
DULL CARE
DULL CARE

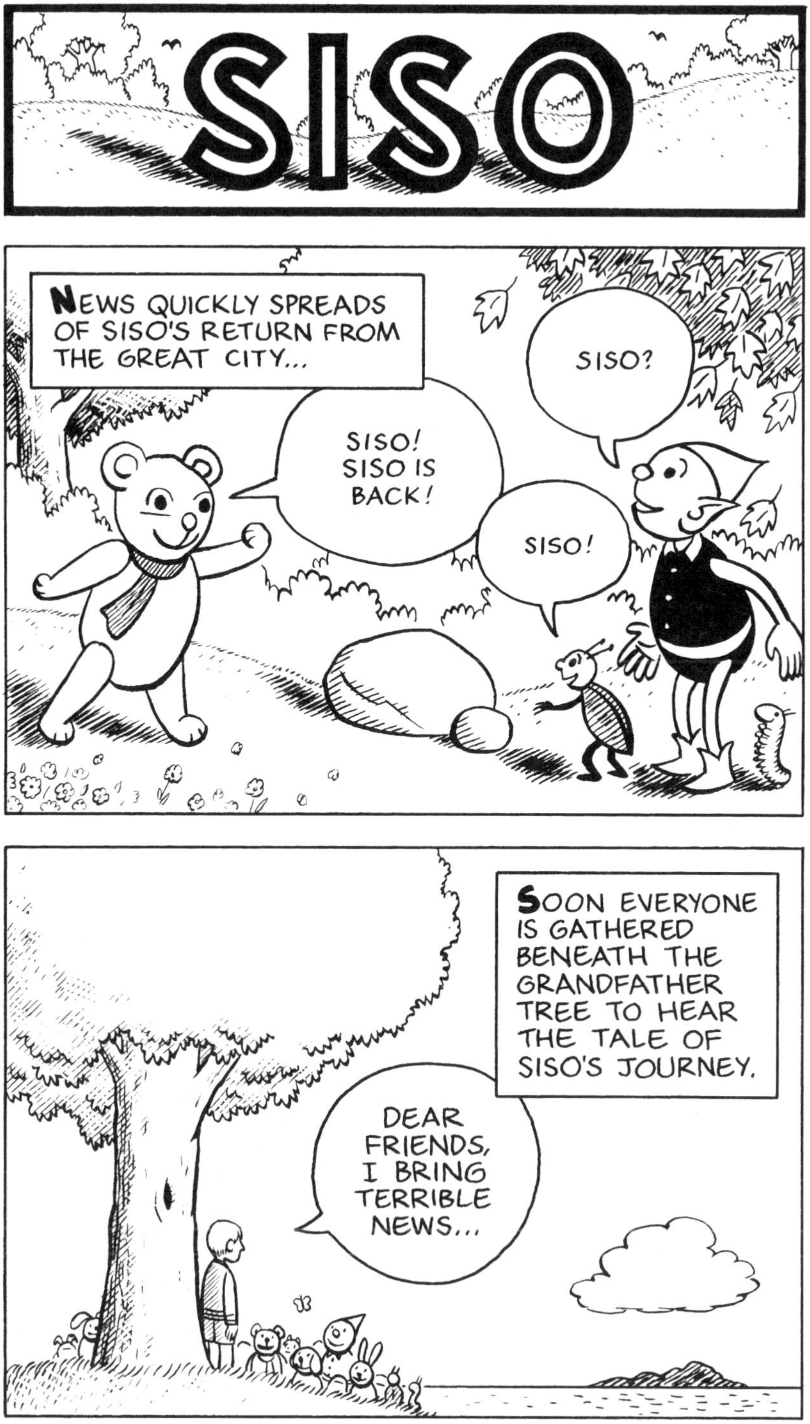
SISO
NEWS QUICKLY SPREADS OF SISO'S RETURN FROM THE GREAT CITY...
SISO! SISO IS BACK!
SISO?
SISO!
SOON EVERYONE IS GATHERED BENEATH THE GRANDFATHER TREE TO HEAR THE TALE OF SISO'S JOURNEY.
DEAR FRIENDS, I BRING TERRIBLE NEWS...

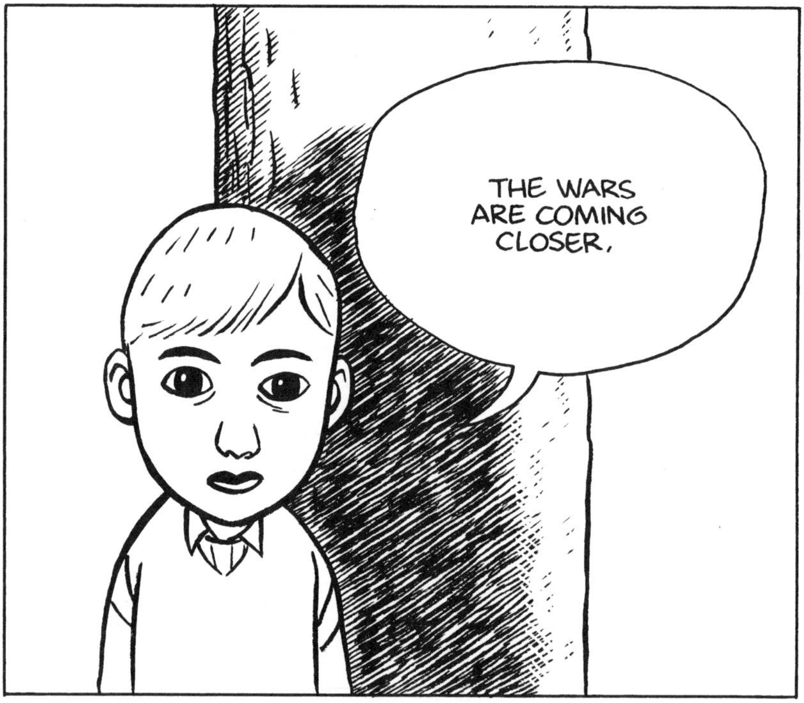
THE WARS ARE COMING CLOSER.

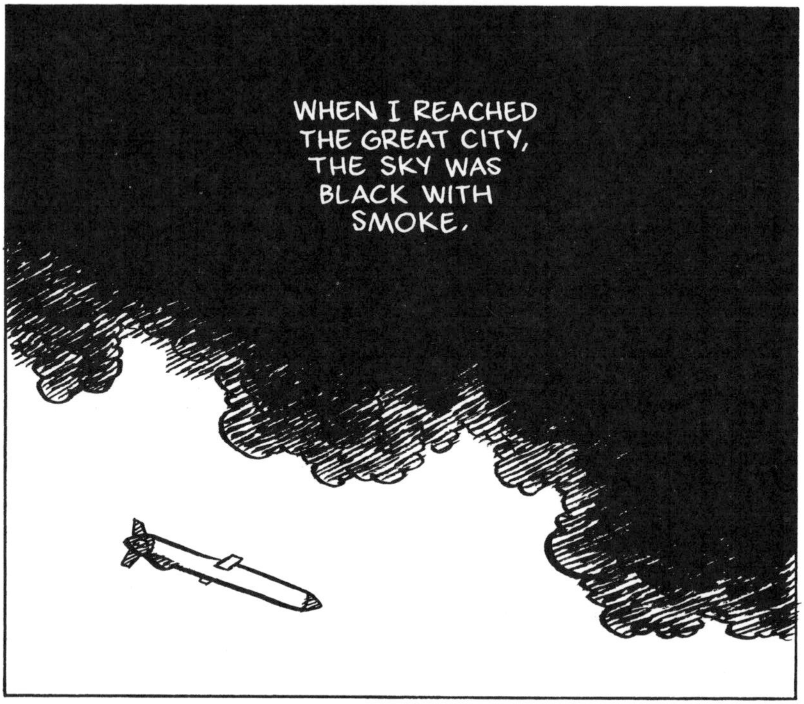
WHEN I REACHED THE GREAT CITY, THE SKY WAS BLACK WITH SMOKE.

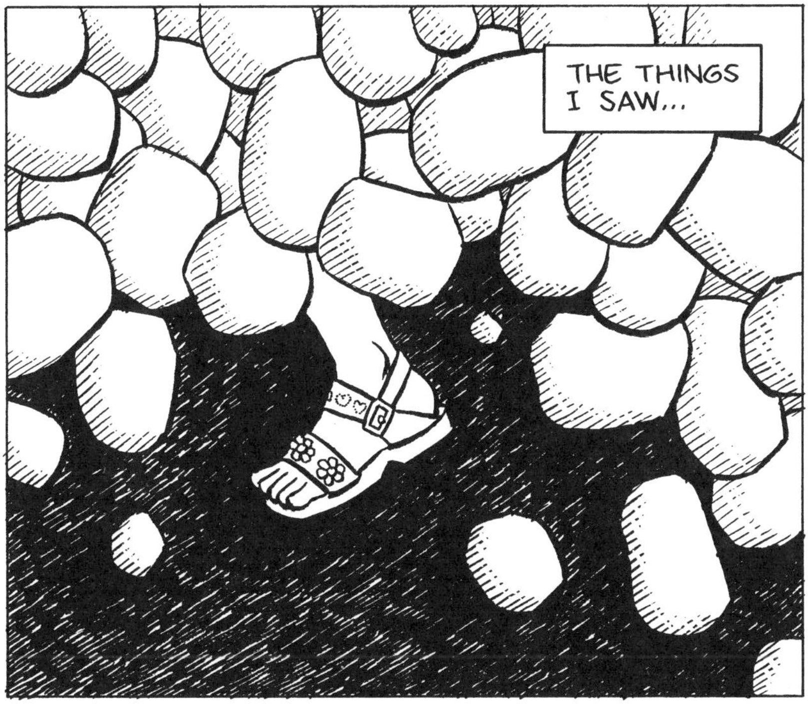
THE THINGS I SAW...

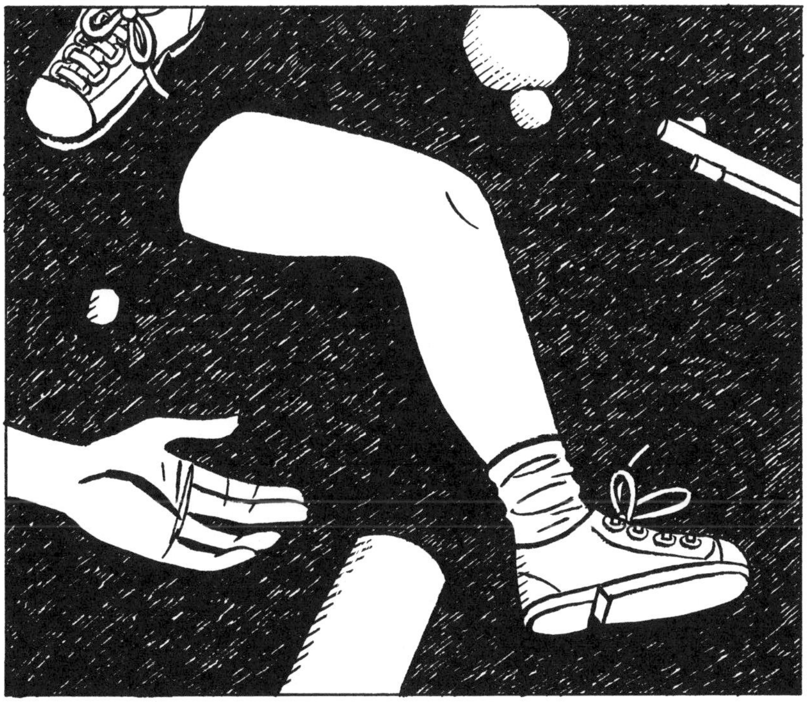

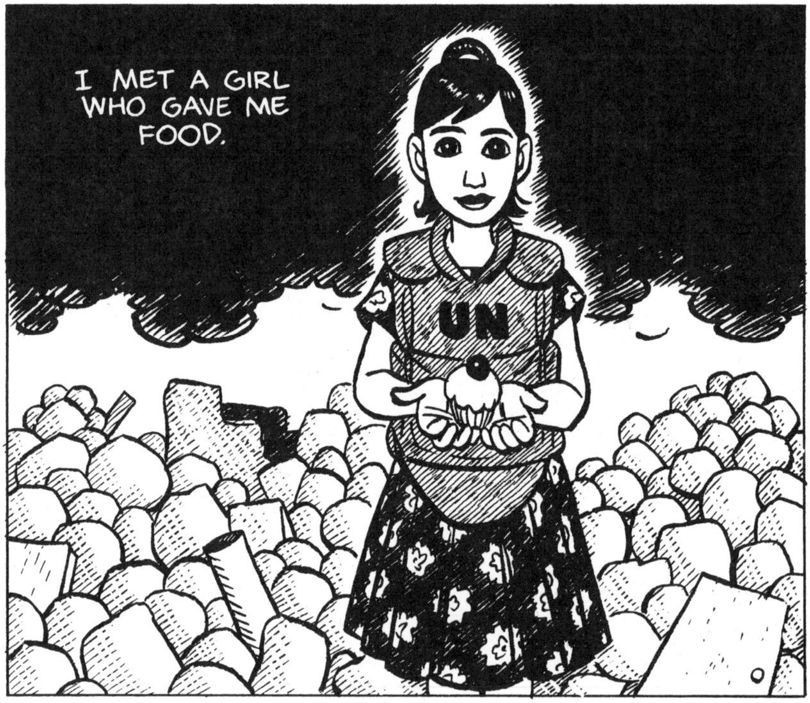
I MET A GIRL WHO GAVE ME FOOD.
UN

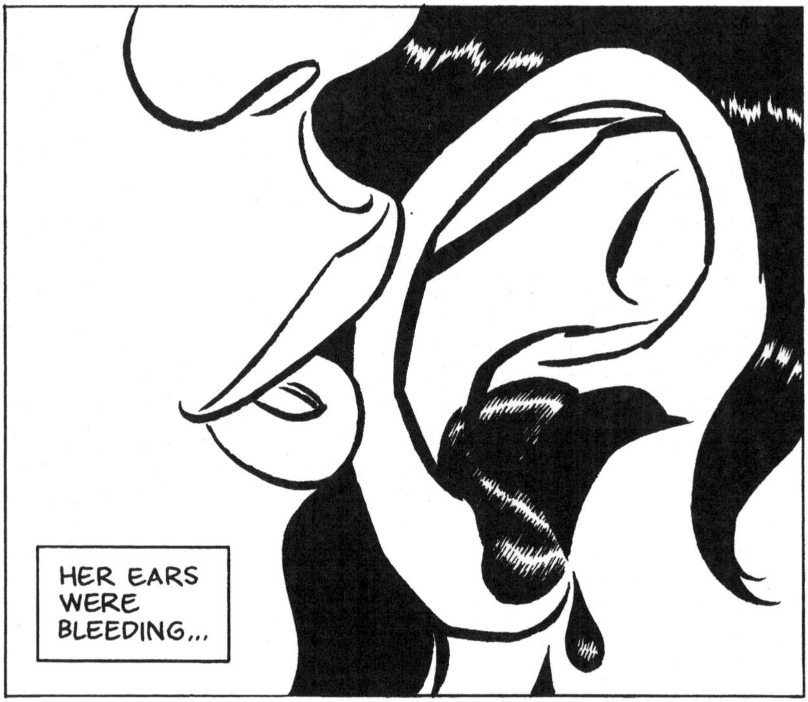
HER EARS WERE BLEEDING...

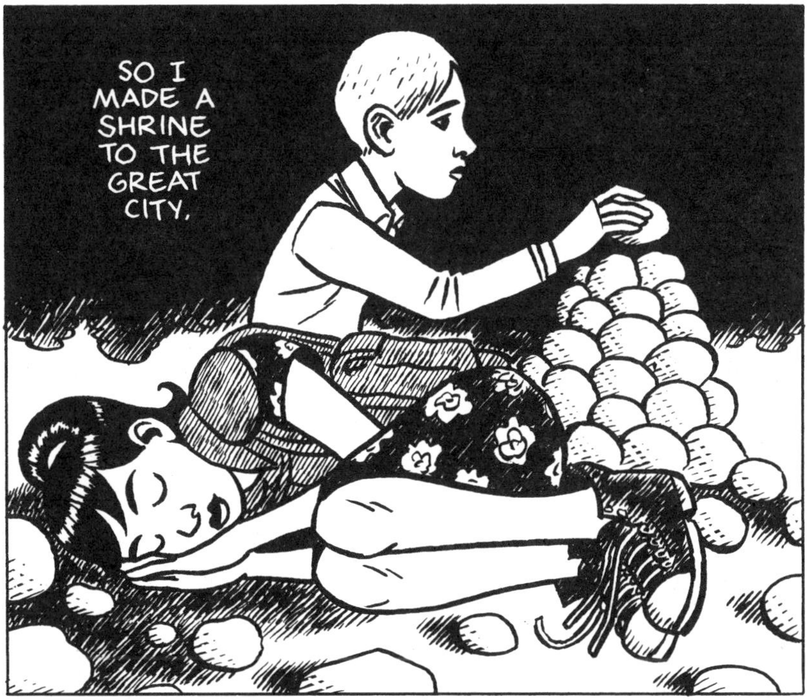
SO I MADE A SHRINE TO THE GREAT CITY,

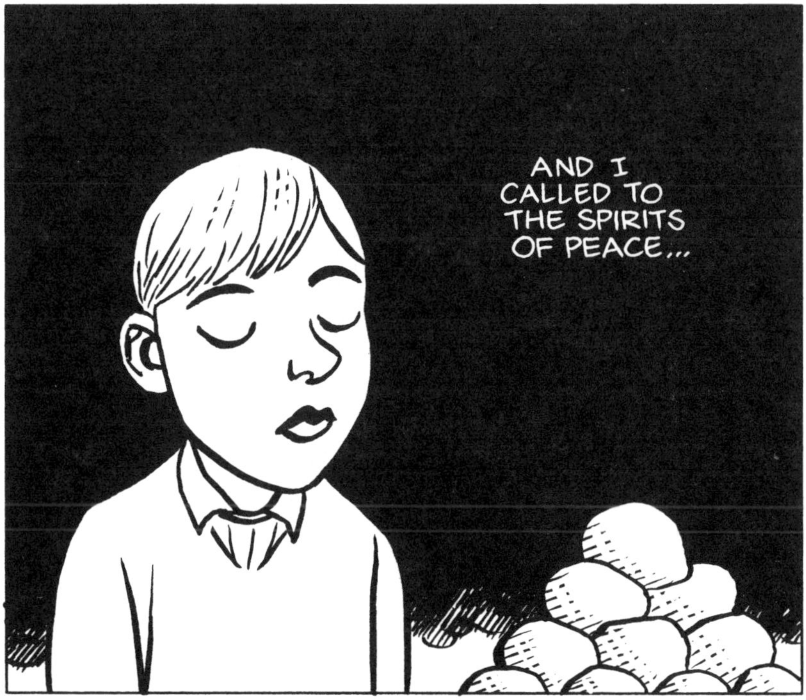
AND I CALLED TO THE SPIRITS OF PEACE...

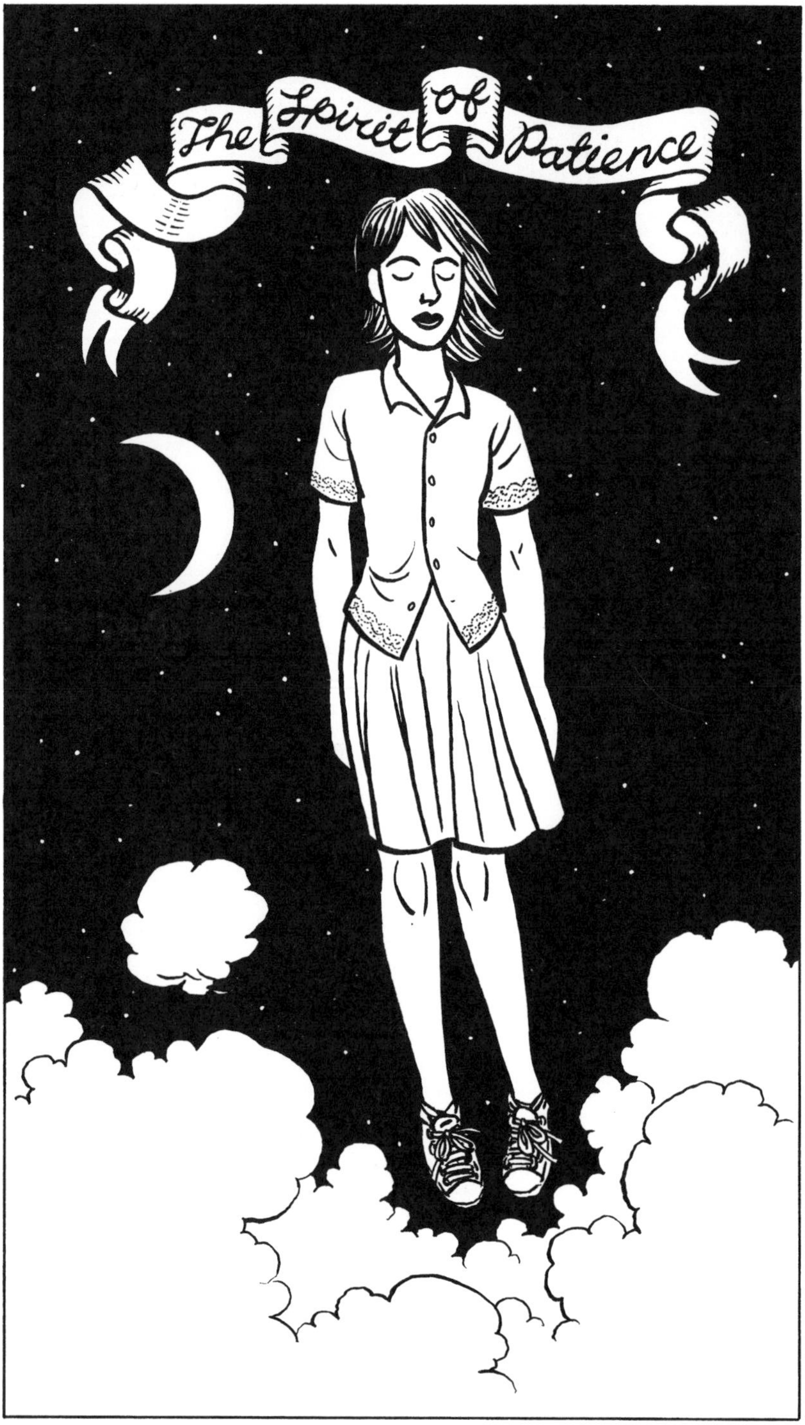
The Spirit of Patience

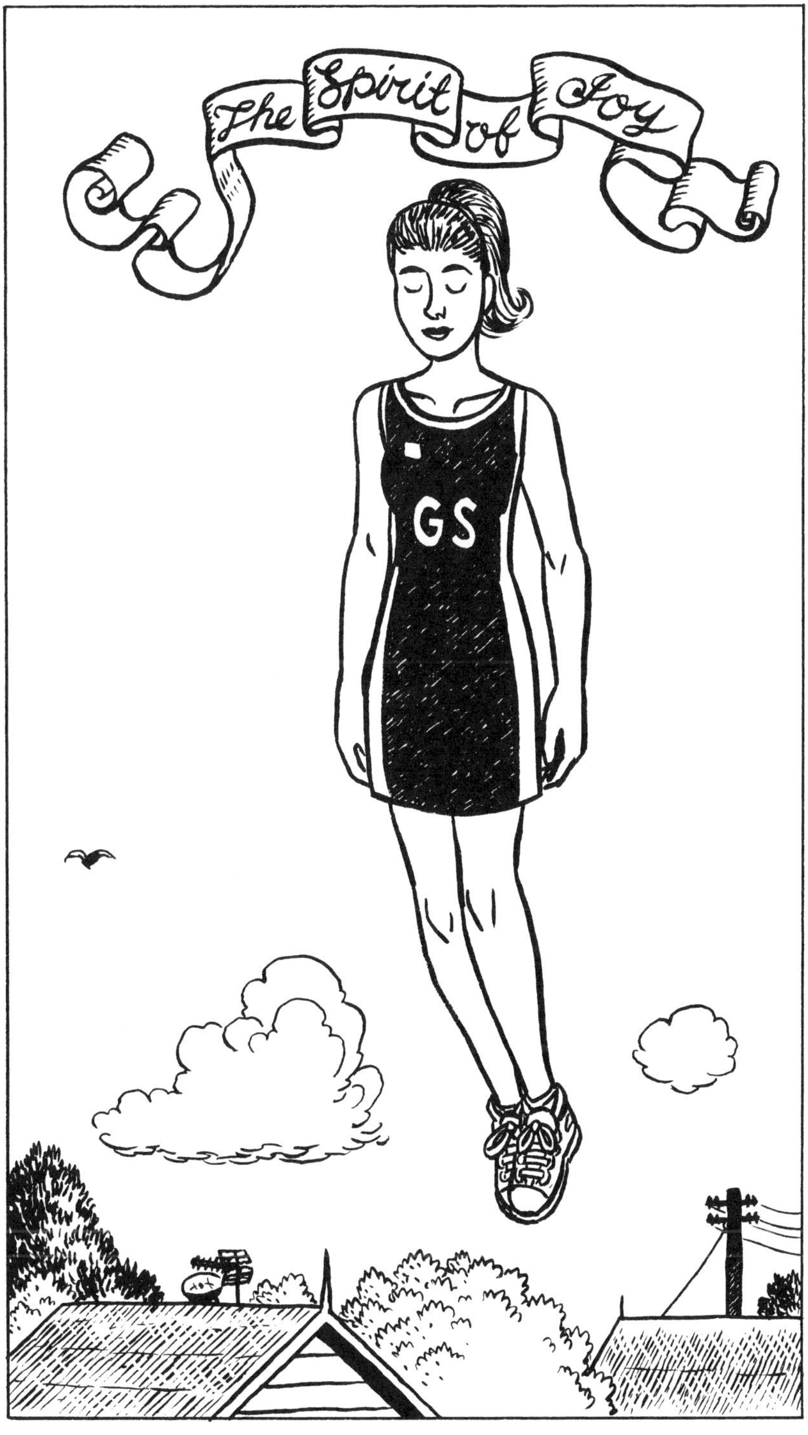
The Spirit of Joy
GS

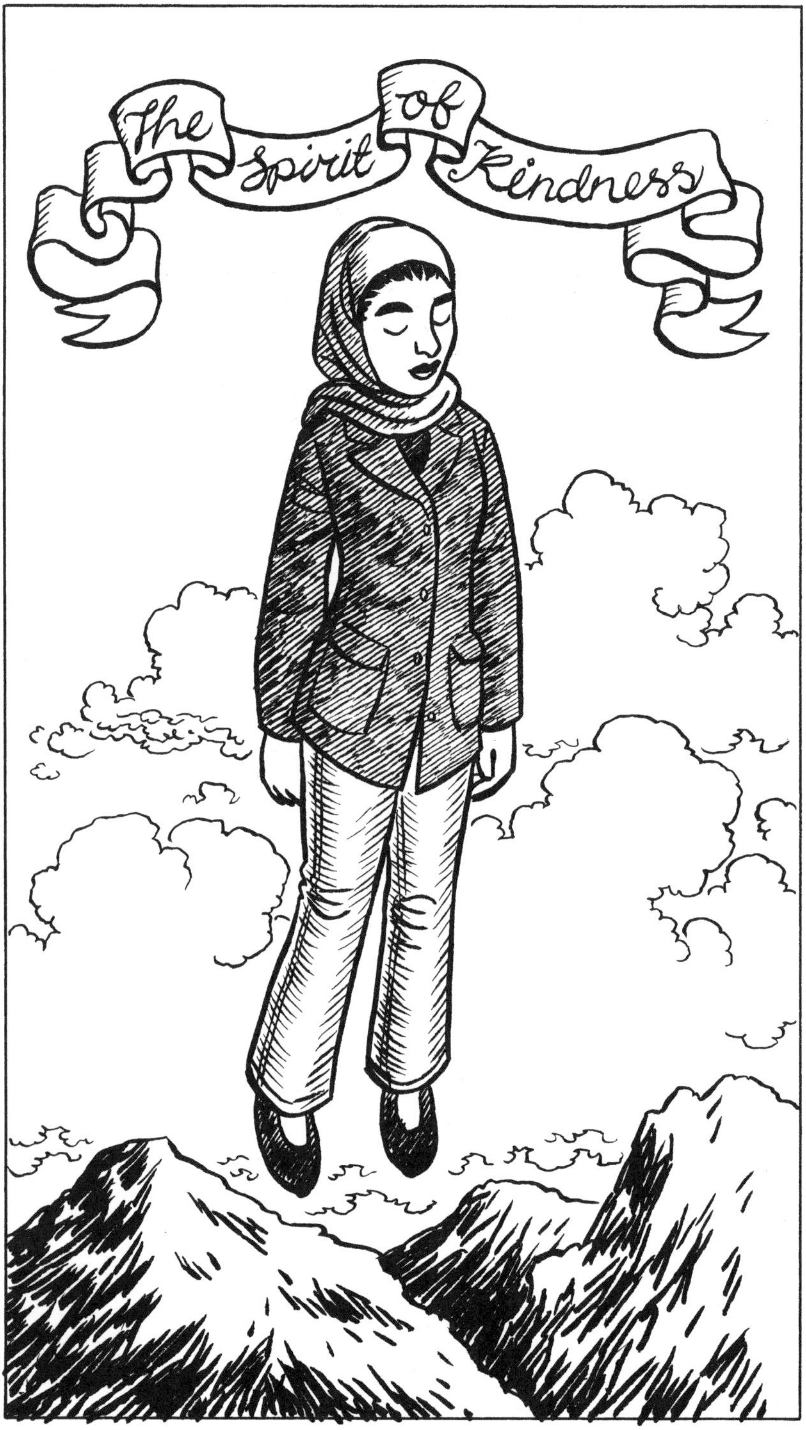
The Spirit of Kindness

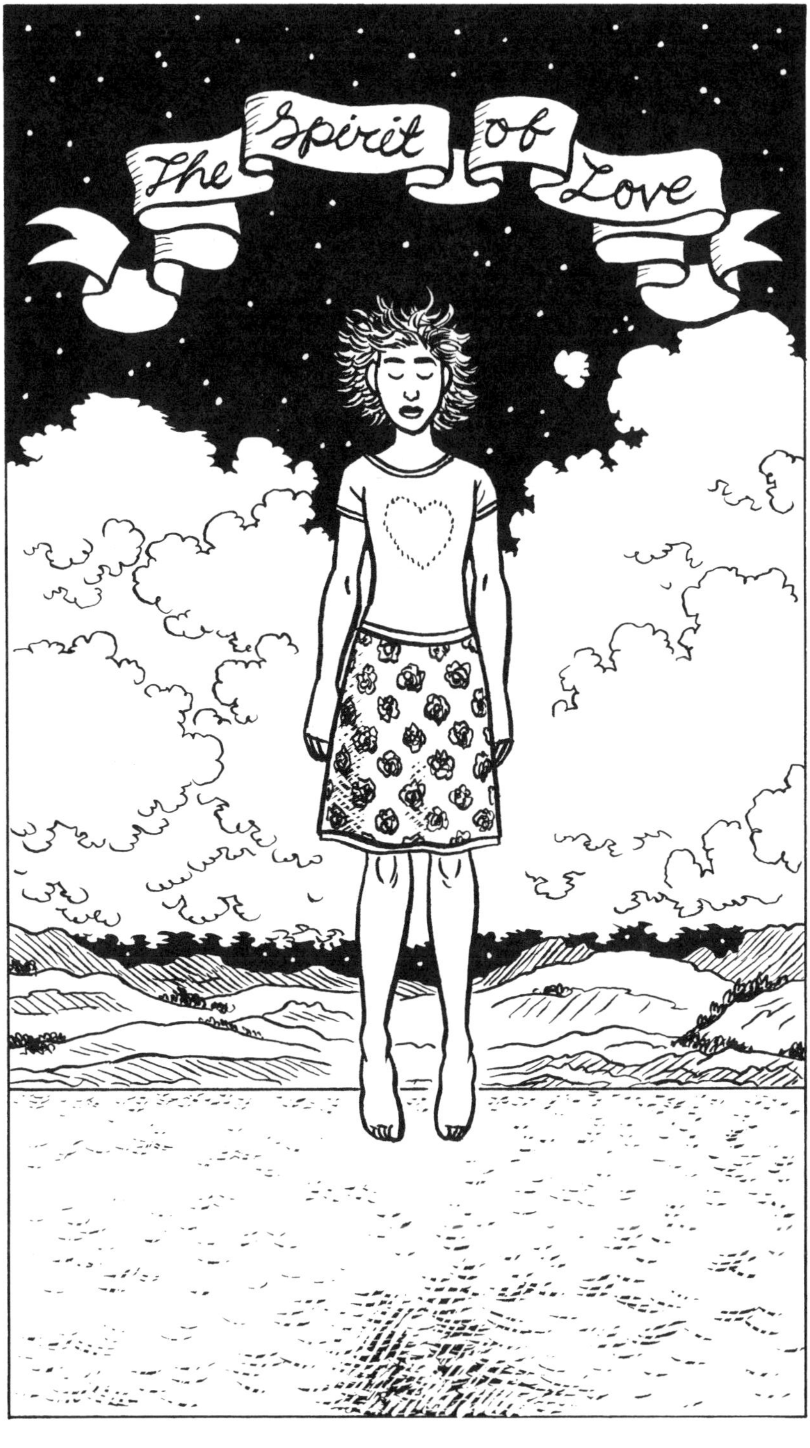
The Spirit of Love

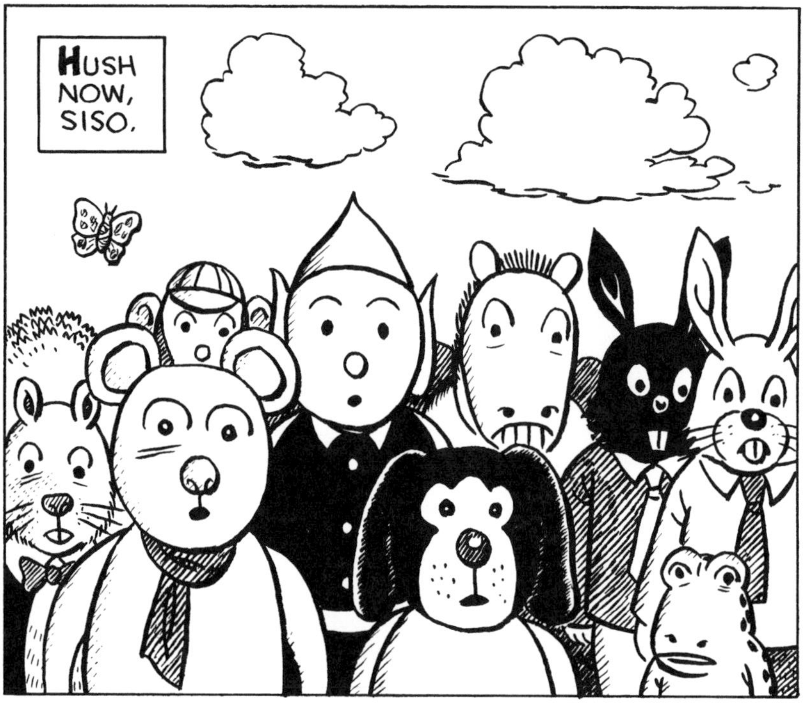
HUSH NOW, SISO.

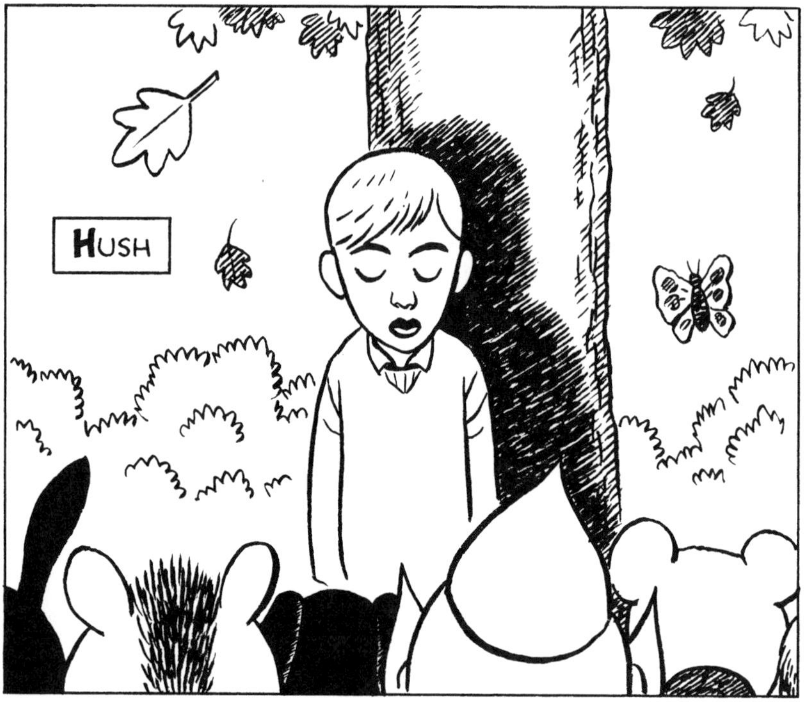
HUSH

# THE PHYSICS ENGINE

by DYLAN HORROCKS

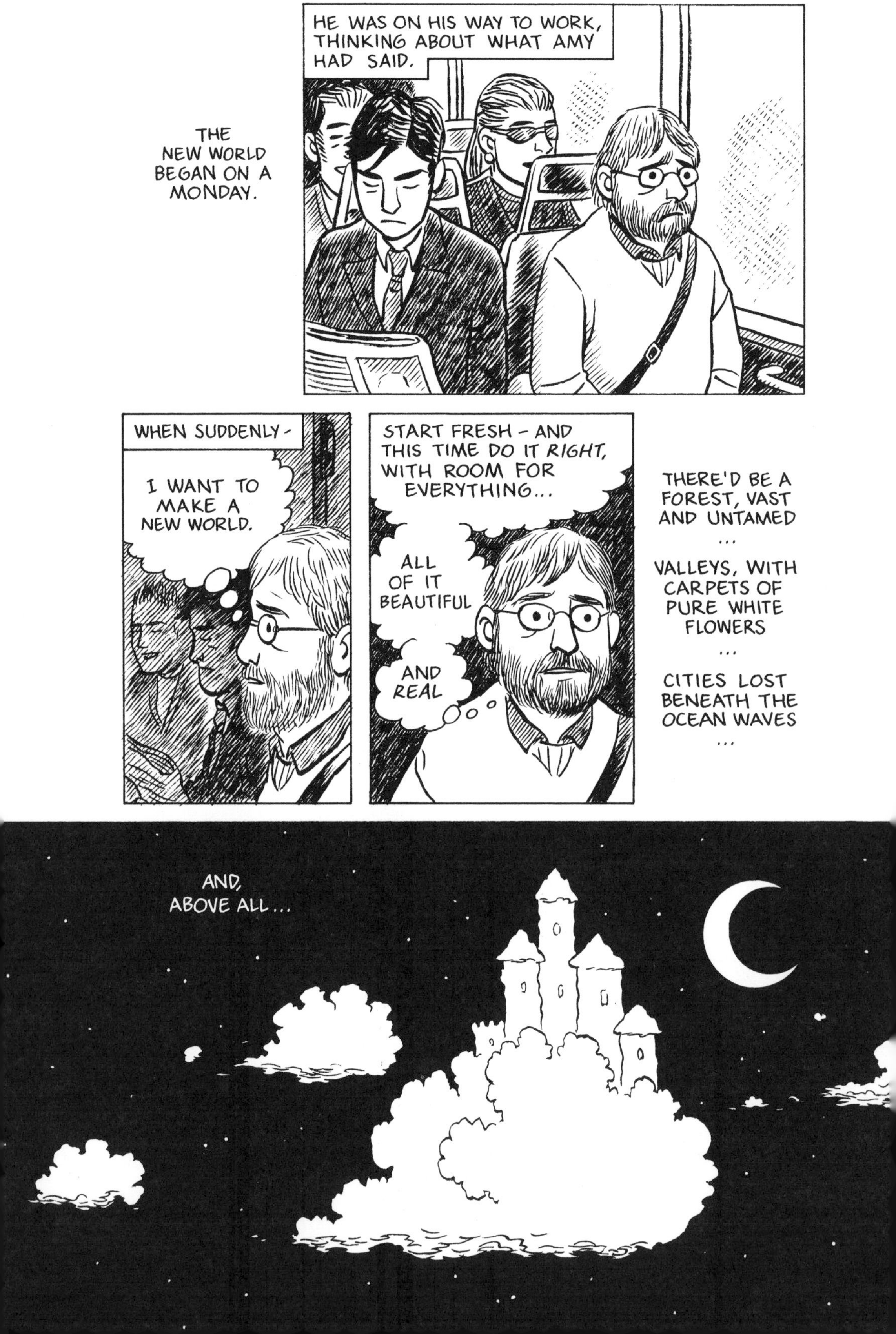
THE NEW WORLD BEGAN ON A MONDAY.
HE WAS ON HIS WAY TO WORK, THINKING ABOUT WHAT AMY HAD SAID.
WHEN SUDDENLY-
I WANT TO MAKE A NEW WORLD.
START FRESH - AND THIS TIME DO IT *RIGHT*, WITH ROOM FOR EVERYTHING...
ALL OF IT BEAUTIFUL
AND REAL
THERE'D BE A FOREST, VAST AND UNTAMED
...
VALLEYS, WITH CARPETS OF PURE WHITE FLOWERS
...
CITIES LOST BENEATH THE OCEAN WAVES
...
AND, ABOVE ALL...

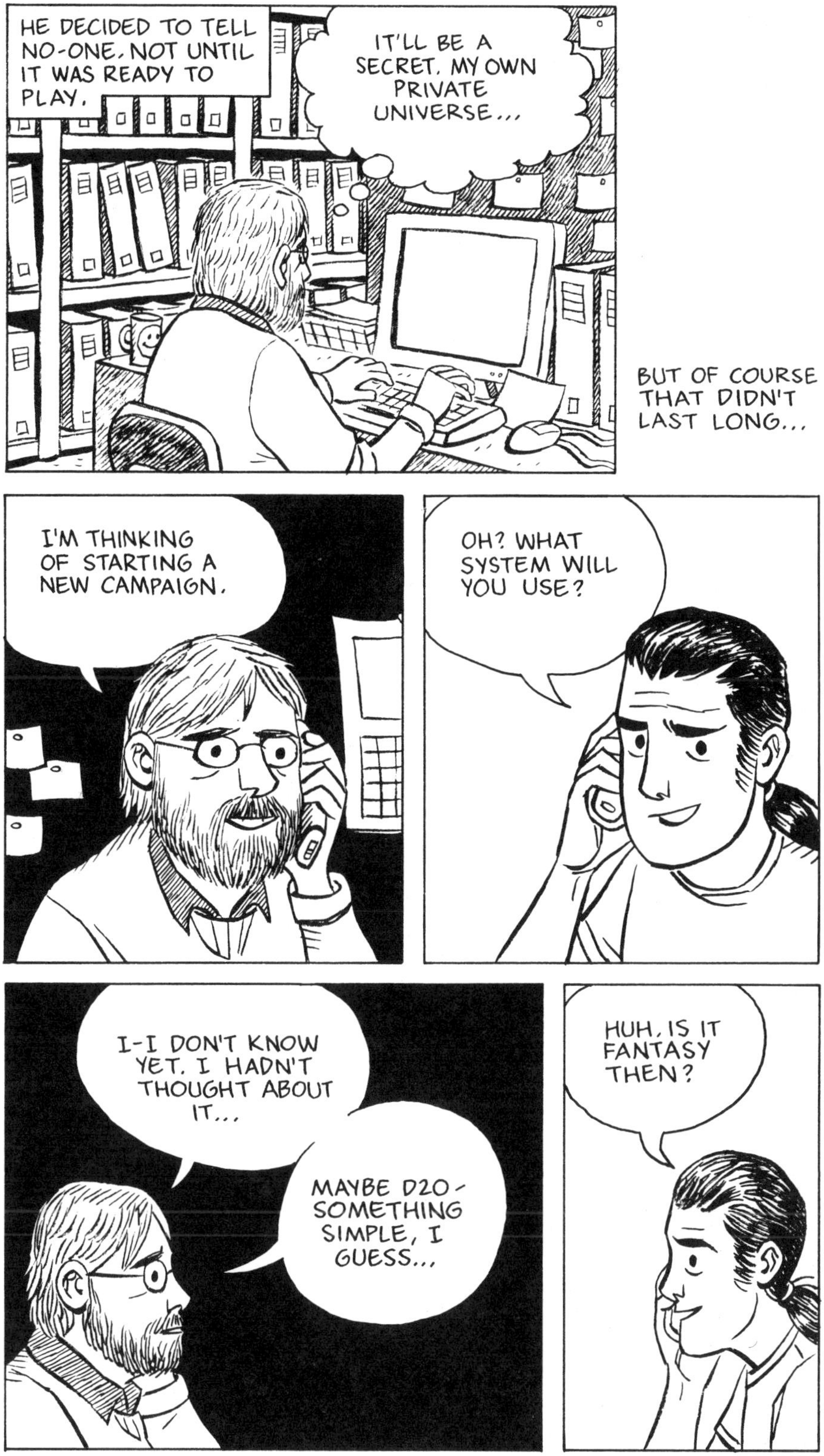
HE DECIDED TO TELL NO-ONE. NOT UNTIL IT WAS READY TO PLAY.
IT'LL BE A SECRET. MY OWN PRIVATE UNIVERSE...
BUT OF COURSE THAT DIDN'T LAST LONG...
I'M THINKING OF STARTING A NEW CAMPAIGN.
OH? WHAT SYSTEM WILL YOU USE?
I-I DON'T KNOW YET. I HADN'T THOUGHT ABOUT IT...
MAYBE D20-SOMETHING SIMPLE, I GUESS...
HUH. IS IT FANTASY THEN?

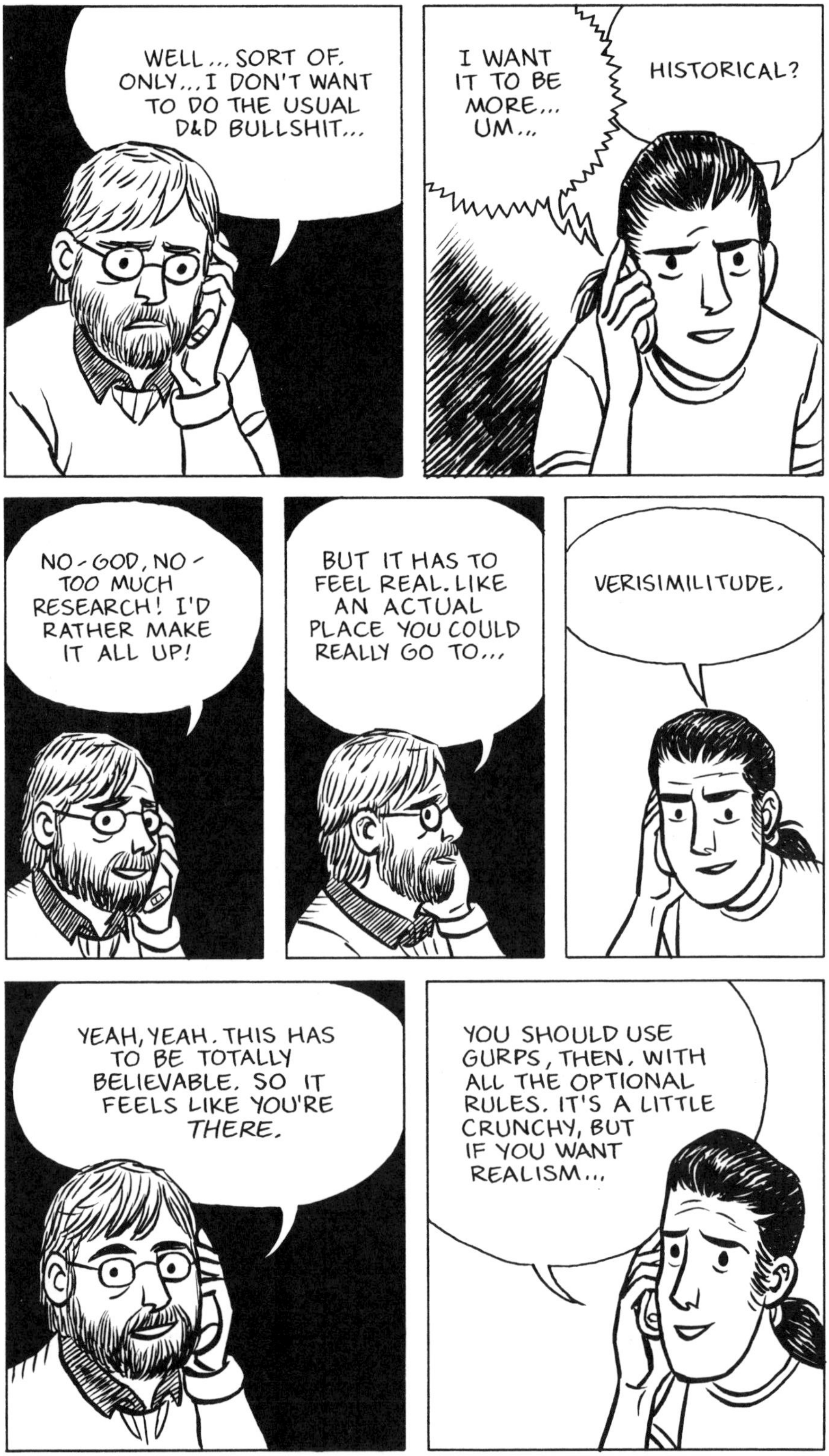
WELL... SORT OF. ONLY... I DON'T WANT TO DO THE USUAL D&D BULLSHIT...
I WANT IT TO BE MORE... UM...
HISTORICAL?
NO - GOD, NO - TOO MUCH RESEARCH! I'D RATHER MAKE IT ALL UP!
BUT IT HAS TO FEEL REAL. LIKE AN ACTUAL PLACE YOU COULD REALLY GO TO...
VERISIMILITUDE.
YEAH, YEAH. THIS HAS TO BE TOTALLY BELIEVABLE. SO IT FEELS LIKE YOU'RE *THERE*.
YOU SHOULD USE GURPS, THEN, WITH ALL THE OPTIONAL RULES. IT'S A LITTLE CRUNCHY, BUT IF YOU WANT REALISM...

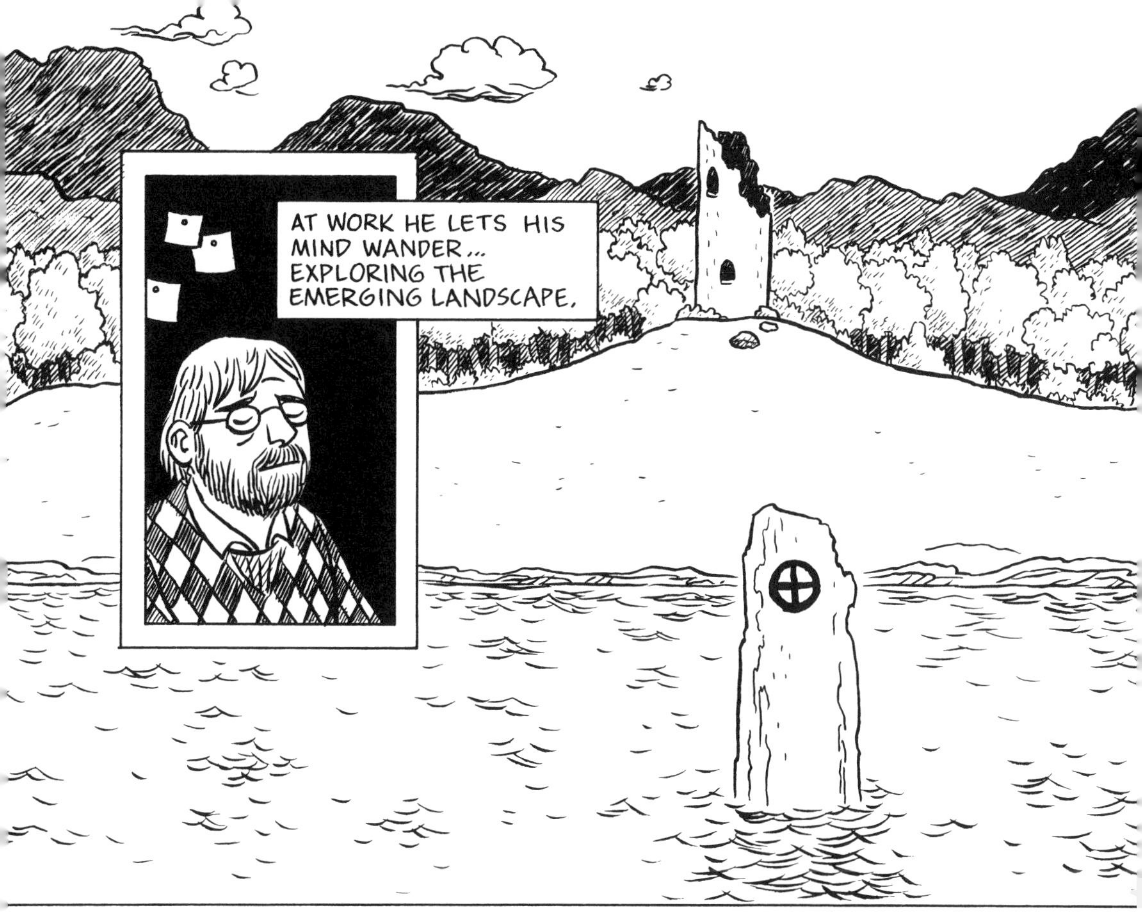
AT WORK HE LETS HIS MIND WANDER... EXPLORING THE EMERGING LANDSCAPE.

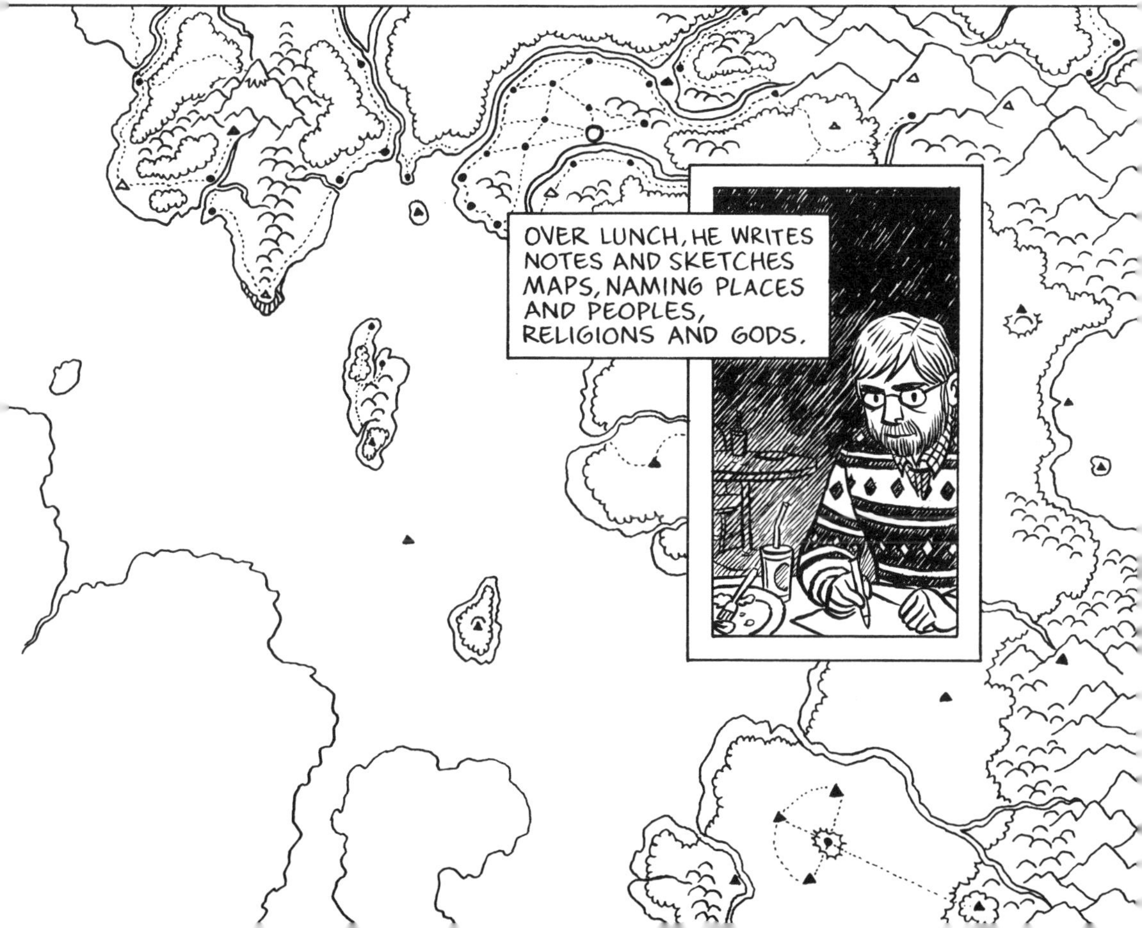
OVER LUNCH, HE WRITES NOTES AND SKETCHES MAPS, NAMING PLACES AND PEOPLES, RELIGIONS AND GODS.

FRIDAY IS DAVE'S GAME.

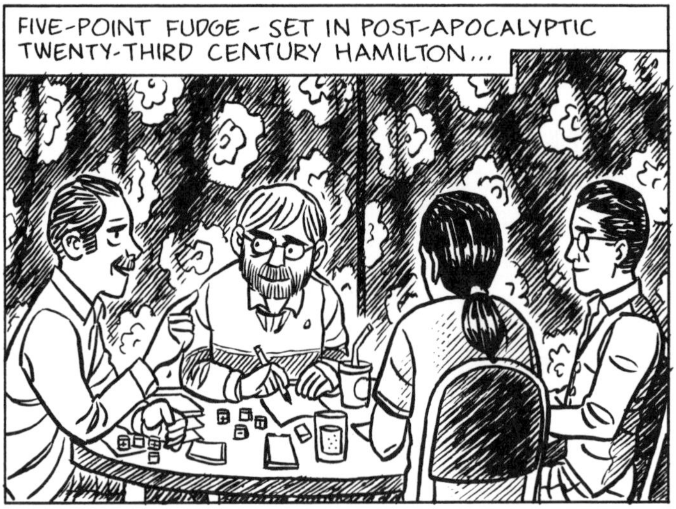
FIVE-POINT FUDGE - SET IN POST-APOCALYPTIC TWENTY-THIRD CENTURY HAMILTON...

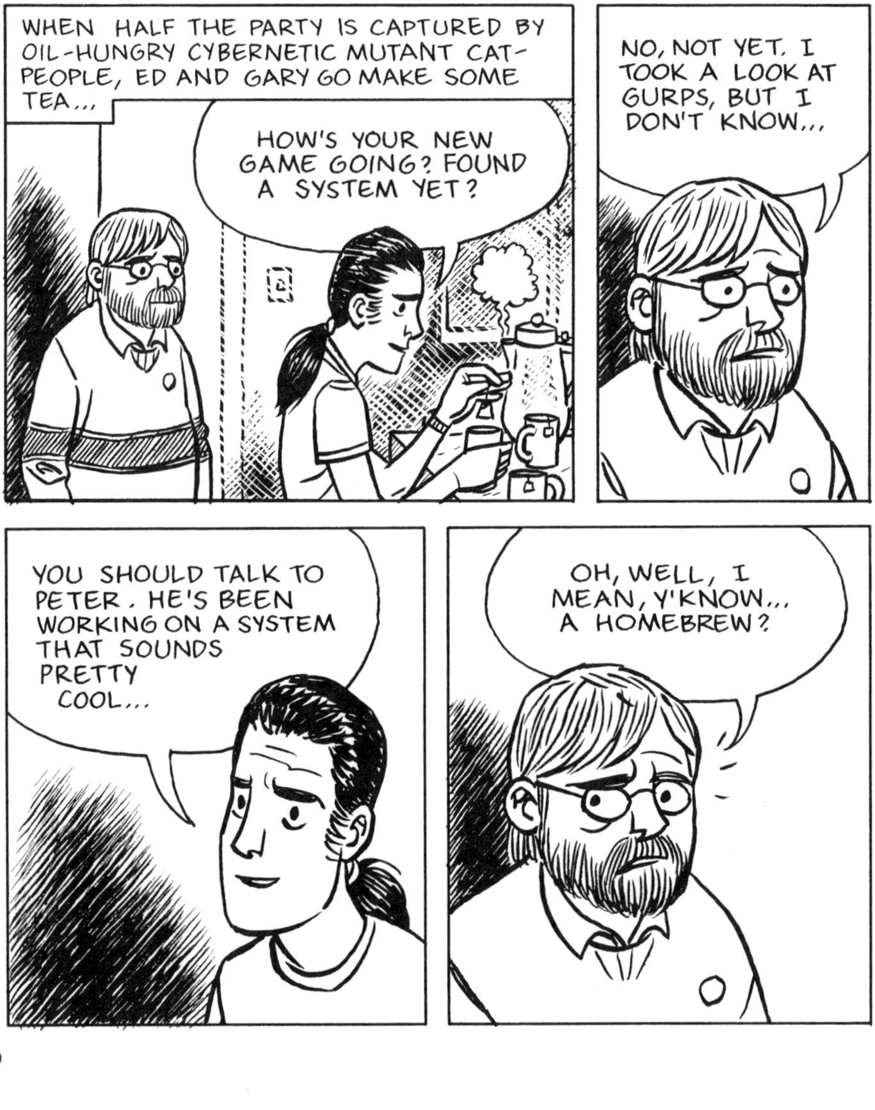
WHEN HALF THE PARTY IS CAPTURED BY OIL-HUNGRY CYBERNETIC MUTANT CAT-PEOPLE, ED AND GARY GO MAKE SOME TEA...
HOW'S YOUR NEW GAME GOING? FOUND A SYSTEM YET?
NO, NOT YET. I TOOK A LOOK AT GURPS, BUT I DON'T KNOW...
YOU SHOULD TALK TO PETER. HE'S BEEN WORKING ON A SYSTEM THAT SOUNDS PRETTY COOL...
OH, WELL, I MEAN, Y'KNOW... A HOMEBREW?

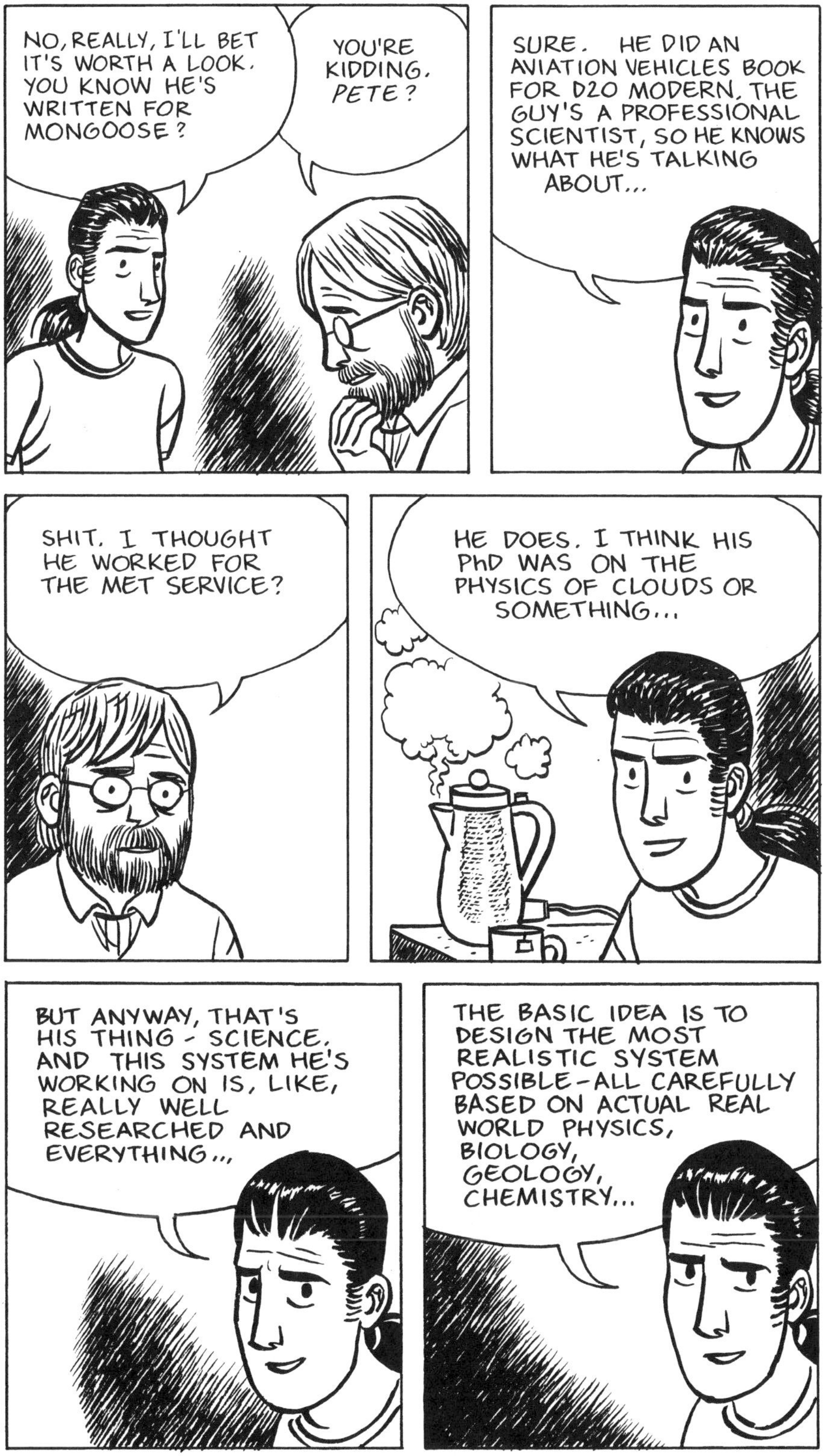
NO, REALLY, I'LL BET IT'S WORTH A LOOK. YOU KNOW HE'S WRITTEN FOR MONGOOSE?
YOU'RE KIDDING, PETE?
SURE. HE DID AN AVIATION VEHICLES BOOK FOR D20 MODERN. THE GUY'S A PROFESSIONAL SCIENTIST, SO HE KNOWS WHAT HE'S TALKING ABOUT...
SHIT. I THOUGHT HE WORKED FOR THE MET SERVICE?
HE DOES. I THINK HIS PhD WAS ON THE PHYSICS OF CLOUDS OR SOMETHING...
BUT ANYWAY, THAT'S HIS THING - SCIENCE. AND THIS SYSTEM HE'S WORKING ON IS, LIKE, REALLY WELL RESEARCHED AND EVERYTHING...
THE BASIC IDEA IS TO DESIGN THE MOST REALISTIC SYSTEM POSSIBLE - ALL CAREFULLY BASED ON ACTUAL REAL WORLD PHYSICS, BIOLOGY, GEOLOGY, CHEMISTRY...

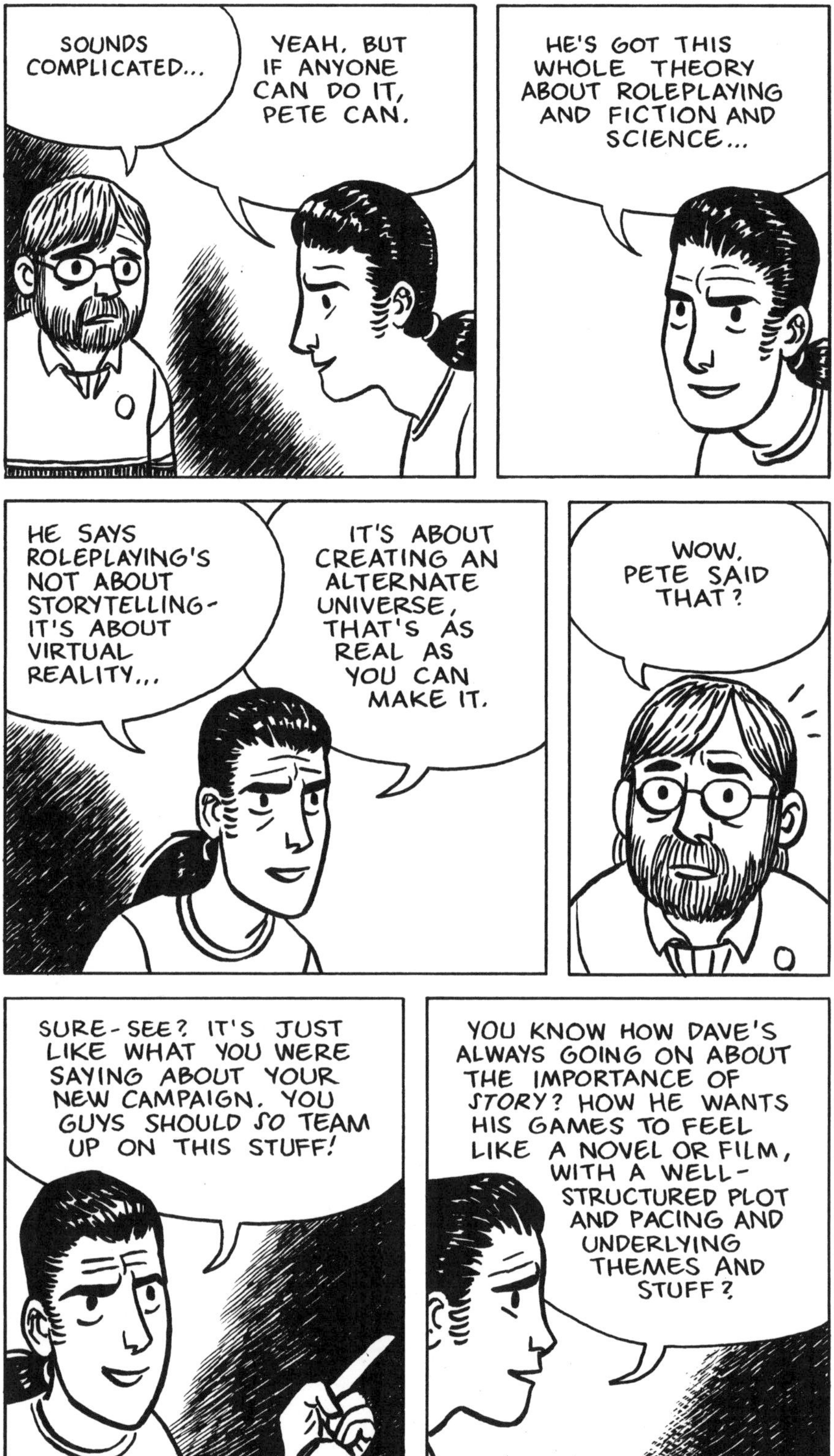
SOUNDS COMPLICATED...
YEAH, BUT IF ANYONE CAN DO IT, PETE CAN.
HE'S GOT THIS WHOLE THEORY ABOUT ROLEPLAYING AND FICTION AND SCIENCE...
HE SAYS ROLEPLAYING'S NOT ABOUT STORYTELLING- IT'S ABOUT VIRTUAL REALITY...
IT'S ABOUT CREATING AN ALTERNATE UNIVERSE, THAT'S AS REAL AS YOU CAN MAKE IT.
WOW. PETE SAID THAT?
SURE- SEE? IT'S JUST LIKE WHAT YOU WERE SAYING ABOUT YOUR NEW CAMPAIGN. YOU GUYS SHOULD SO TEAM UP ON THIS STUFF!
YOU KNOW HOW DAVE'S ALWAYS GOING ON ABOUT THE IMPORTANCE OF STORY? HOW HE WANTS HIS GAMES TO FEEL LIKE A NOVEL OR FILM, WITH A WELL-STRUCTURED PLOT AND PACING AND UNDERLYING THEMES AND STUFF?

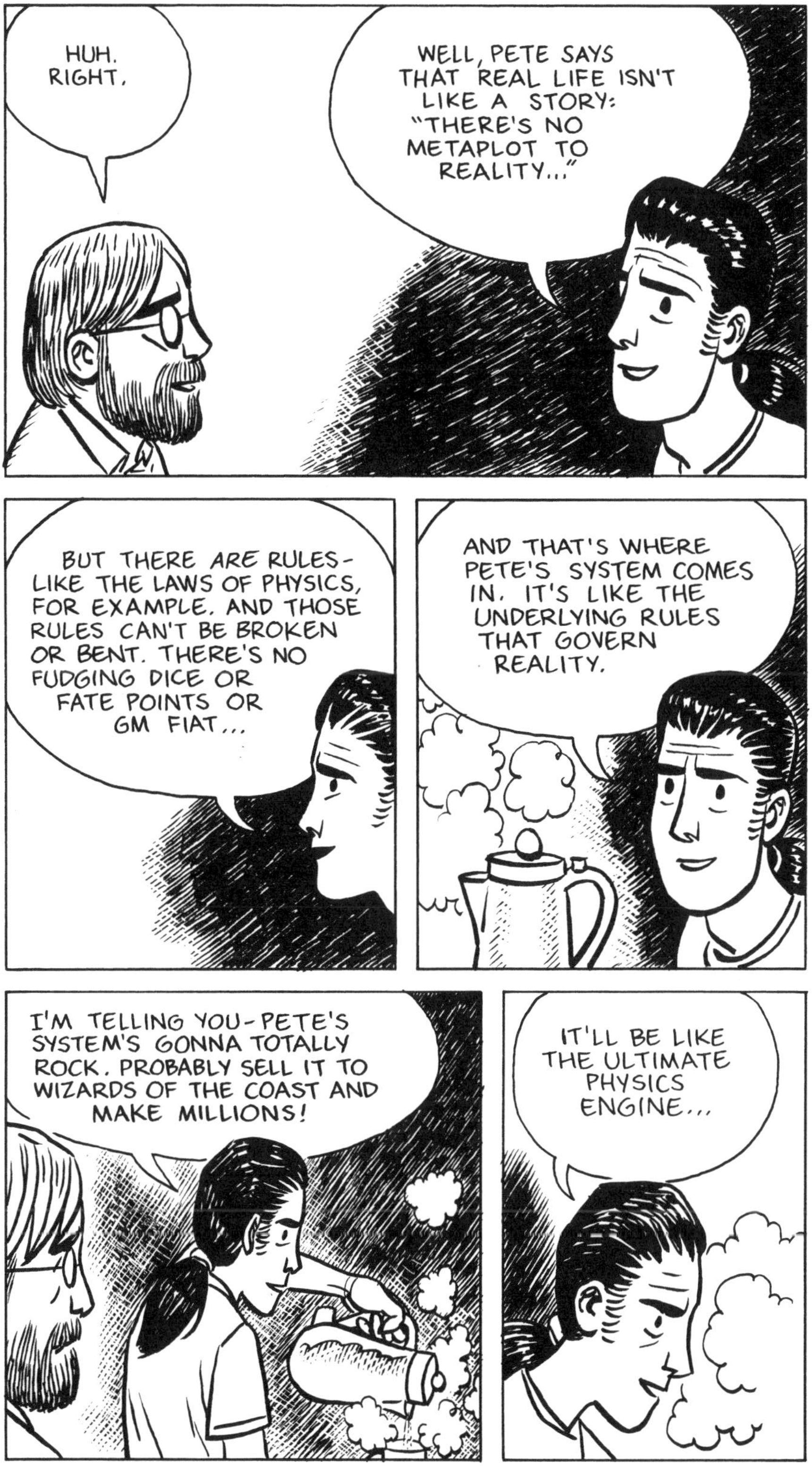
HUH. RIGHT.
WELL, PETE SAYS THAT REAL LIFE ISN'T LIKE A STORY: "THERE'S NO METAPLOT TO REALITY..."
BUT THERE ARE RULES-LIKE THE LAWS OF PHYSICS, FOR EXAMPLE. AND THOSE RULES CAN'T BE BROKEN OR BENT. THERE'S NO FUDGING DICE OR FATE POINTS OR GM FIAT...
AND THAT'S WHERE PETE'S SYSTEM COMES IN. IT'S LIKE THE UNDERLYING RULES THAT GOVERN REALITY.
I'M TELLING YOU-PETE'S SYSTEM'S GONNA TOTALLY ROCK. PROBABLY SELL IT TO WIZARDS OF THE COAST AND MAKE MILLIONS!
IT'LL BE LIKE THE ULTIMATE PHYSICS ENGINE...

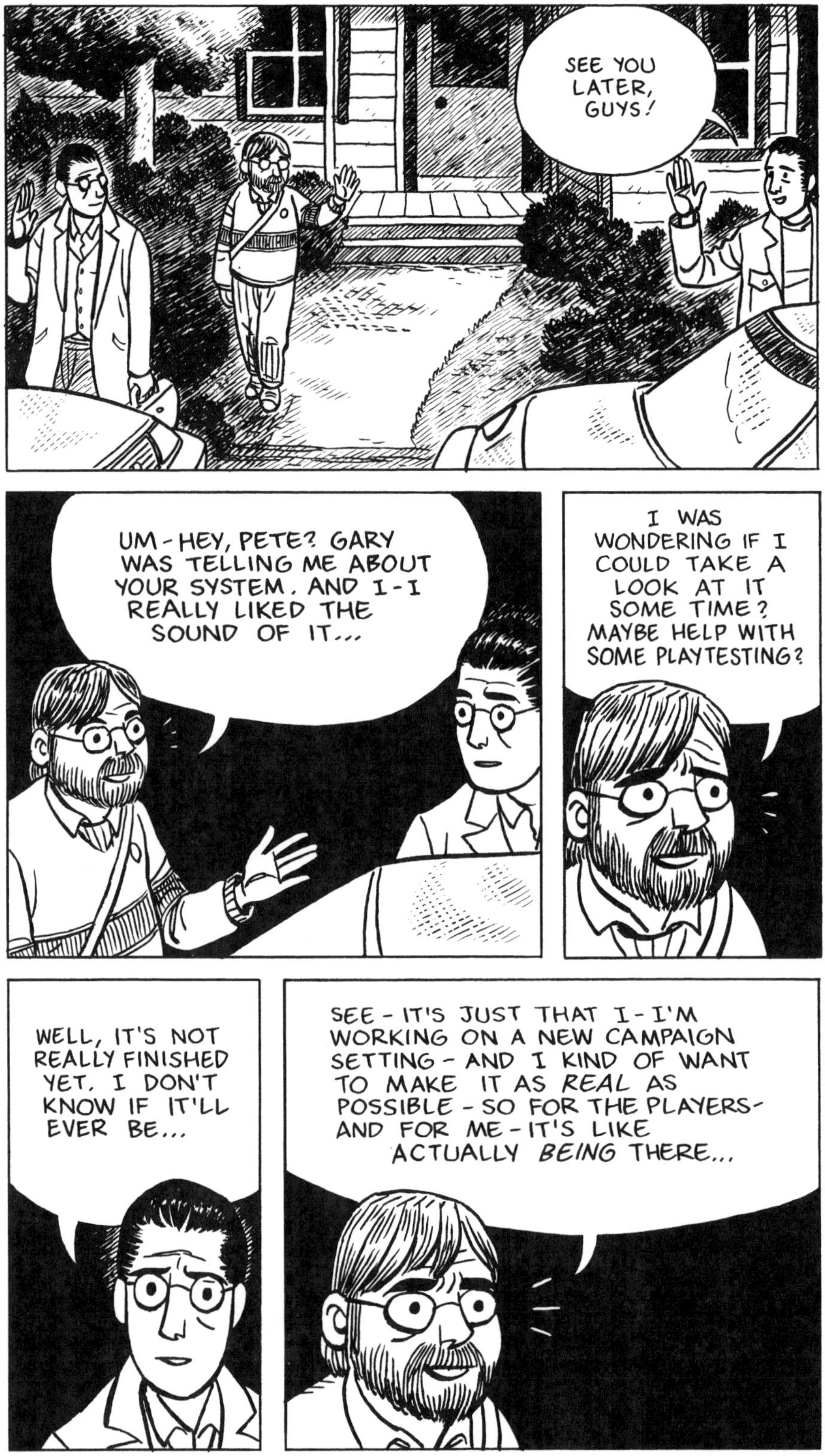
SEE YOU LATER, GUYS!
UM - HEY, PETE? GARY WAS TELLING ME ABOUT YOUR SYSTEM. AND I - I REALLY LIKED THE SOUND OF IT...
I WAS WONDERING IF I COULD TAKE A LOOK AT IT SOME TIME? MAYBE HELP WITH SOME PLAYTESTING?
WELL, IT'S NOT REALLY FINISHED YET. I DON'T KNOW IF IT'LL EVER BE...
SEE - IT'S JUST THAT I - I'M WORKING ON A NEW CAMPAIGN SETTING - AND I KIND OF WANT TO MAKE IT AS *REAL* AS POSSIBLE - SO FOR THE PLAYERS - AND FOR ME - IT'S LIKE ACTUALLY *BEING* THERE...

OH? THAT DOES SOUND INTERESTING...

AND SO-I-UM-I WAS THINKING-FROM WHAT GARY SAID-YOUR SYSTEM SOUNDS PERFECT FOR WHAT I WANT TO DO, YOU KNOW-TO HELP GIVE IT THAT FEELING OF... VERISIMILITUDE...

UH HUH, RIGHT.

SO-UM-I WANTED TO ASK YOU-- HOW-HOW DOES YOUR MAGIC SYSTEM WORK?

UM-WELL-THERE IS NO...

'CAUSE THERE'S SOMETHING I'M REALLY LOOKING FORWARD TO HAVING IN MY WORLD...

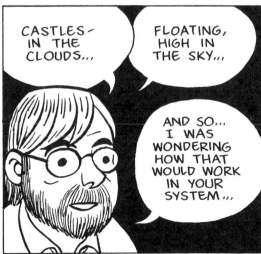

CASTLES-IN THE CLOUDS...

FLOATING, HIGH IN THE SKY...

AND SO... I WAS WONDERING HOW THAT WOULD WORK IN YOUR SYSTEM...

UH...

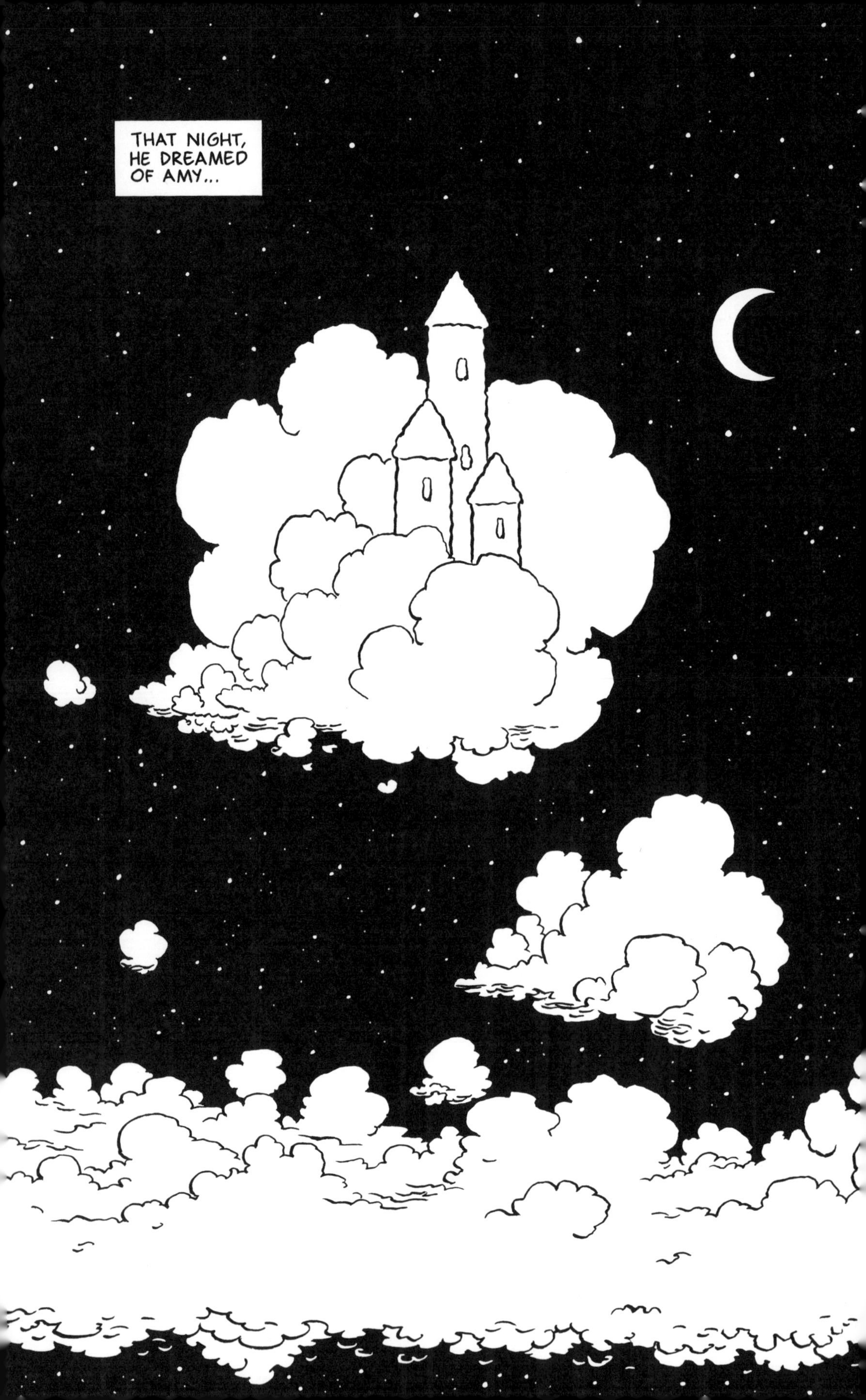
THAT NIGHT, HE DREAMED OF AMY...

# NOTES

PAGE 2:

'READY TO PLAY': i.e. TO USE IN A ROLE-PLAYING GAME. ROLE-PLAYING GAMES (RPGs) FIRST EVOLVED OUT OF TABLETOP WARGAMING IN THE LATE 1960s. THE FIRST PUBLISHED RPG WAS DUNGEONS & DRAGONS (1974). ONE PLAYER (THE GAME MASTER, OR GM) OVERSEES THE GAME, WHILE THE OTHER PLAYERS EACH CREATE A CHARACTER. AS THE GAME UNFOLDS, THE GM DESCRIBES THE SITUATION IN WHICH THE PLAYERS' CHARACTERS FIND THEMSELVES. EACH PLAYER DECIDES HOW HIS OR HER CHARACTER REACTS AND WHAT THEY WILL TRY TO DO. THE RESULT IS A KIND OF IMPROVISED COLLABORATIVE STORY, AS THE PLAYERS INTERACT WITH THE GM'S IMAGINARY WORLD.

'...A NEW CAMPAIGN': AMONG ROLE-PLAYING GAMERS (RPGers), A CAMPAIGN IS AN ONGOING GAME, PLAYED OUT OVER A SERIES OF INDIVIDUAL SESSIONS, SOMETIMES LASTING SEVERAL YEARS. THE TERM IS A LEGACY OF RPGs' WARGAMING ORIGINS.

'WHAT SYSTEM WILL YOU USE?': A ROLE-PLAYING GAME SYSTEM IS THE SET OF RULES THAT GOVERNS CHARACTER CREATION AND THE WAY IN WHICH EVENTS AND ACTIONS PLAY OUT. FOR EXAMPLE, IF A CHARACTER ATTEMPTS TO LEAP FROM A FIRST FLOOR BALCONY ON TO THE ROOF OF A PASSING CARRIAGE, THE SYSTEM WILL PROVIDE A METHOD FOR DETERMINING WHETHER SHE IS SUCCESSFUL (AND, IF NOT, THE CONSEQUENCES). MOST, BUT NOT ALL, RPG SYSTEMS USE DICE TO RESOLVE SITUATIONS WHERE PROBABILITY PLAYS A PART.

'MAYBE D20': D20 IS AN RPG SYSTEM FIRST DESIGNED FOR THE THIRD EDITION OF DUNGEONS & DRAGONS (2000) AND SUBSEQUENTLY USED FOR A NUMBER OF POPULAR GAMES, INCLUDING D20 MODERN, STAR WARS D20 AND SPYCRAFT. D20 IS NAMED FOR THE 20-SIDED DICE USED TO DETERMINE THE OUTCOME OF MOST ACTIONS.

PAGE 3:

'THE USUAL D&D BULLSHIT': D&D IS SHORTHAND FOR DUNGEONS & DRAGONS, FIRST DESIGNED BY GARY GYGAX AND DAVE ARNESON IN 1974 AND STILL THE MOST POPULAR RPG, WITH MILLIONS OF PLAYERS WORLD-WIDE. THE MOST RECENT EDITION (3.5) WAS DESIGNED BY MONTE COOK, SKIP WILLIAMS AND JONATHAN TWEET (AMONG OTHERS) AND WAS PUBLISHED IN 2002. MANY OF THE MOST WIDELY RECOGNISED TROPES OF RPGs (AND SUBSEQUENTLY COMPUTER GAMES) COME FROM D&D, INCLUDING HIT POINTS, CHARACTER CLASSES AND LEVELS, DUNGEON-BASED ADVENTURES AND ICONIC MONSTERS SUCH AS THE BEHOLDER, THE MIND-FLAYER AND DROW.

'YOU SHOULD USE GURPS': THE GENERIC UNIVERSAL ROLE-PLAYING SYSTEM (GURPS) WAS FIRST DESIGNED BY STEVE JACKSON IN 1986. IT IS NOW IN ITS 4TH EDITION (PUBLISHED IN 2004), BUT THE ESSENTIAL SYSTEM REMAINS THE SAME (POINT-BUY CLASSLESS AND LEVEL-LESS CHARACTER GENERATION; RELATIVELY 'REALISTIC' RULES; THE USE OF THREE SIX-SIDED DICE, WHICH GIVES A BELL-SHAPED PROBABILITY CURVE, IN CONTRAST TO D20'S FLAT LINE).

'WITH ALL THE OPTIONAL RULES': GURPS INCLUDES MANY OPTIONAL RULES, WHICH CAN BE USED TO ADD MORE DETAIL AND REALISM.

'IT'S A LITTLE CRUNCHY': RPGers DISTINGUISH BETWEEN 'CRUNCH' (THE ACTUAL RULES SYSTEM) AND 'FLUFF' (THE NON-RULES-BASED ELEMENTS OF AN RPG

GAME WORLD, SUCH AS HISTORY, CULTURES, SCENERY, ETC). A 'CRUNCHY'- OR 'RULES HEAVY'- SYSTEM IS ONE WHICH IS PARTICULARLY COMPLEX AND DETAILED.

PAGE 5:

'5-POINT FUDGE': FUDGE (FREE-FORM UNIVERSAL DO-IT-YOURSELF GAMING ENGINE) IS A RULES-LIGHT RPG SYSTEM DESIGNED IN 1992 BY STEFFAN O'SULLIVAN AND DISTRIBUTED FREELY ON THE INTERNET. WHERE MOST SYSTEMS USE NUMBERS TO DEFINE A CHARACTER'S ABILITIES (e.g. STRENGTH 18, CLIMB SKILL +4), FUDGE USES ADJECTIVES (e.g. 'GREAT' STRENGTH, 'MEDIOCRE' CLIMBER). THE ONLY DICE USED ARE SPECIAL FUDGE DICE, WHICH BEAR NO NUMBERS, BUT INSTEAD GIVE A RESULT OF '+', '−' OR 'O'. CONSEQUENTLY, FUDGE IS POPULAR WITH RPGers WHO WANT TO AVOID NUMBER-CRUNCHING AND FOCUS INSTEAD ON CHARACTER, STORY AND IMMERSION IN THE 'GAME REALITY.' '5-POINT FUDGE' IS A WIDELY-USED CHARACTER-GENERATION SYSTEM FOR FUDGE.

'WHEN HALF THE PARTY...': A PARTY IS A GROUP OF PLAYER-CHARACTERS, AS IN 'A PARTY OF EXPLORERS OR ADVENTURERS.'

'...A HOMEBREW?': A HOMEBREW SYSTEM IS ONE THAT HAS BEEN DESIGNED BY AN INDIVIDUAL PLAYER FOR THEIR OWN USE, AND USUALLY UNPUBLISHED.

PAGE 6:

'WRITTEN FOR MONGOOSE': MONGOOSE PUBLISHING IS A UK-BASED RPG PUBLISHER.

'D20 MODERN': A VARIANT ON D20 DESIGNED FOR USE IN MODERN, RATHER THAN FANTASY, SETTINGS.

'WORKED FOR THE MET SERVICE': METSERVICE IS NEW ZEALAND'S MAIN METEOROLICAL ORGANISATION, PROVIDING FORECASTS AND OTHER INFORMATION TO THE GOVERNMENT, PRIVATE COMPANIES AND THE PUBLIC.

PAGE 8:

'METAPLOT': IN RPG TERMINOLOGY, 'METAPLOT' REFERS TO THE OVER-ARCHING NARRATIVE PLOT THAT BINDS A CAMPAIGN (OR SERIES OF ADVENTURES) TOGETHER. WHEN USED IN REFERENCE TO COMMERCIALLY-PUBLISHED GAME WORLDS (SUCH AS THE FORGOTTEN REALMS OR DRAGONLANCE), IT IS THE EVOLVING STORY THAT SHAPES THAT WORLD OVER TIME, WHICH GAMERS MAY TRY TO REFLECT IN THEIR INDIVIDUAL CAMPAIGNS.

'THERE'S NO FUDGING DICE': WHEN A GM 'FUDGES THE DICE', HE OR SHE IGNORES A DIE-ROLL RESULT WHICH WOULD 'DERAIL THE PLOT' OR OTHERWISE INTERFERE WITH A SATISFYING GAME EXPERIENCE FOR THE PLAYERS.

'FATE POINTS': SOME RPG SYSTEMS ALLOW PLAYERS TO 'SPEND' POINTS IN ORDER TO CIRCUMVENT THE GAME'S NORMAL MECHANICS - e.g. TO AVOID DEATH IN A SITUATION THAT WOULD OTHERWISE BE FATAL.

'GM FIAT': WHEN A GM ARBITRARILY DECREES A PARTICULAR OUTCOME OR EVENT WITH NO REFERENCE TO THE RULE SYSTEM OR DICE.

'WIZARDS OF THE COAST': THE PUBLISHERS OF DUNGEONS & DRAGONS, D20 MODERN AND OTHER POPULAR RPGs. TODAY THEY ARE A FULLY-OWNED SUBSIDIARY OF THE TOY GIANT HASBRO, INC.

'THE ULTIMATE PHYSICS ENGINE': A 'PHYSICS ENGINE' IS AN RPG RULE SYSTEM DESIGNED TO SIMULATE REAL-WORLD PHYSICS. THE TERM IS BORROWED FROM DISCUSSIONS OF COMPUTER GAME SOFTWARE DESIGN.

PAGE 9:

'PLAYTESTING': PLAYING A GAME IN ORDER TO FIND FLAWS IN THE SYSTEM BEFORE IT IS PUBLISHED.

PAGE 10:

'MAGIC SYSTEM': IN A FANTASY RPG, THE RULES THAT DESCRIBE AND DETERMINE 'HOW MAGIC WORKS.'

# TO THE I-LAND

## THE COMICS OF BARRY LINTON

### AN APPRECIATION BY DYLAN HORROCKS

BARRY LINTON WAS BORN IN AUCKLAND IN THE YEAR 5707,\* THEN "RAISED IN CHRISTCHURCH, A TEENAGER IN WAIKATO." HE BEGAN DRAWING CARTOONS WHILE STILL AT SCHOOL: SINGLE PANEL DRAWINGS, OFTEN FEATURING RECURRING CHARACTERS LIKE DUKE, A TEDDY BOY BIKER. OVER TIME, THESE CHARACTERS BECAME MORE FULLY DEVELOPED, UNTIL LINTON WAS DRAWING WHOLE PAGES OF SINGLE-PANEL CARTOONS: "IT WOULD LOOK LIKE A COMIC, EVEN IF IT DIDN'T HAVE A STORY."

AFTER WORKING FOR A WHILE IN A SHOE SHOP AND THEN DESIGNING WINDOW DISPLAYS FOR A HAMILTON DEPARTMENT STORE, LINTON DECIDED TO GO TO ART SCHOOL. HE SPENT TWO YEARS AT THE ELAM SCHOOL OF FINE ARTS IN AUCKLAND ("ONLY ONE OFFICIALLY") BEFORE DROPPING OUT AND HITTING "THE HA HA HIGHWAY," HITCHHIKING AND TRAVELLING AROUND THE COUNTRY. THE NEXT FEW YEARS WERE A BLUR OF HICK TOWNS, DRUNKEN PARTIES AND HIPPY COMMUNES, WHICH WENT ON "TILL I'D LOST ALL TRACK OF TIME AND VIRTUALLY ALL KNOWLEDGE OF WHERE I WAS AT..."

---

\*Rather than use the Christian Dating System, Linton prefers the ancient Sumerian Calendar of Nippur, begun in 3760 B.C., making it one of the oldest in the world. Hence 2000 A.D. equates to 5760 after Nippur.

EVENTUALLY LINTON RETURNED TO AUCKLAND FIRED UP BY HIS TRAVELS AND BEGAN DRAWING COMICS FOR THE UNIVERSITY NEWSPAPER AND OTHER ALTERNATIVE RAGS. THIS EARLY WORK WAS REMINISCIENT OF ROBERT CRUMB'S PSYCHEDELIC 'STREAM OF CONSCIOUSNESS' COMICS: "JUST NONSENSICAL SPEECH BALLOONS."

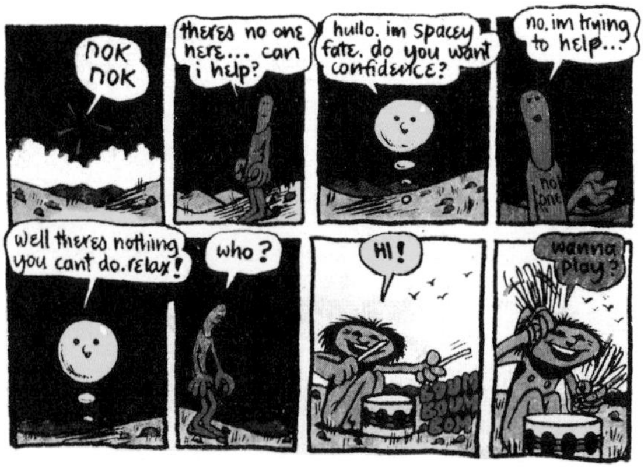
nok nok
theres no one here... can i help?
hullo. im spacey fate. do you want confidence?
no. im trying to help...
well theres nothing you cant do. relax!
who?
HI!
wanna play?

ONE OF LINTON'S FRIENDS WAS JOE WYLIE, AN ANIMATOR WHO'D STUDIED ART WITH MONKS IN NEPAL. LINTON AND WYLIE USED TO SIT AT THE KITCHEN TABLE TOGETHER AND DRAW.

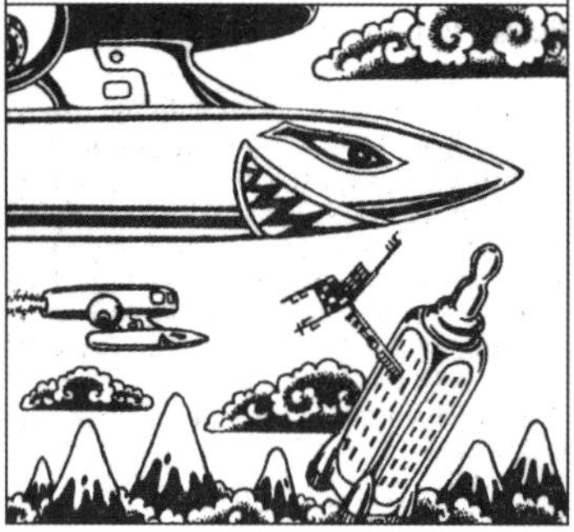

WYLIE

ANOTHER FRIEND, TERRY HOGAN, WAS FLATTING WITH COLIN WILSON, A YOUNG ARTIST WHO DREAMED OF STARTING UP A NEW ZEALAND COMICS MAGAZINE.

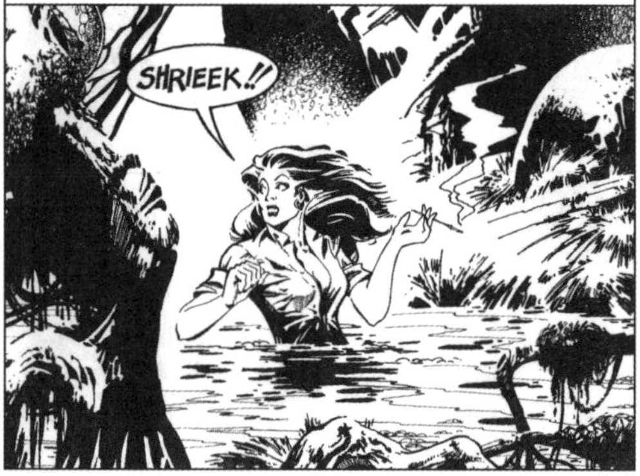
SHRIEEK!!

WILSON

IN 5727, THEY GOT TOGETHER TO CREATE *STRIPS*, WHICH LASTED FOR TEN YEARS AND 23 ISSUES...

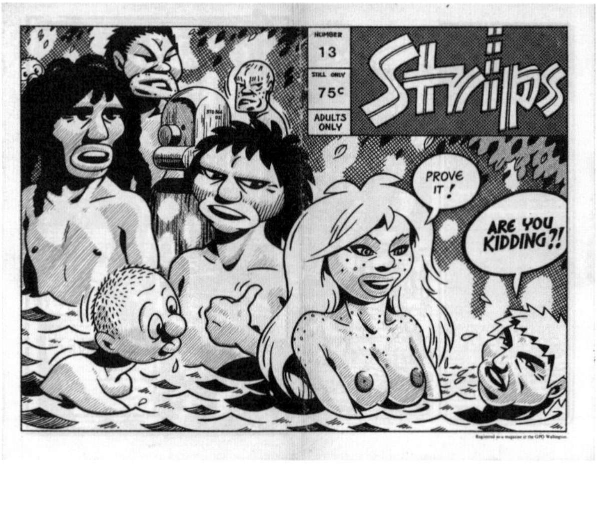
NUMBER
13
STILL ONLY
75c
ADULTS ONLY
Strips
PROVE IT!
ARE YOU KIDDING?!

LINTON'S *STRIPS* STORIES ARE DRAWN IN A POWERFUL EXPRESSIVE STYLE HE DESCRIBES AS "BRUTALLY DYNAMIC." THEY WERE ALSO HIS FIRST REAL STORIES - WITH PLOTS AND A RECURRING CAST OF CHARACTERS, INCLUDING:

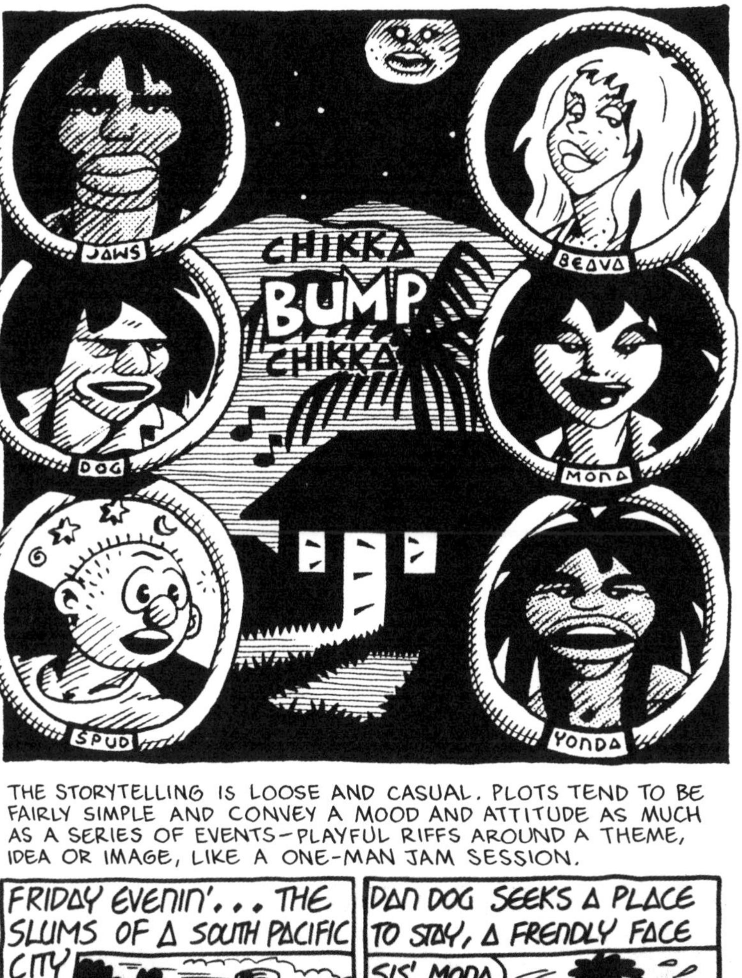
JAWS
BEAVA
CHIKKA
BUMP
CHIKKA
DOG
MONA
SPUD
YONDA

THE STORYTELLING IS LOOSE AND CASUAL. PLOTS TEND TO BE FAIRLY SIMPLE AND CONVEY A MOOD AND ATTITUDE AS MUCH AS A SERIES OF EVENTS - PLAYFUL RIFFS AROUND A THEME, IDEA OR IMAGE, LIKE A ONE-MAN JAM SESSION.

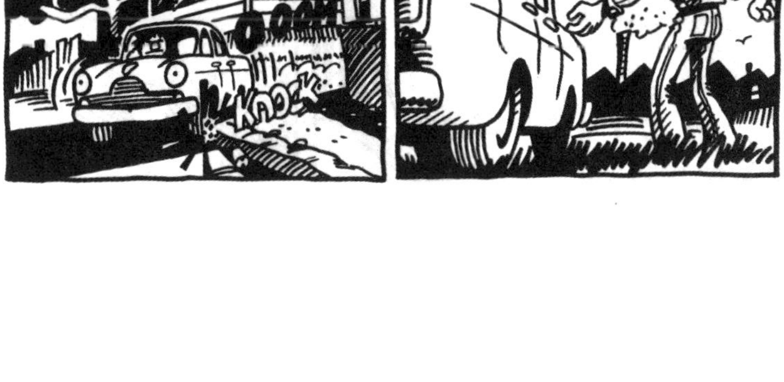
FRIDAY EVENIN'... THE SLUMS OF A SOUTH PACIFIC CITY
KNOCK
DAN DOG SEEKS A PLACE TO STAY, A FRENDLY FACE
SIS' MONA

LINTON USES LANGUAGE MUSICALLY, TOO. WORDS FADE IN AND OUT, IMPROVISED OVER THE PICTURES IN SHORT BROKEN PHRASES...

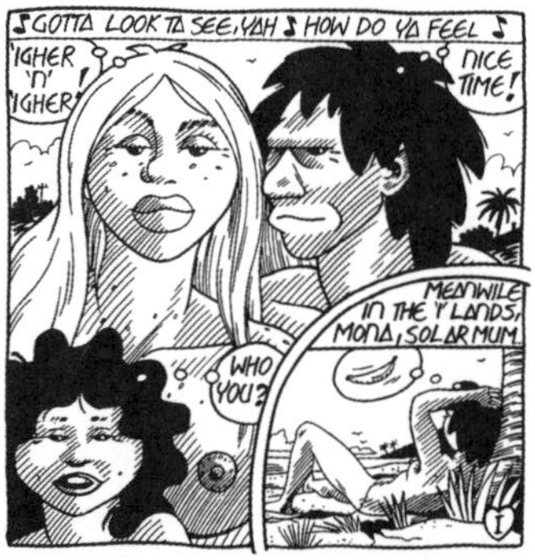

♪ GOTTA LOOK TA SEE, YAH ♪ HOW DO YA FEEL ♪
'IGHER 'N' 'IGHER
NICE TIME!
MEANWILE IN THE 'I' LANDS, MONA, SOLAR MUM
WHO YOU?


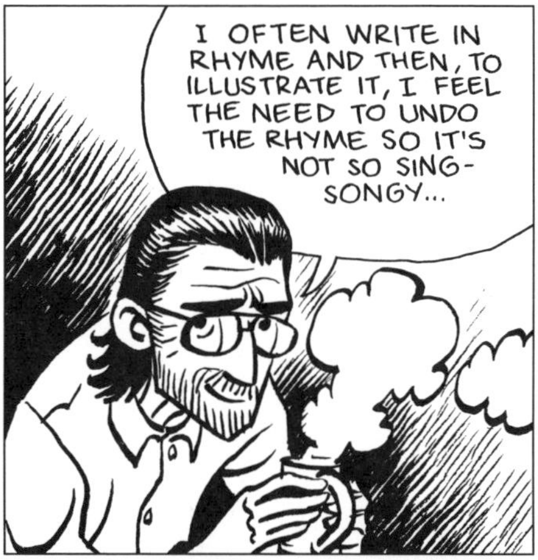

I OFTEN WRITE IN RHYME AND THEN, TO ILLUSTRATE IT, I FEEL THE NEED TO UNDO THE RHYME SO IT'S NOT SO SING-SONGY...


(DURING THE EARLY *STRIPS* YEARS LINTON'S DAY JOB WAS AT WARNER BROS RECORDS AND HE WAS HEAVILY INVOLVED IN THE MUSIC SCENE, DRAWING ALBUM COVERS AND BAND POSTERS...)

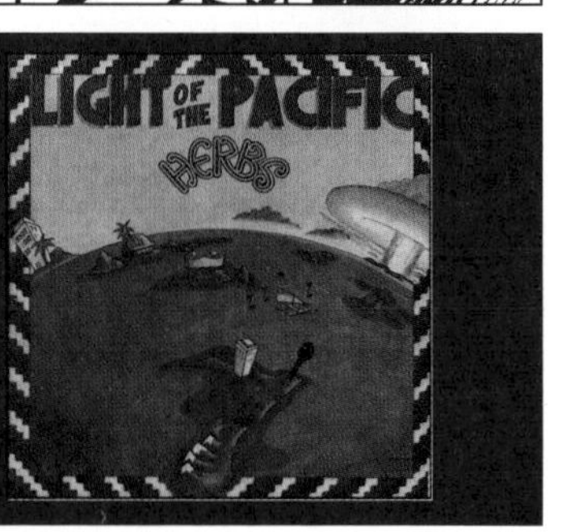

LIGHT OF THE PACIFIC
HERBS


LINTON'S WORK ALWAYS HAS A STRONG SENSE OF PLACE, WHICH HE CONSCIOUSLY SOUGHT FROM EARLY ON...

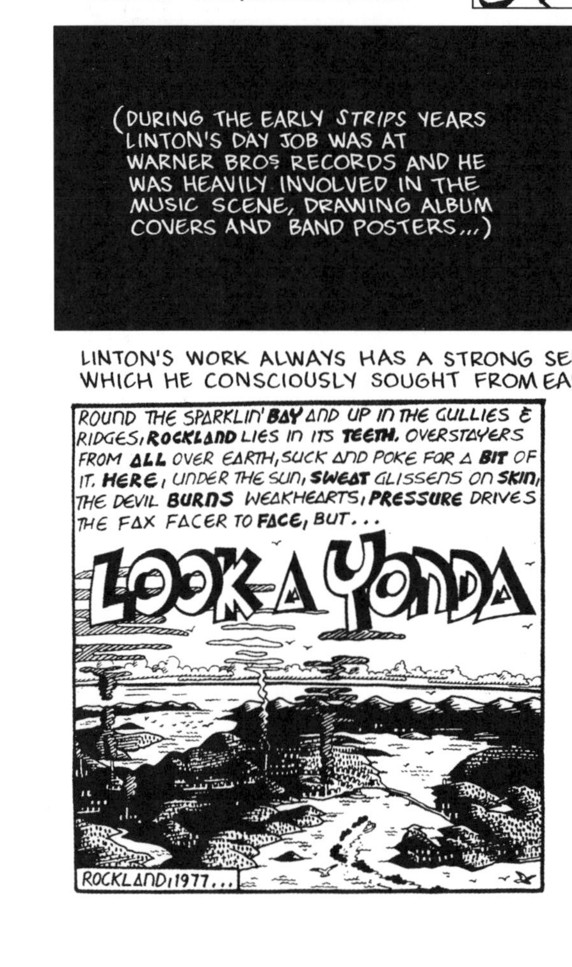

ROUND THE SPARKLIN' **BAY** AND UP IN THE GULLIES & RIDGES, **ROCKLAND** LIES IN ITS **TEETH**. OVERSTAYERS FROM **ALL** OVER EARTH, SUCK AND POKE FOR A **BIT** OF IT. **HERE**, UNDER THE SUN, **SWEAT** GLISSENS ON **SKIN**, THE DEVIL **BURNS** WEAKHEARTS, **PRESSURE** DRIVES THE FAX FACER TO **FACE**, BUT...
LOOK-A YONDA
ROCKLAND, 1977...


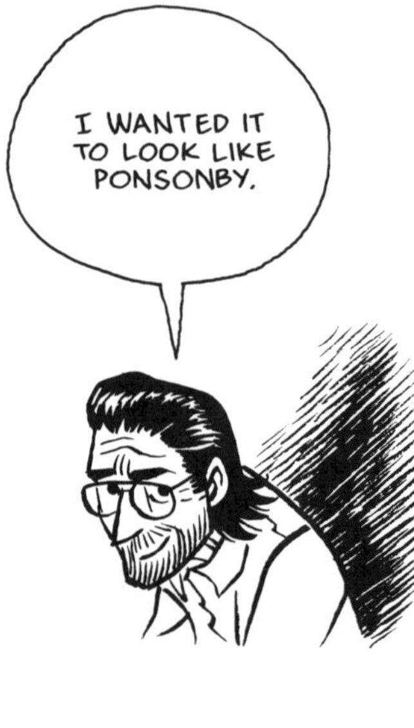

I WANTED IT TO LOOK LIKE PONSONBY.

IT'S ALWAYS HOT AND HUMID IN LINTON'S AUCKLAND (OR "ROCKLAND"). DURING THE DAY EVERYONE LOUNGES AROUND, SWEATY, HORNY AND STONED...

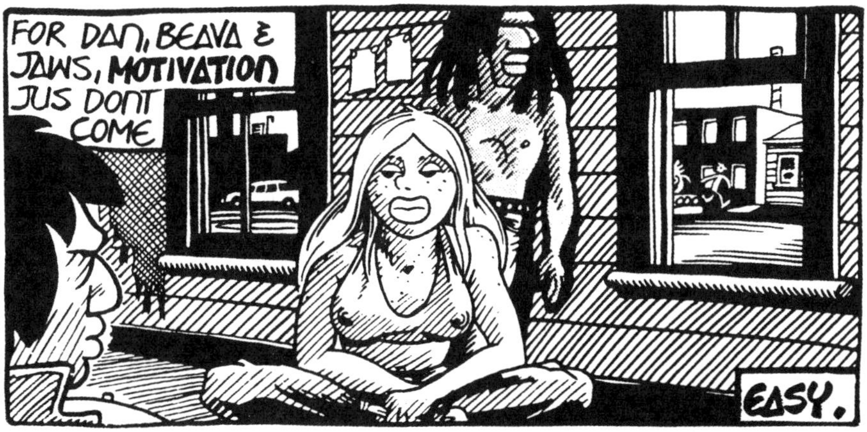
FOR DAN, BEAVA & JAWS, MOTIVATION JUS DONT COME
EASY.

AT NIGHT, THE CITY COMES TO LIFE-DARK AND WILD, HUMMING WITH MUSIC, SEX AND SUDDEN VIOLENCE.

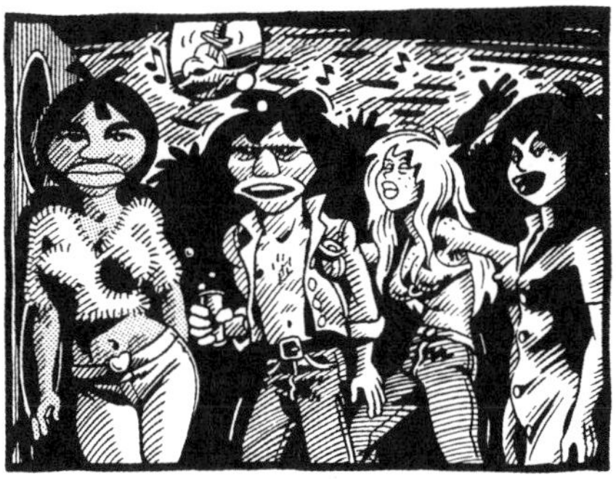

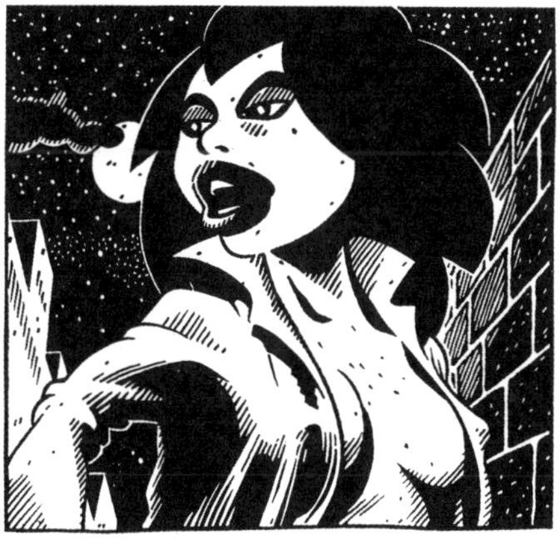

BY THE 5730s LINTON'S STORIES WERE BECOMING MORE COMPLEX, WITH A GROWING ENSEMBLE OF REGULAR CHARACTERS. THEY BEGAN TO REFLECT THE CHANGING SOCIAL LANDSCAPE, INCREASINGLY POPULATED BY SLEAZY BUSINESSMEN, CORRUPT LAWYERS, HUMAN TRAFFICKERS AND DRUG DEALERS...

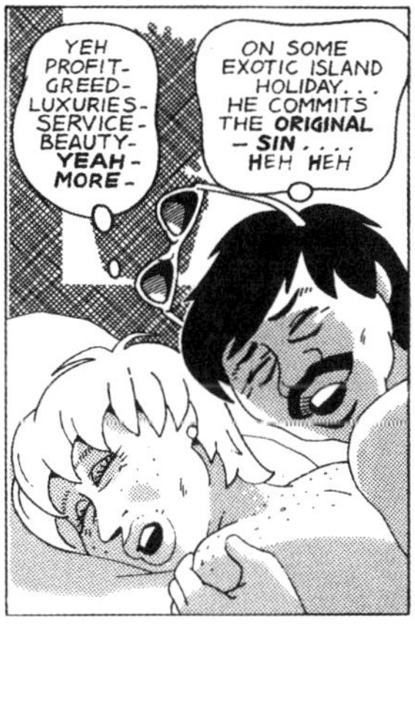
YEH PROFIT-GREED-LUXURIES-SERVICE-BEAUTY-YEAH-MORE-
ON SOME EXOTIC ISLAND HOLIDAY... HE COMMITS THE ORIGINAL -SIN.... HEH HEH

AT THE SAME TIME, HIS DRAWING GREW LIGHTER, THE LINEWORK MORE CAREFUL AND PRECISE...

BY NOW LINTON WAS WORKING AT THE *AUCKLAND STAR*, PRODUCING GRAPHICS AND ILLUSTRATIONS FOR NEWS STORIES AND FEATURES, AN EXPERIENCE WHICH HE SAYS REFINED HIS CRAFT, IMPROVED HIS TECHNICAL SKILLS AND GAVE HIM AN ABIDING LOVE OF MAPS...

TASMAN SEA
DARRAN MTS
HUMBOLT MTS
GLACIERS
MILFORD SOUND
SUTHERLAND FALLS
QUEENSTOWN
FLIGHT ROUTE
TE ANAU
ROAD ROUTE

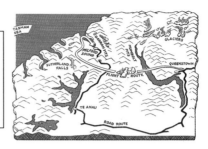

THIS GROWING SOPHISTICATION IN THE DRAFTSMANSHIP WAS ACCOMPANIED BY A GROWING EMOTIONAL SUBTLETY. DAN'S RELATIONSHIP WITH HIS DAUGHTER LINDY COMES TO THE FOREGROUND...

KIISHH
CHAMP
DUMP
THEY SAY YELLOW ROSES
SYMBOLISE GOODBYE
I DIDN'T GIVE YOU THOSE 'CAUSE...
TENDER NEE-EEDS
KIISHH
KRASH
STAY ALIVE...
CHING CHING AJING CHING

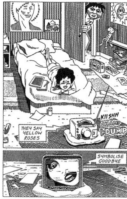

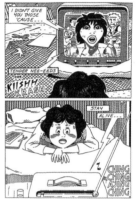

SINCE *STRIPS* FOLDED IN 5737, LINTON'S WORK HAS LACKED A REGULAR HOME. HE HAS, HOWEVER, ACHIEVED SOME WIDER RECOGNITION, WITH COMICS APPEARING IN THE *NZ LISTENER* AND *LANDFALL*...

THE MIGHTY WAIKATO
IN THE 60S, GROWING UP IN HAMILTON WAS LIKE A SEASON-TICKET TO WALLY-WORLD FOR A 15YR OLD 'MAINLANDER'...
I'M CONTINUALLY AMAZED!
©1991 BARRY LINTON

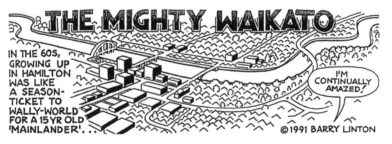

IN 5744 LINTON SELF-PUBLISHED A COLLECTION OF WORK FROM *STRIPS*. IT SOLD OUT QUICKLY AND IS NOW ALMOST IMPOSSIBLE TO FIND...

BARRY LINTON
CHOK CHOK!

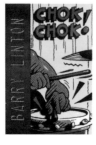

A LATER COLLECTION OF COMICS FROM THE POST-*STRIPS* YEARS IS EVEN RARER...

ONE SHORT LIFE
EVER WONDER WHERE AM I? WHAT TIME IS IT?

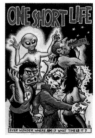

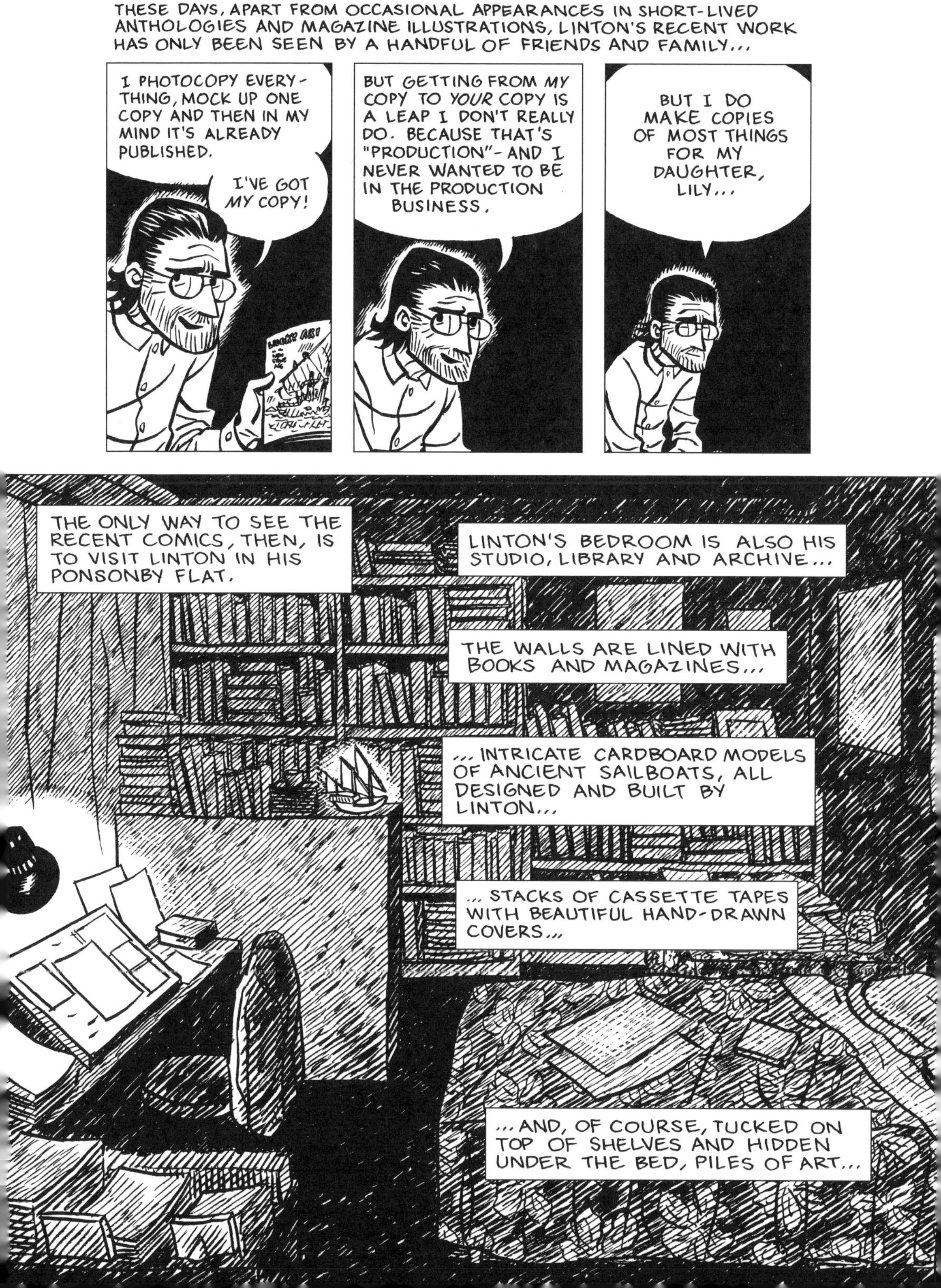
THESE DAYS, APART FROM OCCASIONAL APPEARANCES IN SHORT-LIVED ANTHOLOGIES AND MAGAZINE ILLUSTRATIONS, LINTON'S RECENT WORK HAS ONLY BEEN SEEN BY A HANDFUL OF FRIENDS AND FAMILY...
I PHOTOCOPY EVERYTHING, MOCK UP ONE COPY AND THEN IN MY MIND IT'S ALREADY PUBLISHED.
I'VE GOT MY COPY!
BUT GETTING FROM MY COPY TO YOUR COPY IS A LEAP I DON'T REALLY DO. BECAUSE THAT'S "PRODUCTION"- AND I NEVER WANTED TO BE IN THE PRODUCTION BUSINESS.
BUT I DO MAKE COPIES OF MOST THINGS FOR MY DAUGHTER, LILY...
THE ONLY WAY TO SEE THE RECENT COMICS, THEN, IS TO VISIT LINTON IN HIS PONSONBY FLAT.
LINTON'S BEDROOM IS ALSO HIS STUDIO, LIBRARY AND ARCHIVE...
THE WALLS ARE LINED WITH BOOKS AND MAGAZINES...
... INTRICATE CARDBOARD MODELS OF ANCIENT SAILBOATS, ALL DESIGNED AND BUILT BY LINTON...
... STACKS OF CASSETTE TAPES WITH BEAUTIFUL HAND-DRAWN COVERS...
... AND, OF COURSE, TUCKED ON TOP OF SHELVES AND HIDDEN UNDER THE BED, PILES OF ART...

AROUND THE TIME *STRIPS* FOLDED, LINTON'S WORK UNDERWENT A MAJOR CHANGE. IN MANY OF THESE NEW STORIES, SEXUALITY RETREATED TO THE BACKGROUND. BUT LINTON ALSO BEGAN DRAWING PRIVATE EROTIC COMICS, WHICH WERE NEVER MEANT TO BE PUBLISHED...

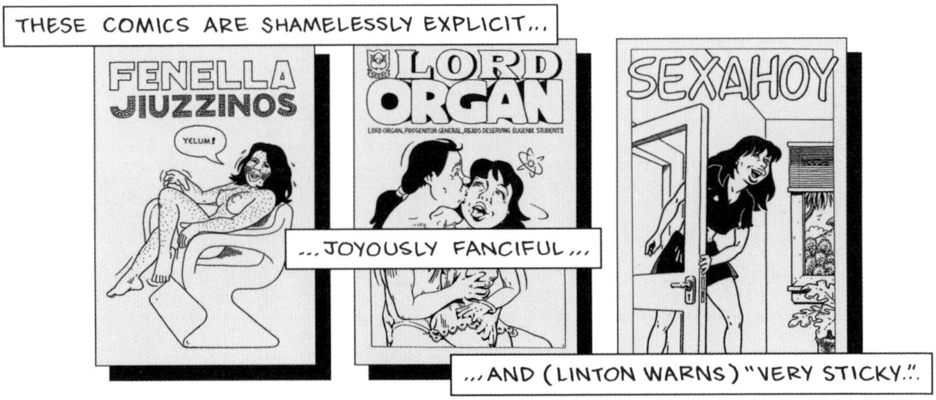

THESE COMICS ARE SHAMELESSLY EXPLICIT...
FENELLA JIUZZINOS
YELUM!
LORD ORGAN
LORD ORGAN, PROGENITOR GENERAL, READS DESERVING EUGENIX STUDENTS
...JOYOUSLY FANCIFUL...
SEXAHOY
...AND (LINTON WARNS) "VERY STICKY."


DURING THE 5740s LINTON BEGAN TO READ ABOUT UFOs, ALIEN ABDUCTION AND WEIRD PHENOMENA: "THE WEIRDER THE BETTER! THE STRANGER THE STORY THE MORE I LIKED IT. THOSE STORIES WORK LIKE MAD ON ME!"

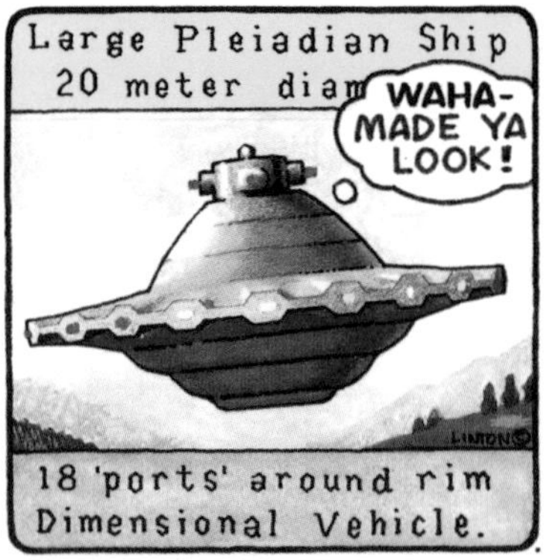

Large Pleiadian Ship
20 meter diam
WAHA-MADE YA LOOK!
LINTON©
18 'ports' around rim
Dimensional Vehicle.


THIS LED TO A SERIES OF COMICS IN WHICH UFOs WERE INCORPORATED INTO A PERSONAL SEARCH FOR SPIRITUAL MEANING...

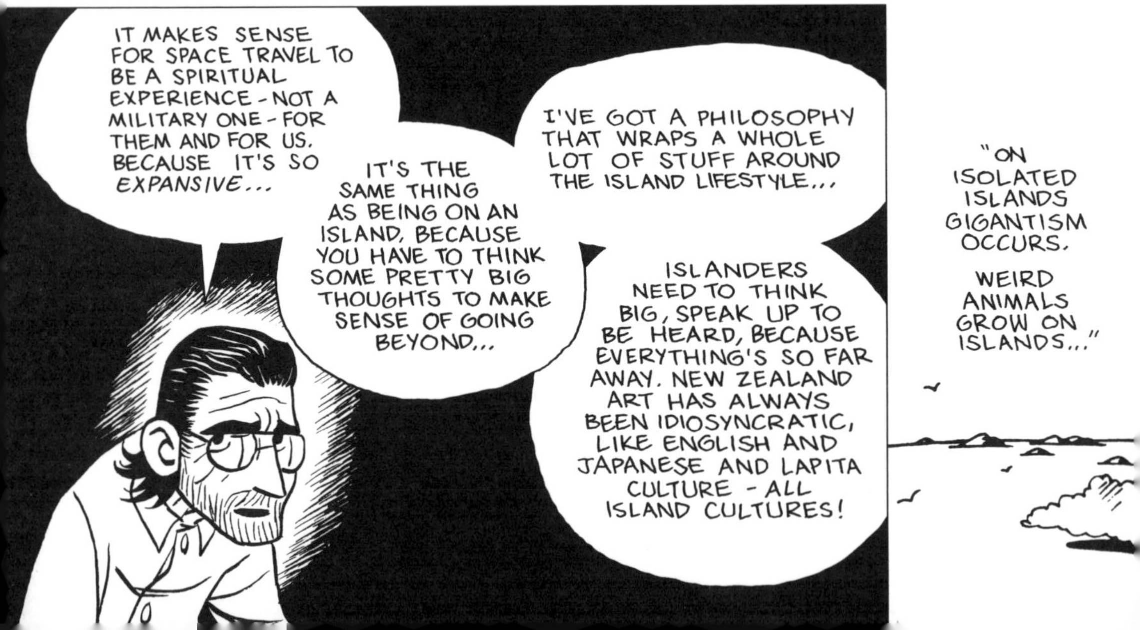

IT MAKES SENSE FOR SPACE TRAVEL TO BE A SPIRITUAL EXPERIENCE - NOT A MILITARY ONE - FOR THEM AND FOR US. BECAUSE IT'S SO *EXPANSIVE*...
IT'S THE SAME THING AS BEING ON AN ISLAND, BECAUSE YOU HAVE TO THINK SOME PRETTY BIG THOUGHTS TO MAKE SENSE OF GOING BEYOND...
I'VE GOT A PHILOSOPHY THAT WRAPS A WHOLE LOT OF STUFF AROUND THE ISLAND LIFESTYLE...
ISLANDERS NEED TO THINK BIG, SPEAK UP TO BE HEARD, BECAUSE EVERYTHING'S SO FAR AWAY. NEW ZEALAND ART HAS ALWAYS BEEN IDIOSYNCRATIC, LIKE ENGLISH AND JAPANESE AND LAPITA CULTURE - ALL ISLAND CULTURES!
"ON ISOLATED ISLANDS GIGANTISM OCCURS.
WEIRD ANIMALS GROW ON ISLANDS..."

TOWARDS THE END OF THE TWENTIETH CENTURY A.D. LINTON FOUND HIMSELF WONDERING WHAT WAS HAPPENING IN THE TWENTIETH CENTURY B.C. HE BEGAN READING ABOUT ANCIENT CIVILISATIONS:

# 20TH CENTURY BC

SUMERIANS...

MAYANS...

AND, EVENTUALLY, HIS FAVOURITE...

CRETE.

KNOSSOS PALACE, ABOUT 2000BC, KRETE'S HIGHLY CULTURED, FAST GROWING, 'FIRST-PALACE' PERIOD.

'LABYRINTH' = HOUSE OF THE AXE ~

LINTON © 2000 AD.

BRONZE AGE CRETE HAS ALL THE ANSWERS, IT'S AN ISLAND CULTURE- EUROPEAN, PROTO-GREEK SPEAKING, VERY GOOD SEAMEN WHO TRAVELLED WIDE AND TRADED WIDE - A MIX WHICH CREATED A HIGHLY CREATIVE, NOT VERY WARLIKE CULTURE, THEY HAD PALACES BUT NOT ARMIES...!

IT LOOKED TO ME LIKE A BLOODY INSPIRATION! WHAT A LIFESTYLE!

I THOUGHT: NO-ONE'S DOING ARCHEOLOGICAL COMICS!

FOR A WHILE, LINTON CONCENTRATED ON DRAWING CAREFUL RECONSTRUCTIONS OF ANCIENT LIFE AND, IN PARTICULAR, ANCIENT WOODEN SAILING SHIPS, WHICH HAD BECOME A PASSION...

NOW, WE KEEP THE PIRATES ⊠ AT BAY, WE TRADE OIL, WINE, TIMBER & ARTS, ROVING THE SEVEN SEAS.

COPPER FROM CYPRUS, AND THESE BEEHIVES ARE FOR THERA, YA?

THEN, MELOS FOR MORE OBSIDIAN!

⊠ WE ARE FASTER AND SHARPER.

THEN LINTON STARTED WORK ON A NEW STORY - THE LONGEST AND MOST AMBITIOUS COMIC HE'S EVER DONE...

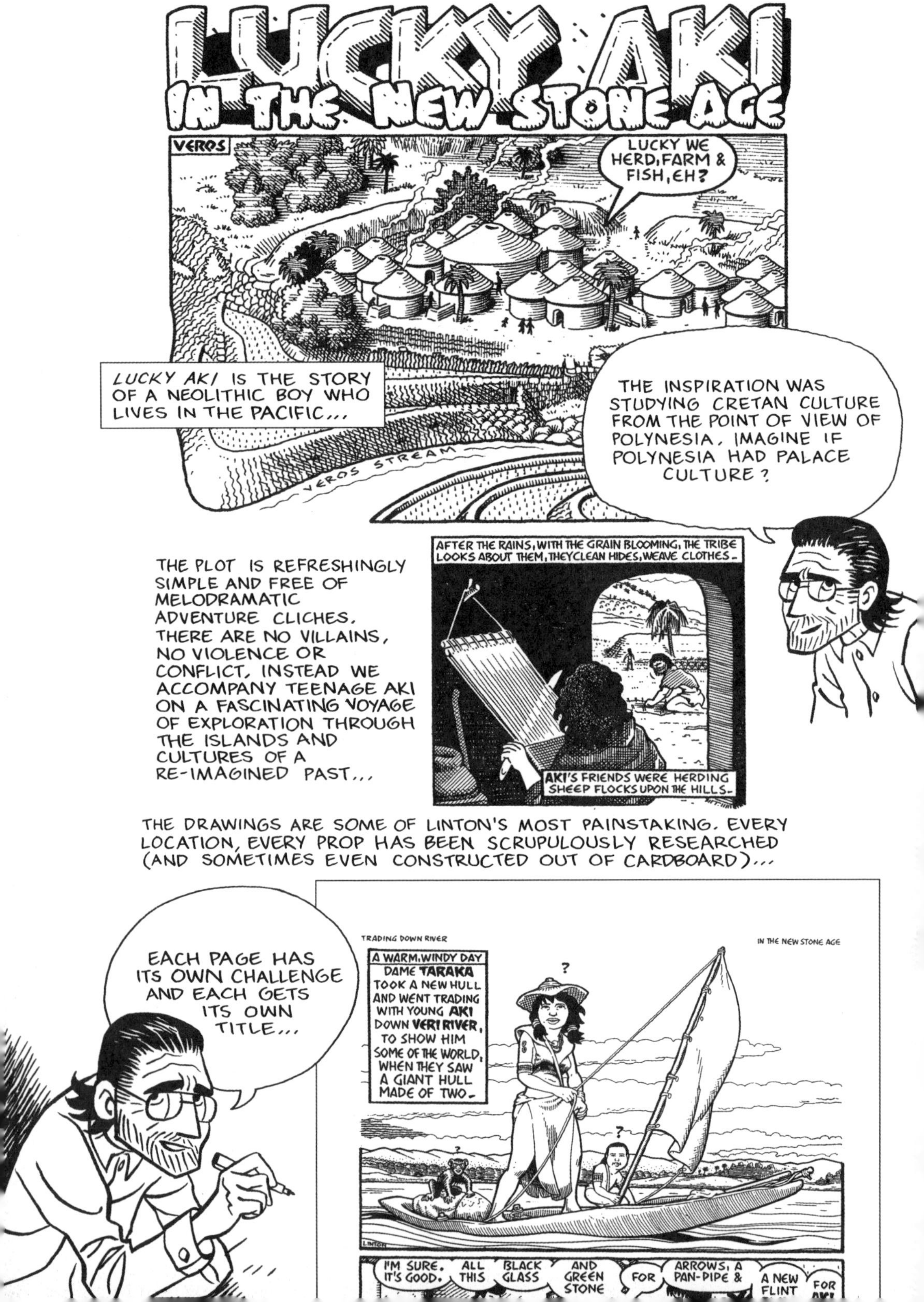
LUCKY AKI
IN THE NEW STONE AGE
VEROS
LUCKY WE HERD, FARM & FISH, EH?
VEROS STREAM
LUCKY AKI IS THE STORY OF A NEOLITHIC BOY WHO LIVES IN THE PACIFIC...
THE INSPIRATION WAS STUDYING CRETAN CULTURE FROM THE POINT OF VIEW OF POLYNESIA. IMAGINE IF POLYNESIA HAD PALACE CULTURE?
THE PLOT IS REFRESHINGLY SIMPLE AND FREE OF MELODRAMATIC ADVENTURE CLICHES. THERE ARE NO VILLAINS, NO VIOLENCE OR CONFLICT. INSTEAD WE ACCOMPANY TEENAGE AKI ON A FASCINATING VOYAGE OF EXPLORATION THROUGH THE ISLANDS AND CULTURES OF A RE-IMAGINED PAST...
AFTER THE RAINS, WITH THE GRAIN BLOOMING, THE TRIBE LOOKS ABOUT THEM. THEY CLEAN HIDES, WEAVE CLOTHES.
AKI'S FRIENDS WERE HERDING SHEEP FLOCKS UPON THE HILLS.
THE DRAWINGS ARE SOME OF LINTON'S MOST PAINSTAKING. EVERY LOCATION, EVERY PROP HAS BEEN SCRUPULOUSLY RESEARCHED (AND SOMETIMES EVEN CONSTRUCTED OUT OF CARDBOARD)...
EACH PAGE HAS ITS OWN CHALLENGE AND EACH GETS ITS OWN TITLE...
TRADING DOWN RIVER
IN THE NEW STONE AGE
A WARM, WINDY DAY
DAME TARAKA TOOK A NEW HULL AND WENT TRADING WITH YOUNG AKI DOWN VERI RIVER, TO SHOW HIM SOME OF THE WORLD, WHEN THEY SAW A GIANT HULL MADE OF TWO.
?
?
?
LINTON
I'M SURE. IT'S GOOD.
ALL THIS
BLACK GLASS
AND GREEN STONE
FOR
ARROWS, A PAN-PIPE &
A NEW FLINT
FOR

LINTON HAS ALREADY FINISHED THE FIRST VOLUME OF AKI'S STORY, COMPLETE WITH MAPS, DIAGRAMS AND DETAILED PLANS OF THE VILLAGES, BUILDINGS AND BOATS HE SEES...

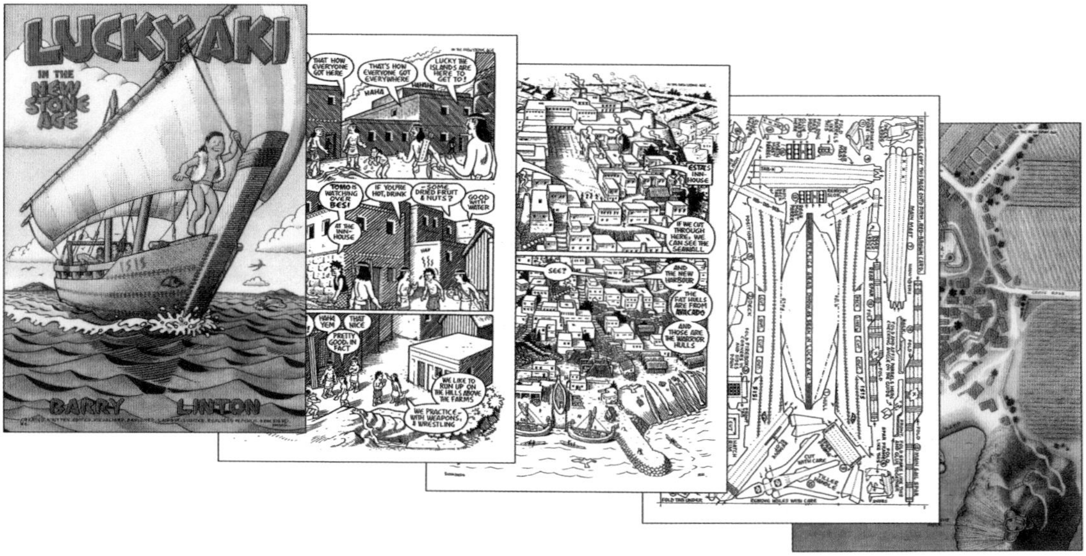
LUCKY AKI
IN THE NEW STONE AGE
BARRY LINTON

FOR ONCE LINTON WAS PERSUADED TO SEND HIS BOOK TO A PUBLISHER. BUT AKI WAS APPARENTLY TOO UNIQUE, PERSONAL AND IDIOSYNCRATIC TO FIT ANY OBVIOUS MARKET NICHE...

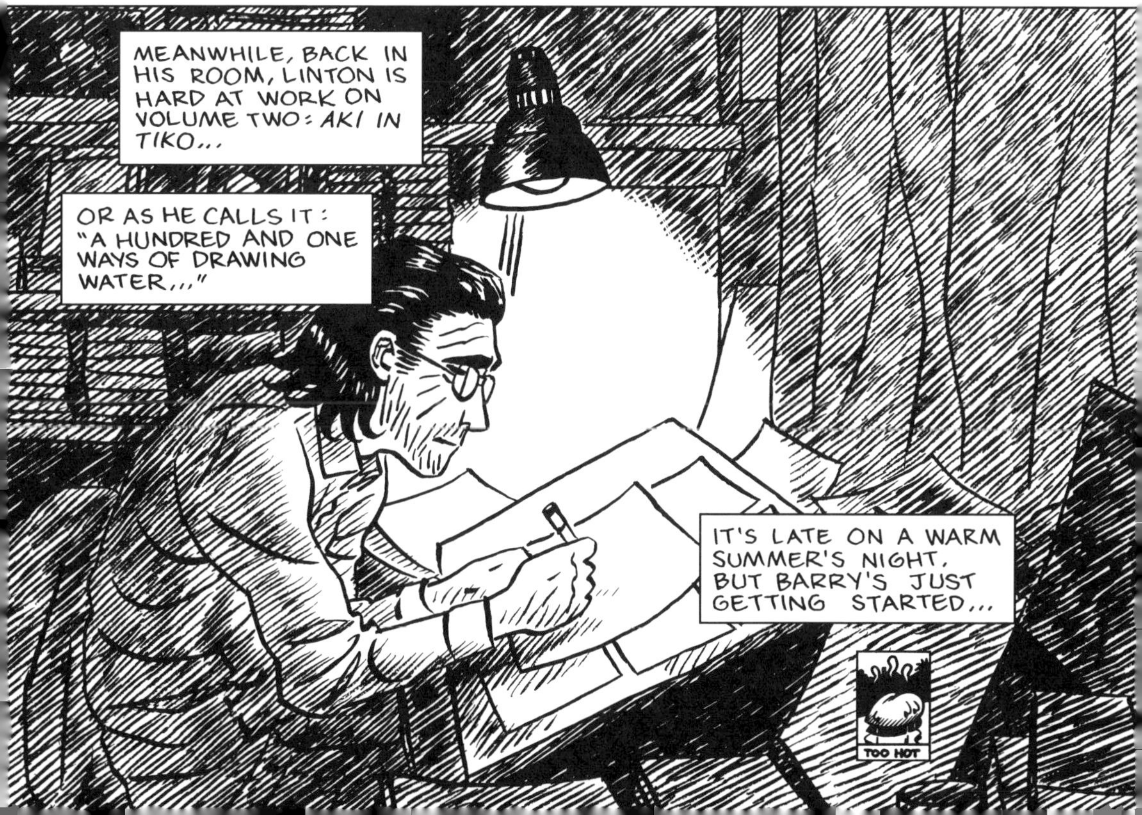
MEANWHILE, BACK IN HIS ROOM, LINTON IS HARD AT WORK ON VOLUME TWO: *AKI IN TIKO*...
OR AS HE CALLS IT: "A HUNDRED AND ONE WAYS OF DRAWING WATER..."
IT'S LATE ON A WARM SUMMER'S NIGHT, BUT BARRY'S JUST GETTING STARTED...
TOO HOT

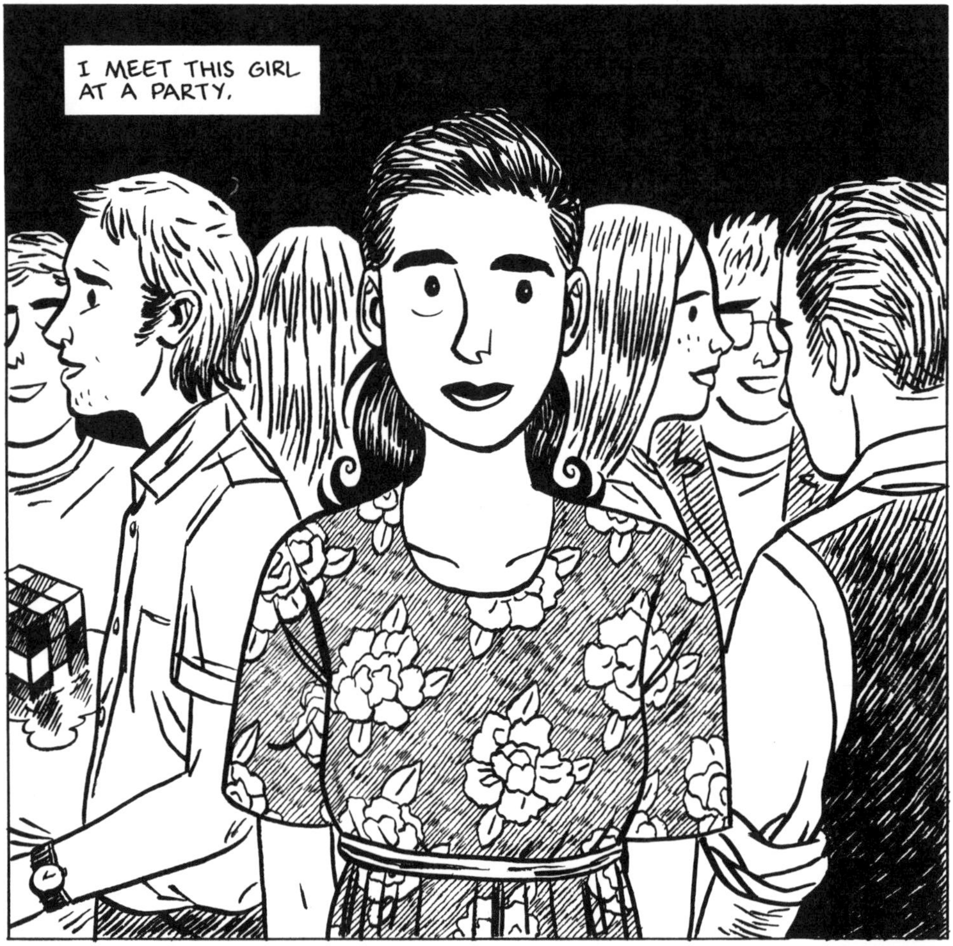
I MEET THIS GIRL AT A PARTY.

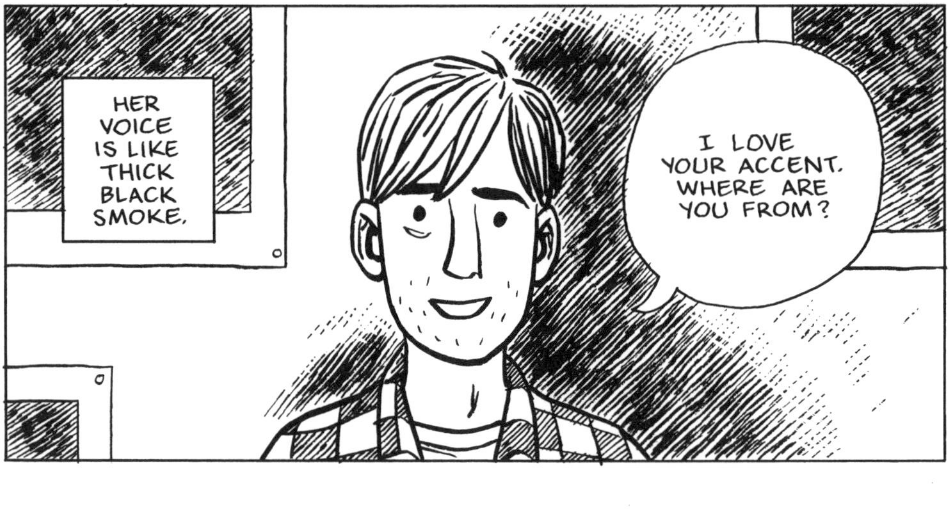
HER VOICE IS LIKE THICK BLACK SMOKE.
I LOVE YOUR ACCENT. WHERE ARE YOU FROM?

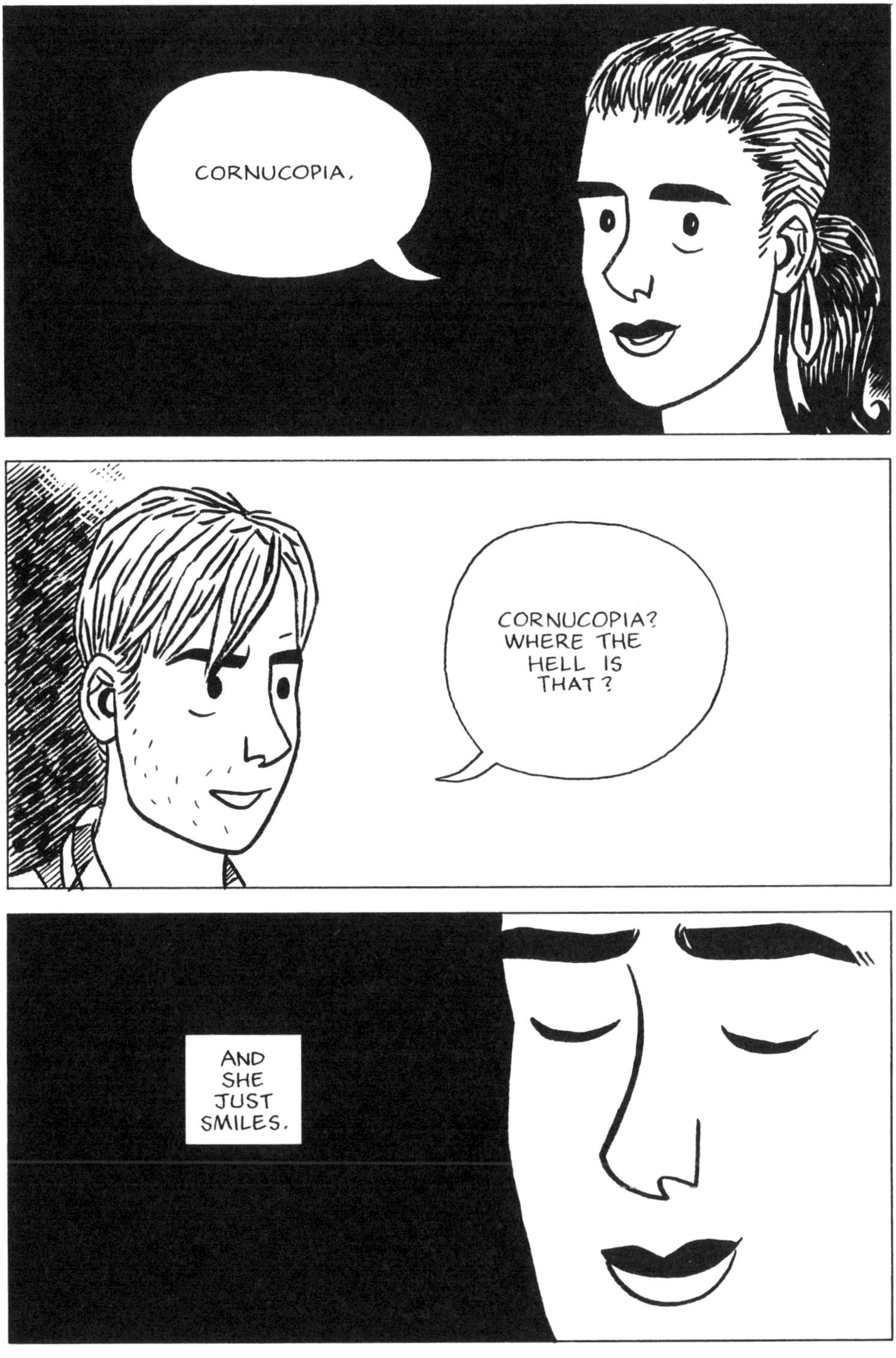
CORNUCOPIA.
CORNUCOPIA? WHERE THE HELL IS THAT?
AND SHE JUST SMILES.

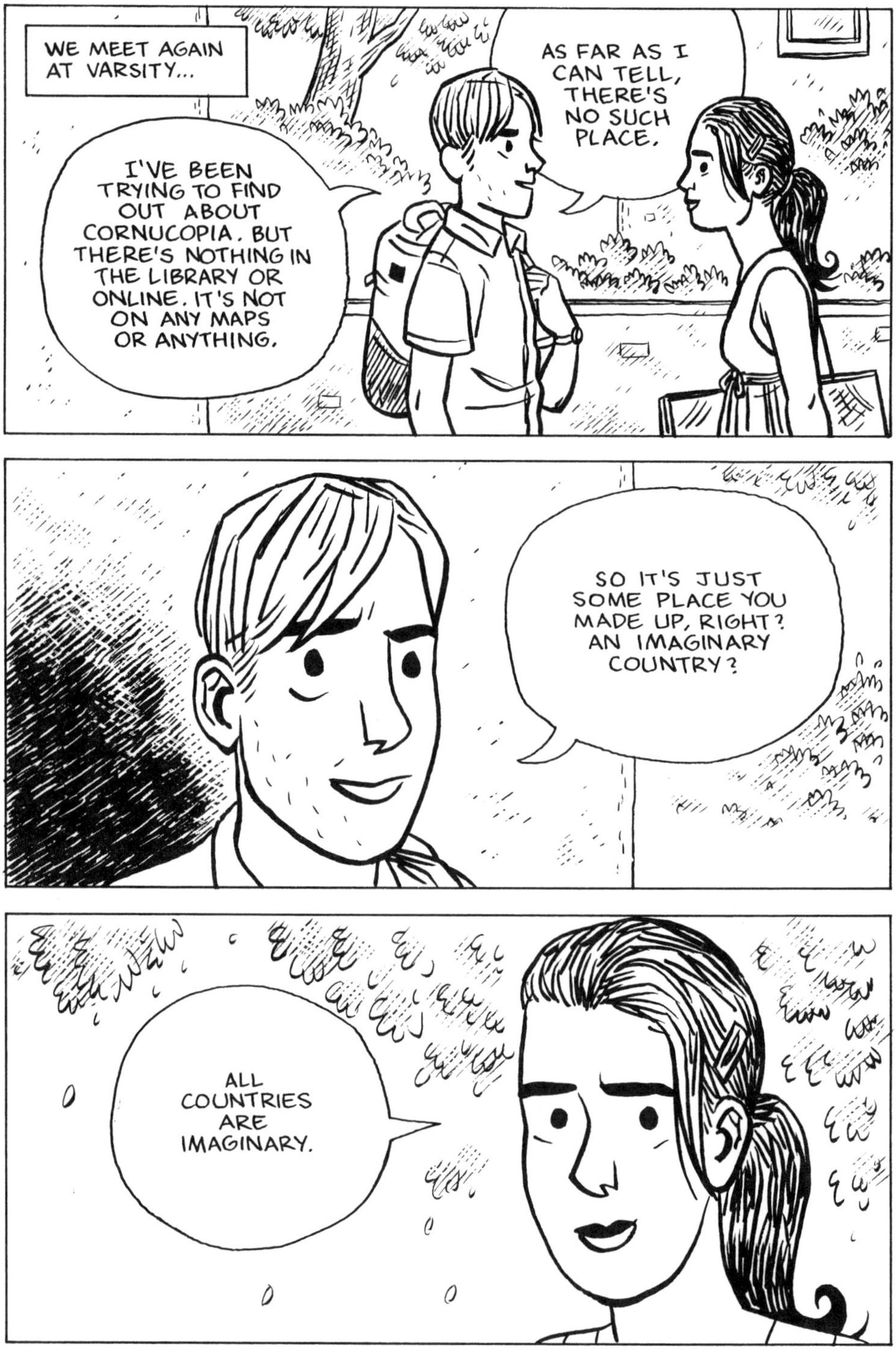
WE MEET AGAIN AT VARSITY...
I'VE BEEN TRYING TO FIND OUT ABOUT CORNUCOPIA. BUT THERE'S NOTHING IN THE LIBRARY OR ONLINE. IT'S NOT ON ANY MAPS OR ANYTHING.
AS FAR AS I CAN TELL, THERE'S NO SUCH PLACE.
SO IT'S JUST SOME PLACE YOU MADE UP, RIGHT? AN IMAGINARY COUNTRY?
ALL COUNTRIES ARE IMAGINARY.

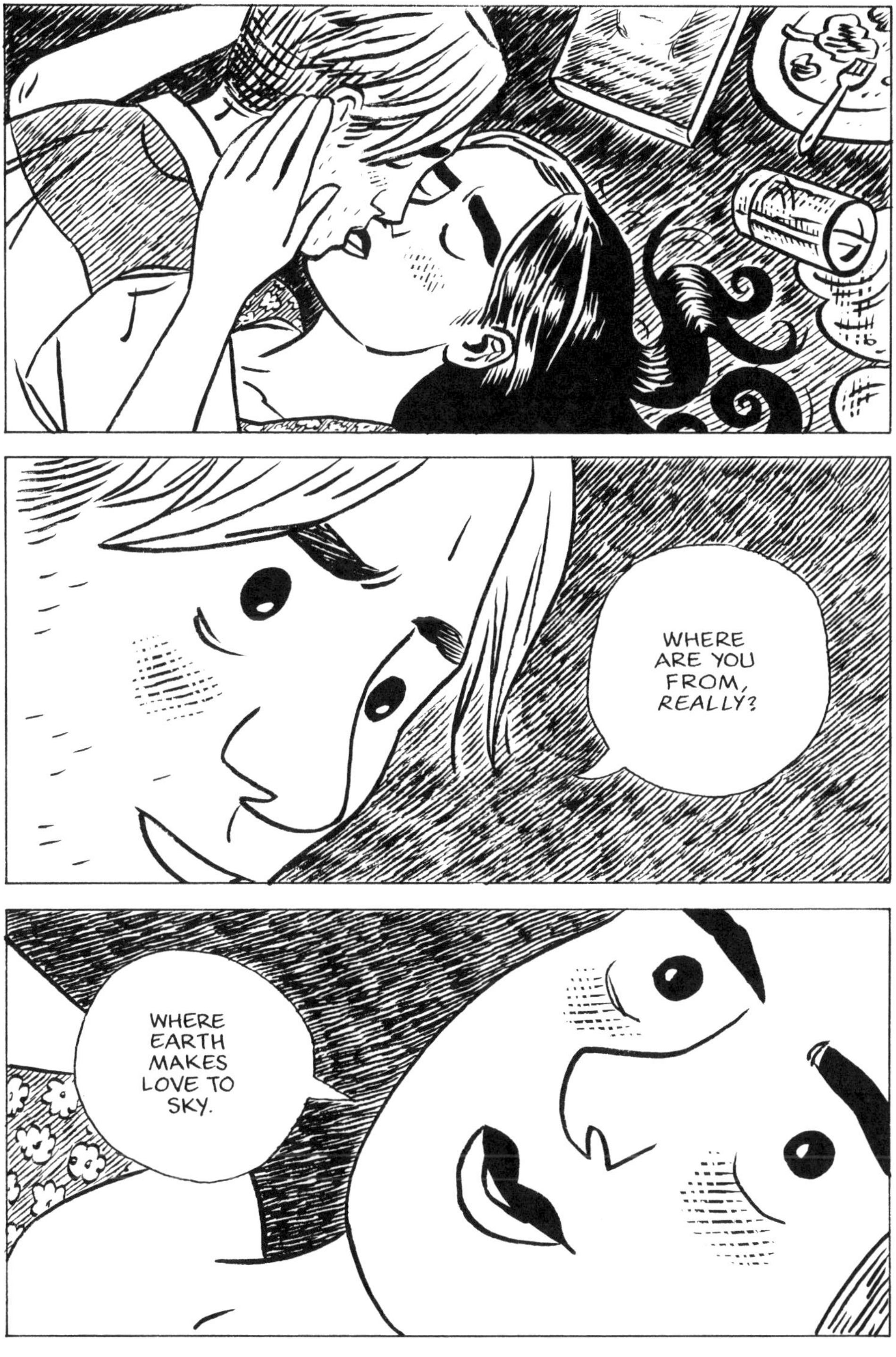
WHERE ARE YOU FROM, *REALLY*?
WHERE EARTH MAKES LOVE TO SKY.

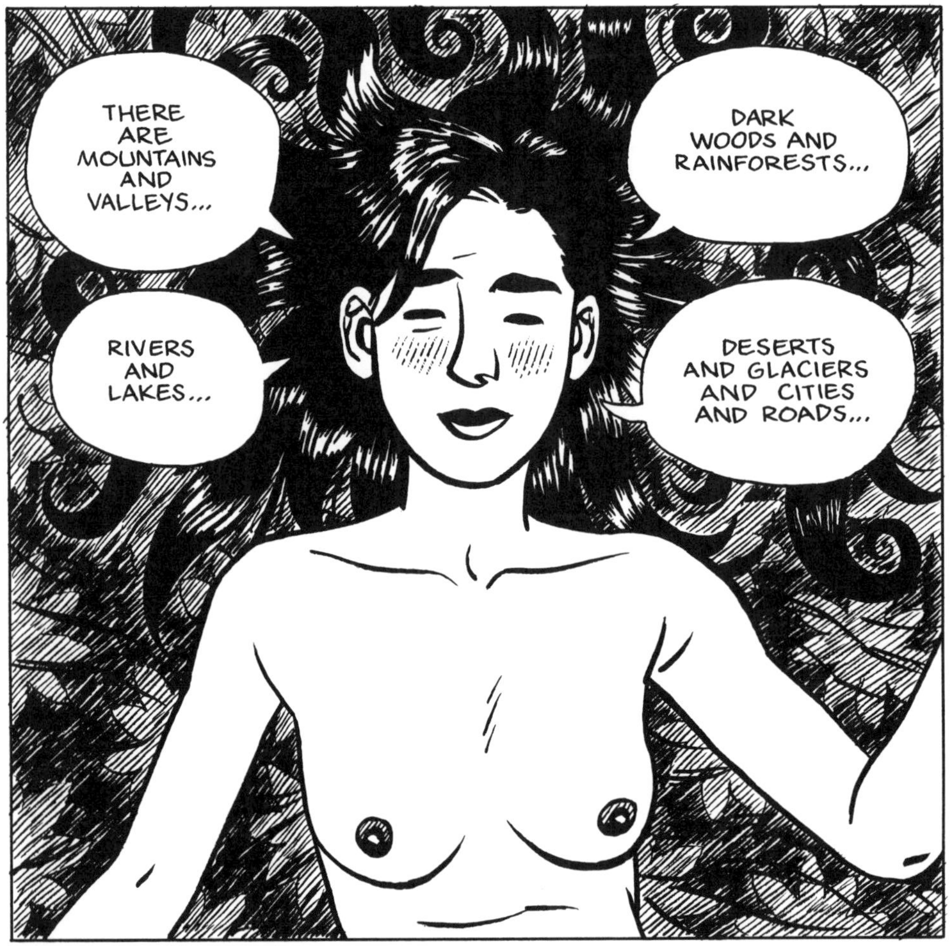
THERE ARE MOUNTAINS AND VALLEYS...
DARK WOODS AND RAINFORESTS...
RIVERS AND LAKES...
DESERTS AND GLACIERS AND CITIES AND ROADS...

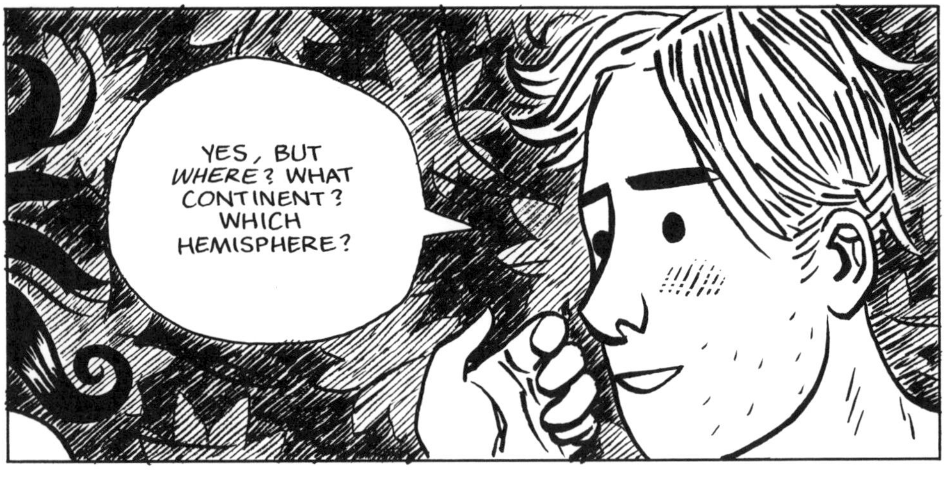
YES, BUT *WHERE*? WHAT CONTINENT? WHICH HEMISPHERE?

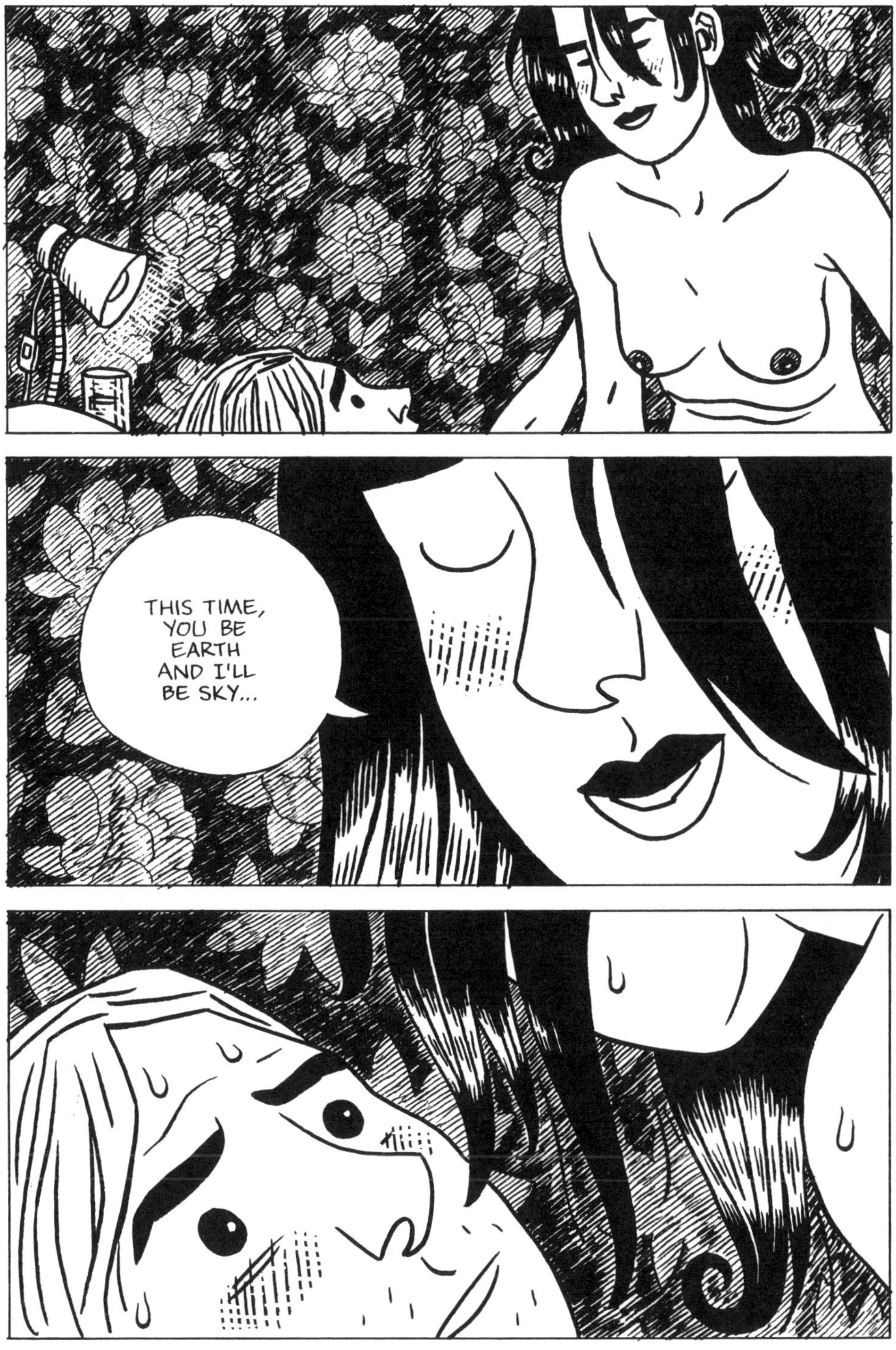
THIS TIME, YOU BE EARTH AND I'LL BE SKY...

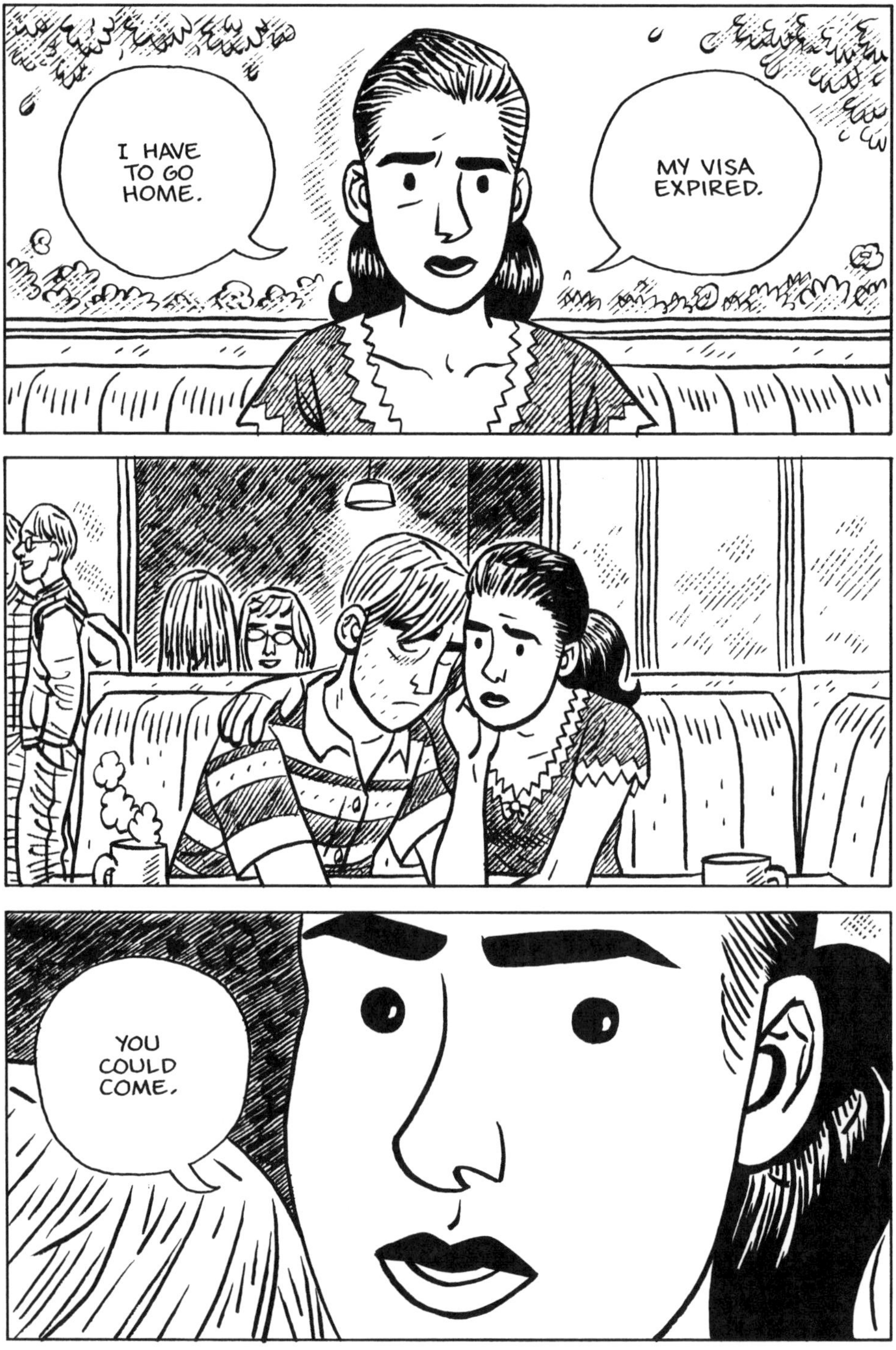
I HAVE TO GO HOME.
MY VISA EXPIRED.
YOU COULD COME.

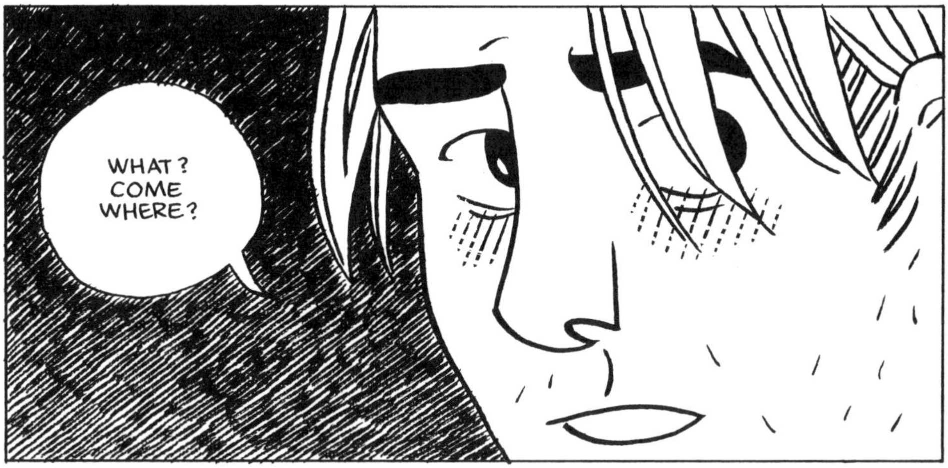
WHAT? COME WHERE?

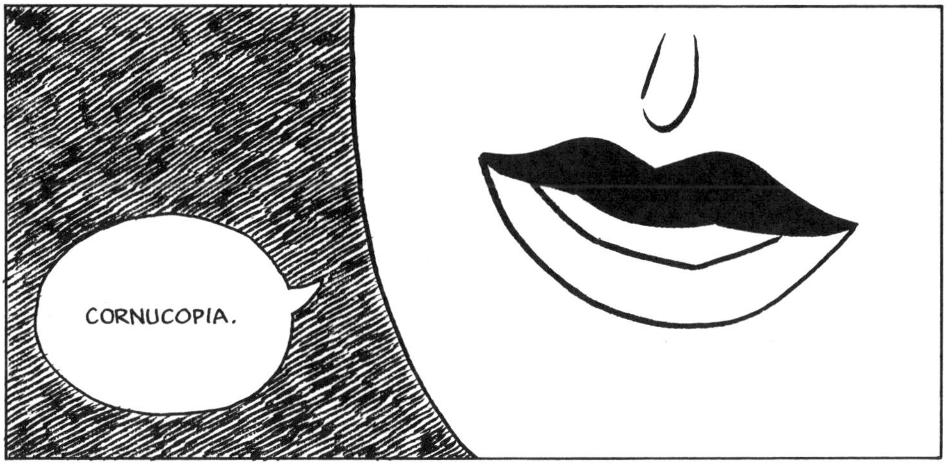
CORNUCOPIA.

AND I COME.

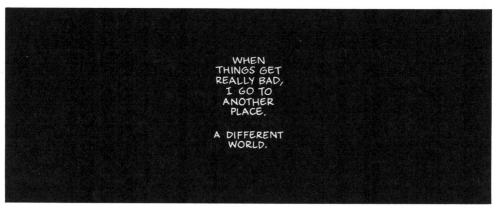

WHEN
THINGS GET
REALLY BAD,
I GO TO
ANOTHER
PLACE.

A DIFFERENT
WORLD.

my
world

IN MY WORLD,
THE POLICE
ARE HELPFUL
AND KIND.

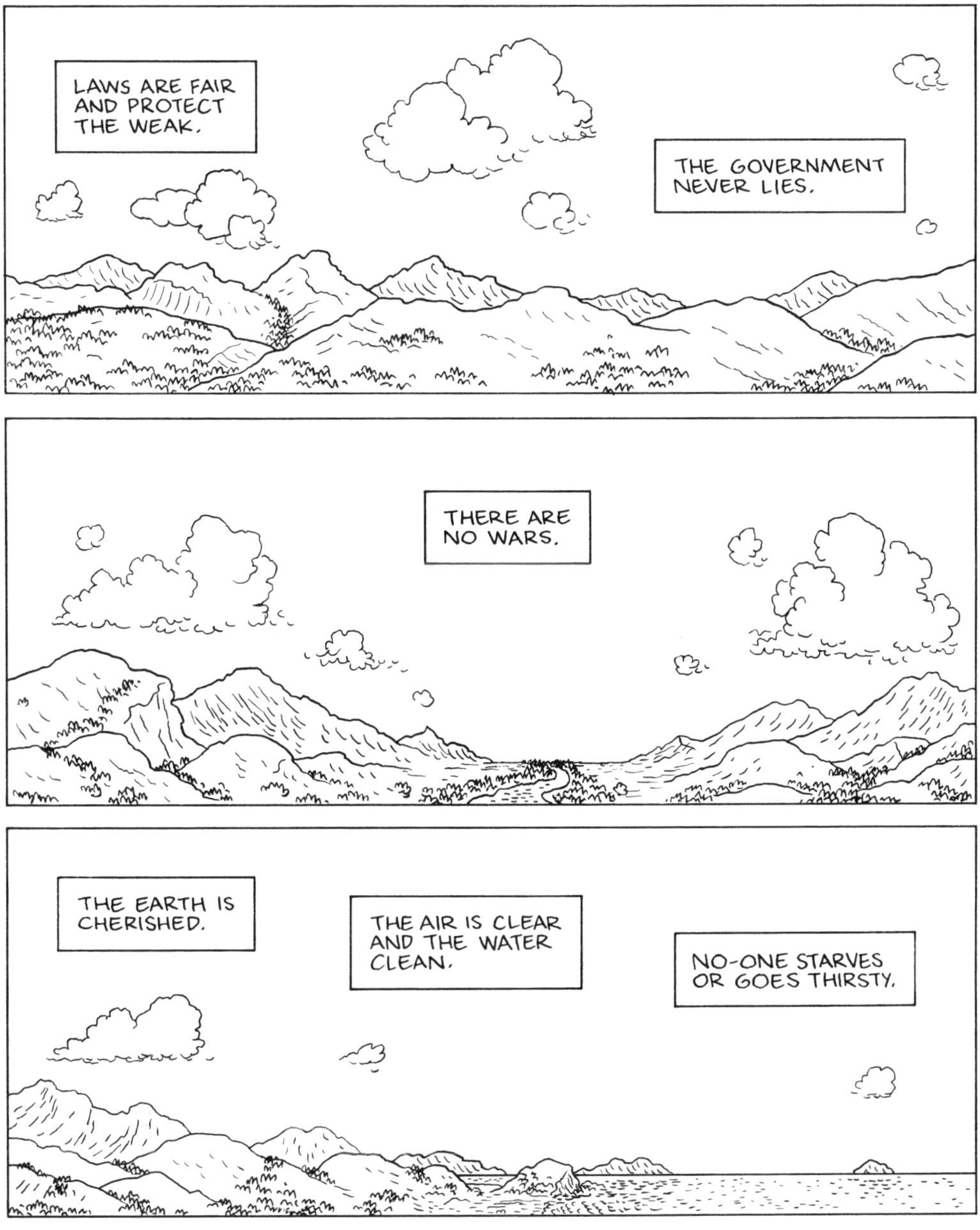
LAWS ARE FAIR AND PROTECT THE WEAK.
THE GOVERNMENT NEVER LIES.
THERE ARE NO WARS.
THE EARTH IS CHERISHED.
THE AIR IS CLEAR AND THE WATER CLEAN.
NO-ONE STARVES OR GOES THIRSTY.

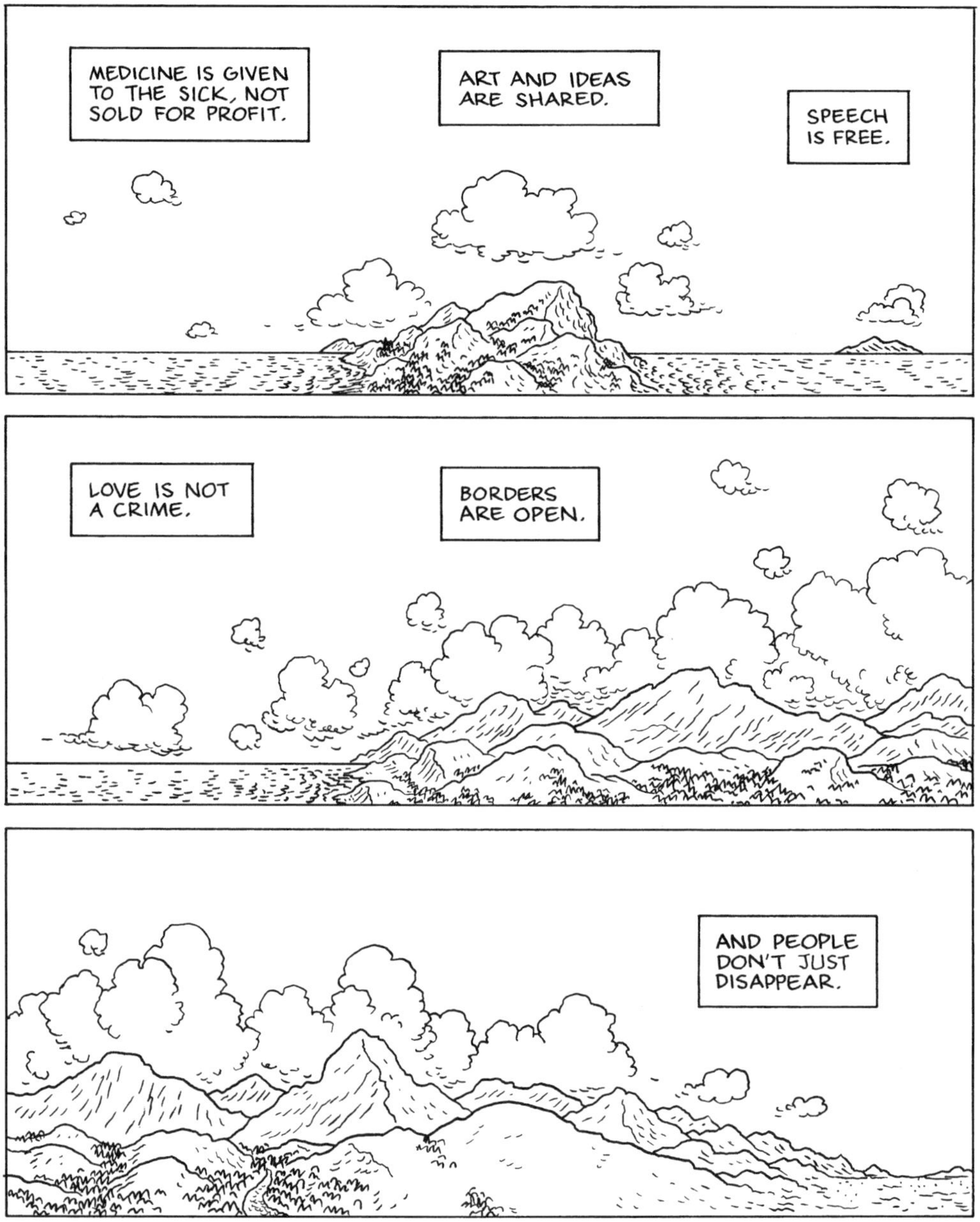
MEDICINE IS GIVEN TO THE SICK, NOT SOLD FOR PROFIT.
ART AND IDEAS ARE SHARED.
SPEECH IS FREE.
LOVE IS NOT A CRIME.
BORDERS ARE OPEN.
AND PEOPLE DON'T JUST DISAPPEAR.

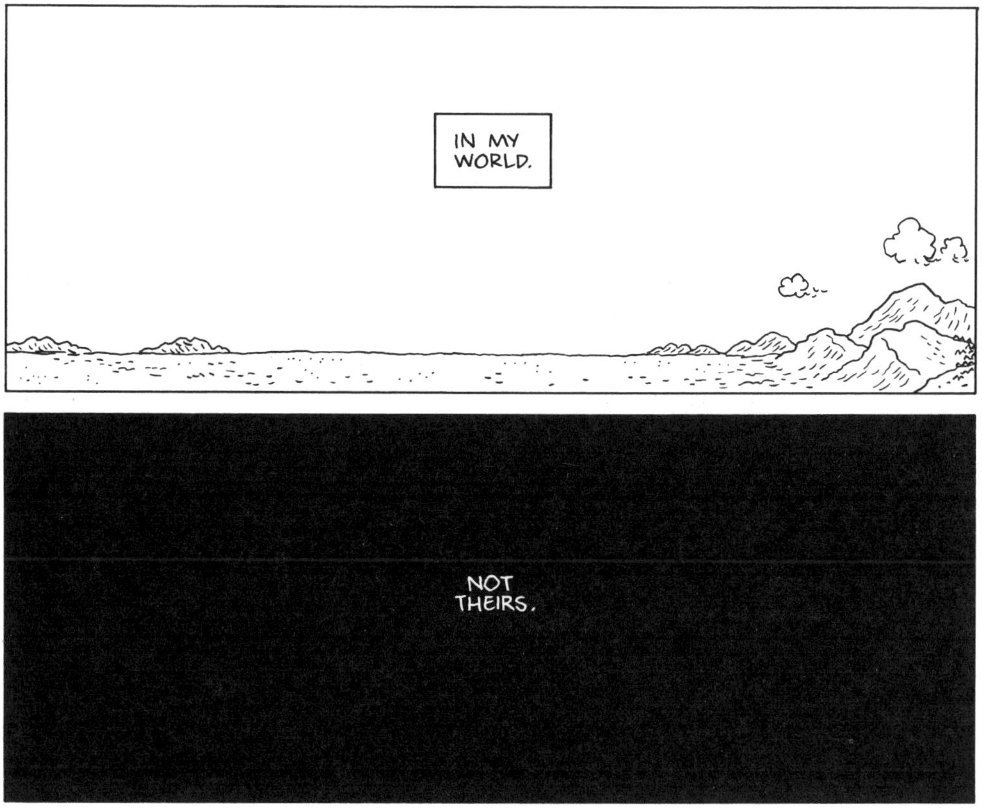
IN MY WORLD.
NOT THEIRS.

"listen: there's a hell
of a good universe next door; let's go"

e.e. cummings

# Things I have done at the mall.

EATEN TOO MUCH.

WORRIED ABOUT MONEY.

READ BOOKS FOR FREE.

GRUMPED AT THE KIDS.

WANTED TO CRY.

SAT IN THE SUN.

KISSED.

BUT TODAY ALL I DO IS DRAW.

DYLAN HORROCKS
Botany Town Centre
4-9-10

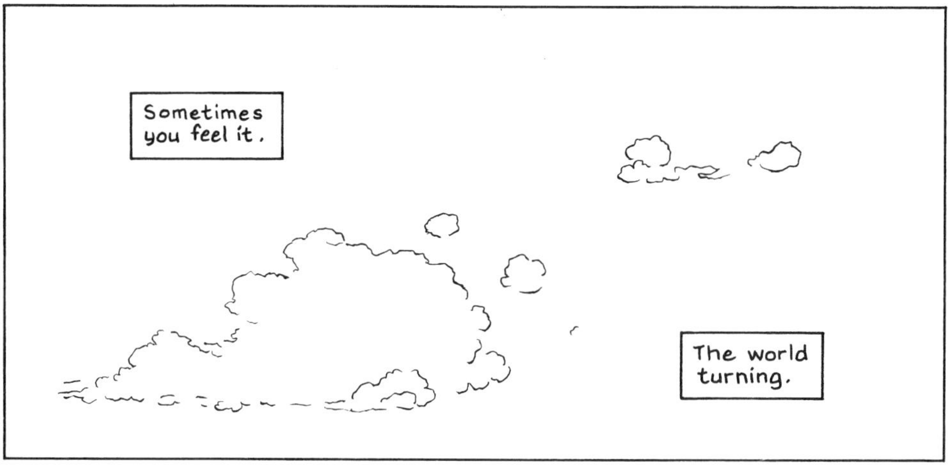
Sometimes you feel it.
The world turning.

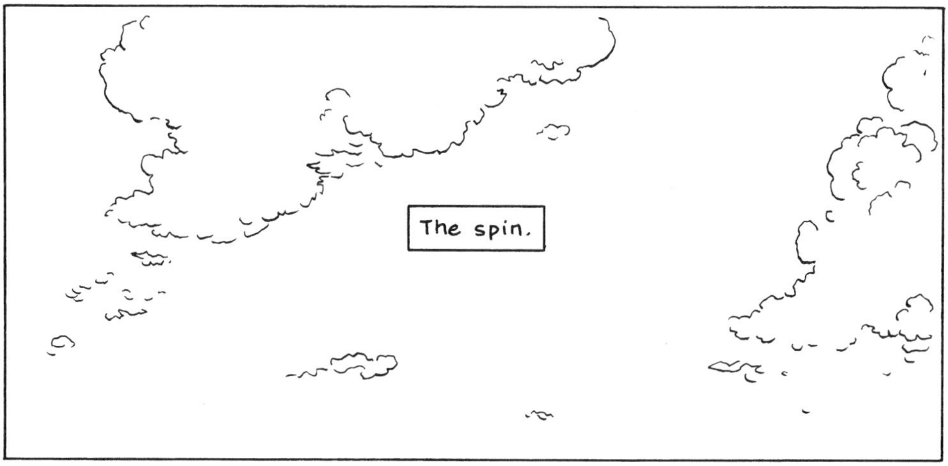
The spin.

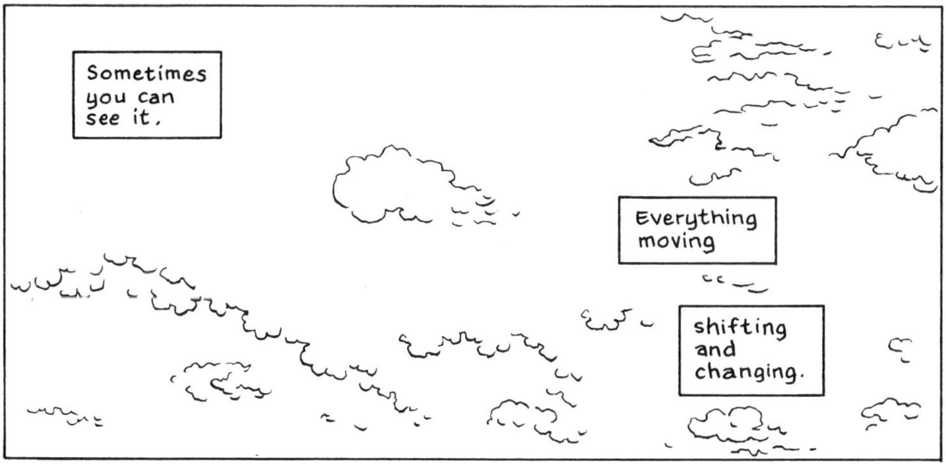
Sometimes you can see it.
Everything moving
shifting and changing.

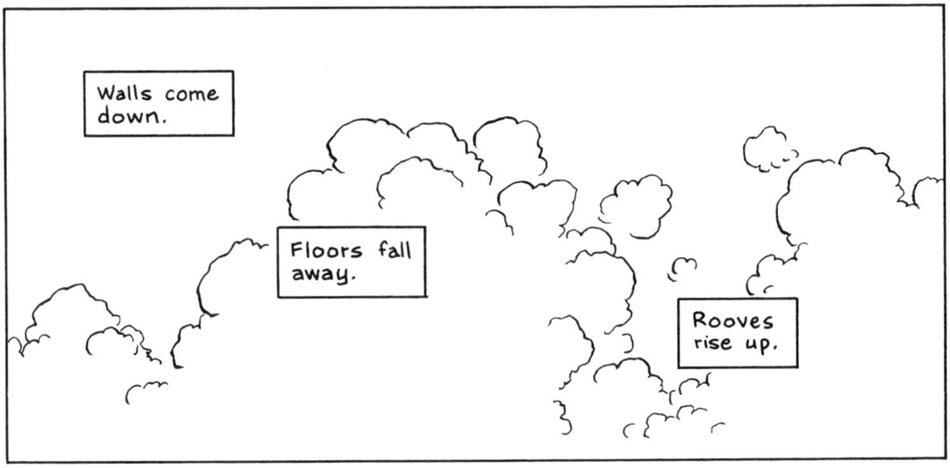
Walls come down.
Floors fall away.
Rooves rise up.

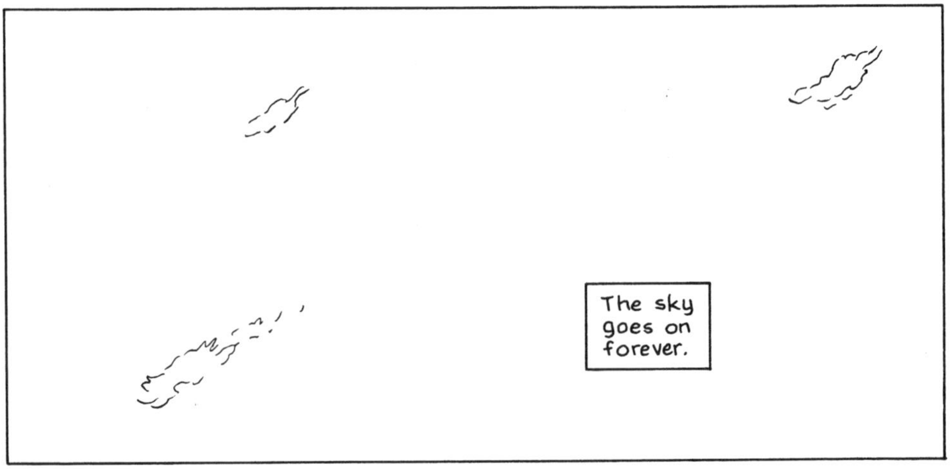
The sky goes on forever.

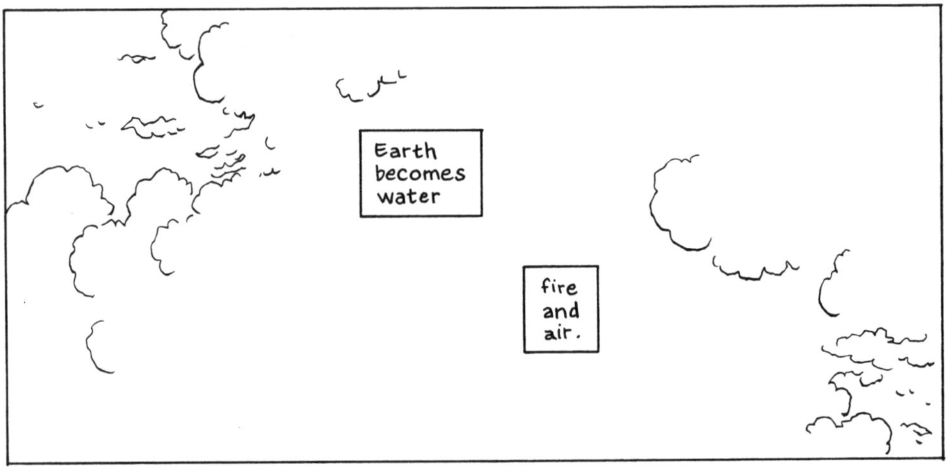
Earth becomes water
fire and air.

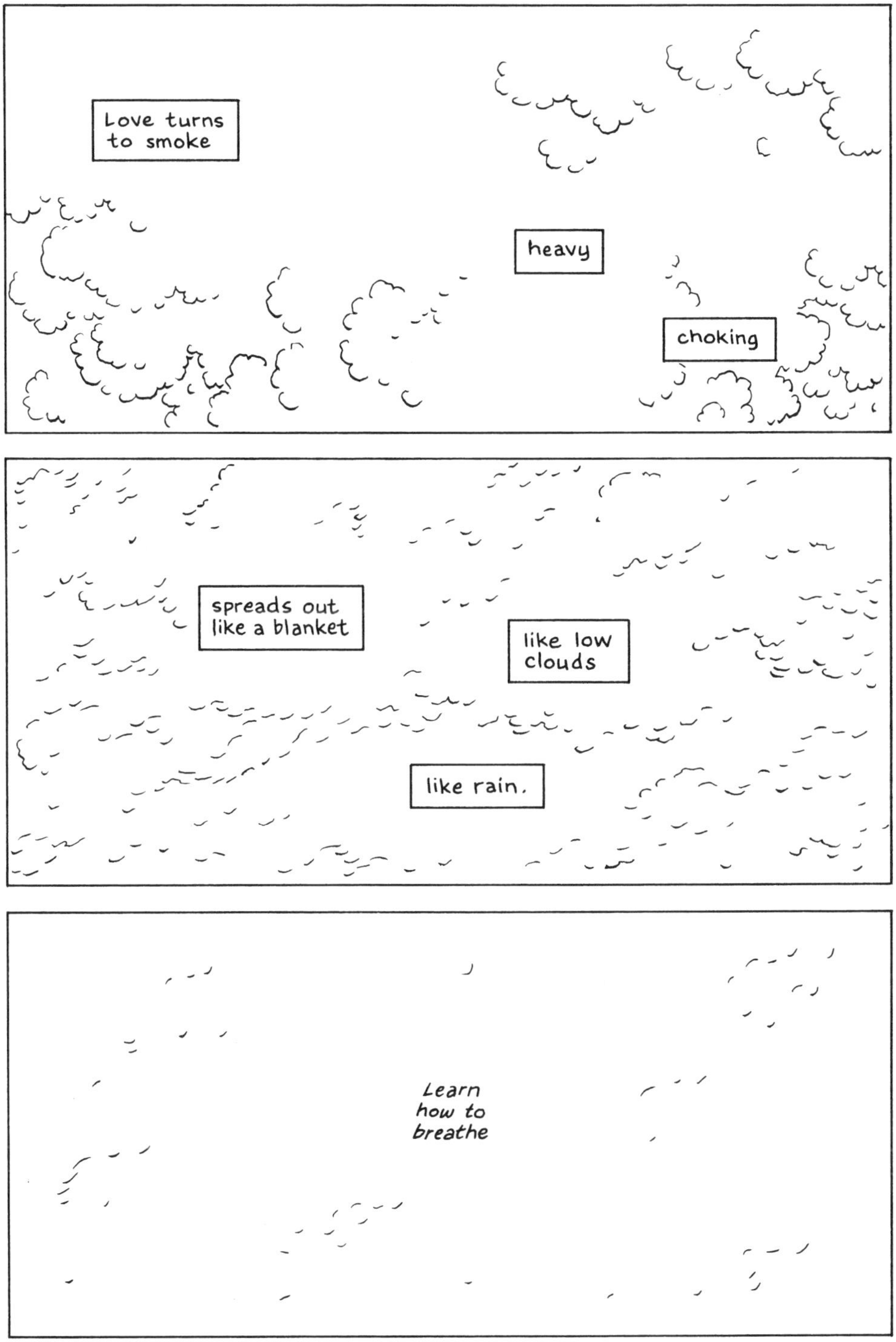
Love turns to smoke
heavy
choking
spreads out like a blanket
like low clouds
like rain.
Learn how to breathe
DYLAN HORROCKS · 21·iii·2011

# A CARTOONIST'S DIARY

SUNDAY 4 MARCH 2012

Up before dawn, so I can drive to Pukekohe to get Louis from a friend's (overnight) party.

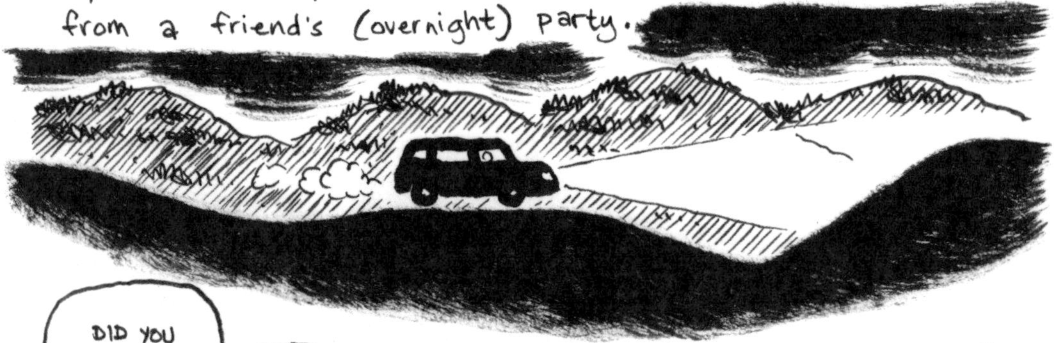

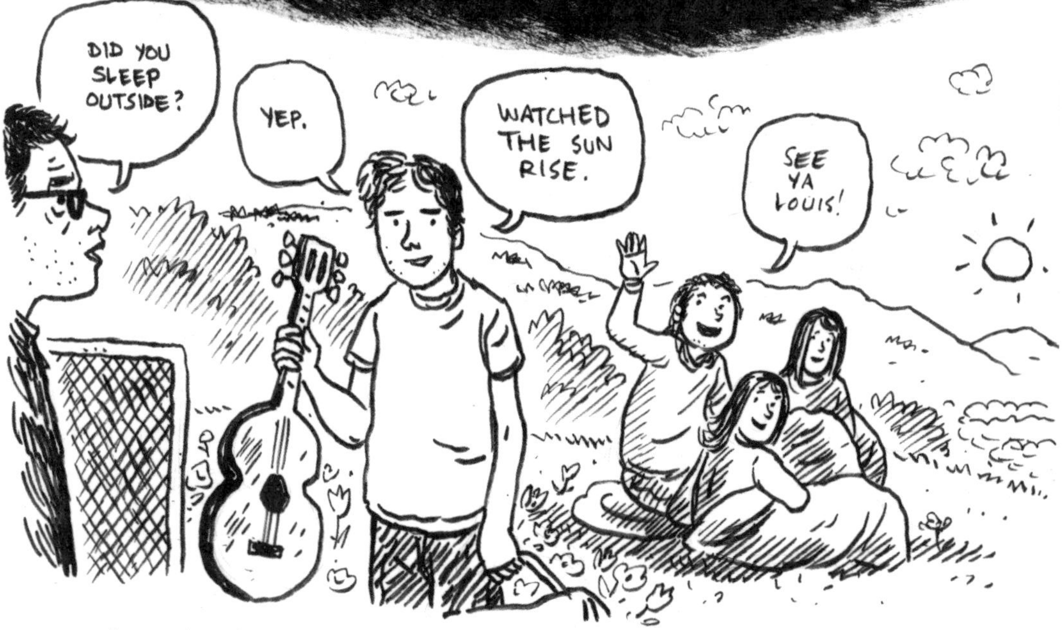
DID YOU SLEEP OUTSIDE?
YEP.
WATCHED THE SUN RISE.
SEE YA LOUIS!

I drop Louis at school. His History Class are heading up North on a field trip – to visit Russell, and Ruapekapeka (where Hone Heke fought the British in 1845-6).

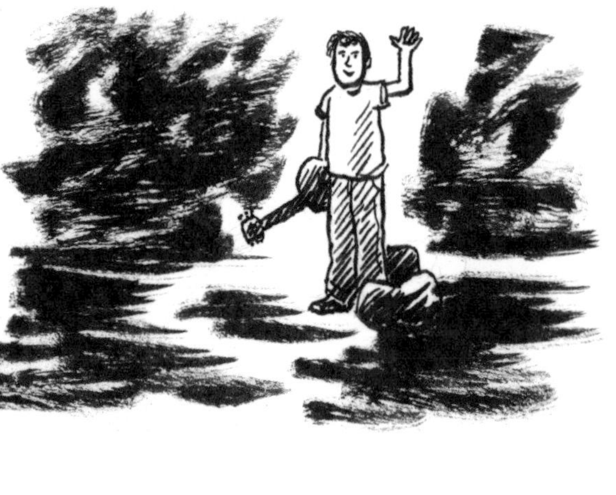

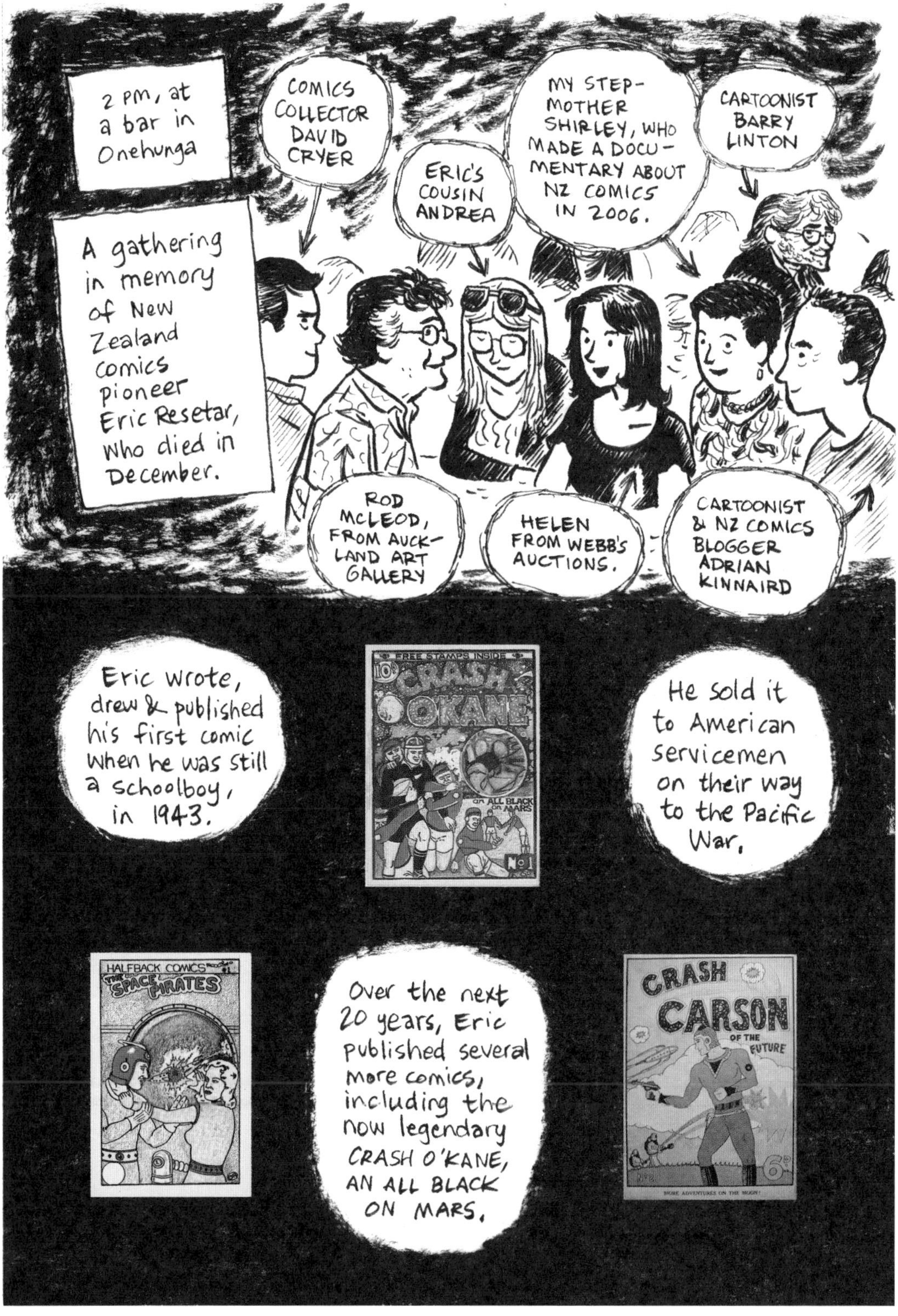

2 pm, at a bar in Onehunga
A gathering in memory of New Zealand comics pioneer Eric Resetar, who died in December.
COMICS COLLECTOR DAVID CRYER
ERIC'S COUSIN ANDREA
MY STEP-MOTHER SHIRLEY, WHO MADE A DOCU-MENTARY ABOUT NZ COMICS IN 2006.
CARTOONIST BARRY LINTON
ROD McLEOD, FROM AUCK-LAND ART GALLERY
HELEN FROM WEBB'S AUCTIONS.
CARTOONIST & NZ COMICS BLOGGER ADRIAN KINNAIRD
Eric wrote, drew & published his first comic when he was still a schoolboy, in 1943.
FREE STAMPS INSIDE
CRASH O'KANE
AN ALL BLACK ON MARS
He sold it to American servicemen on their way to the Pacific War.
HALFBACK COMICS
THE SPACE PIRATES
Over the next 20 years, Eric published several more comics, including the now legendary CRASH O'KANE, AN ALL BLACK ON MARS.
CRASH CARSON OF THE FUTURE
MORE ADVENTURES ON THE MOON!

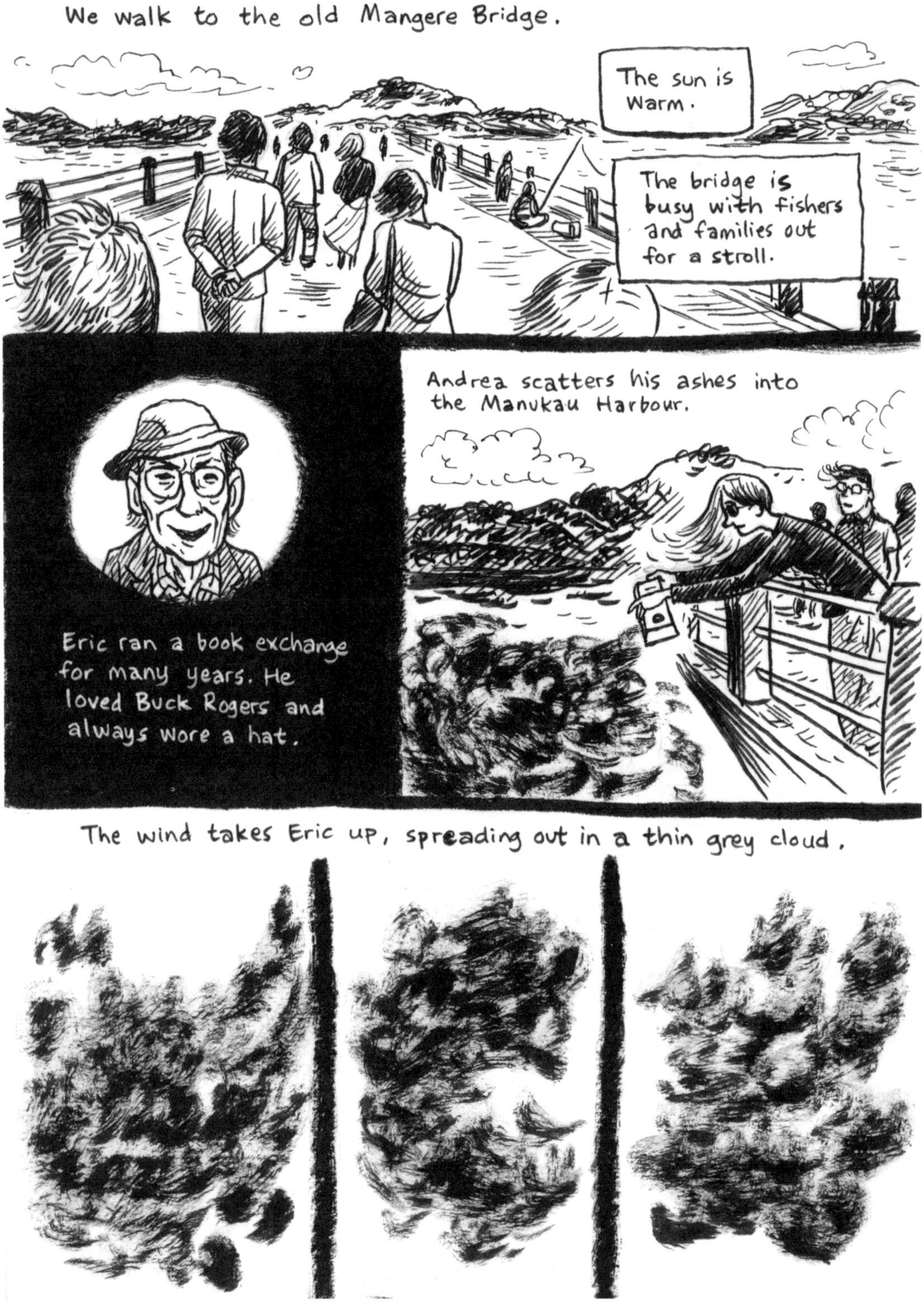
We walk to the old Mangere Bridge.
The sun is warm.
The bridge is busy with fishers and families out for a stroll.
Eric ran a book exchange for many years. He loved Buck Rogers and always wore a hat.
Andrea scatters his ashes into the Manukau Harbour.
The wind takes Eric up, spreading out in a thin grey cloud.

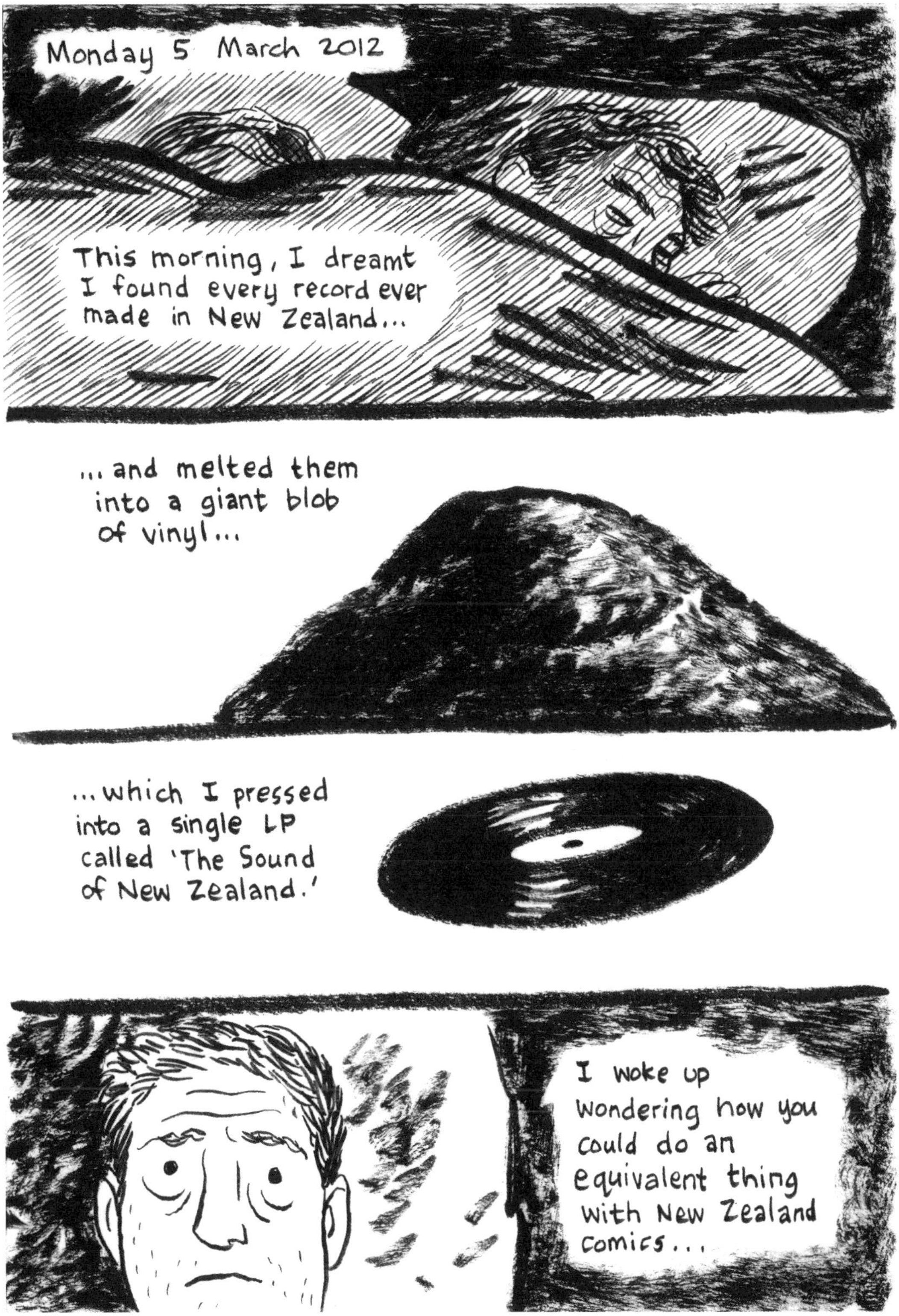
Monday 5 March 2012
This morning, I dreamt I found every record ever made in New Zealand...
...and melted them into a giant blob of vinyl...
...which I pressed into a single LP called 'The Sound of New Zealand.'
I woke up wondering how you could do an equivalent thing with New Zealand comics...

Today is a productive day.

I draw a page of *The Magic Pen*.

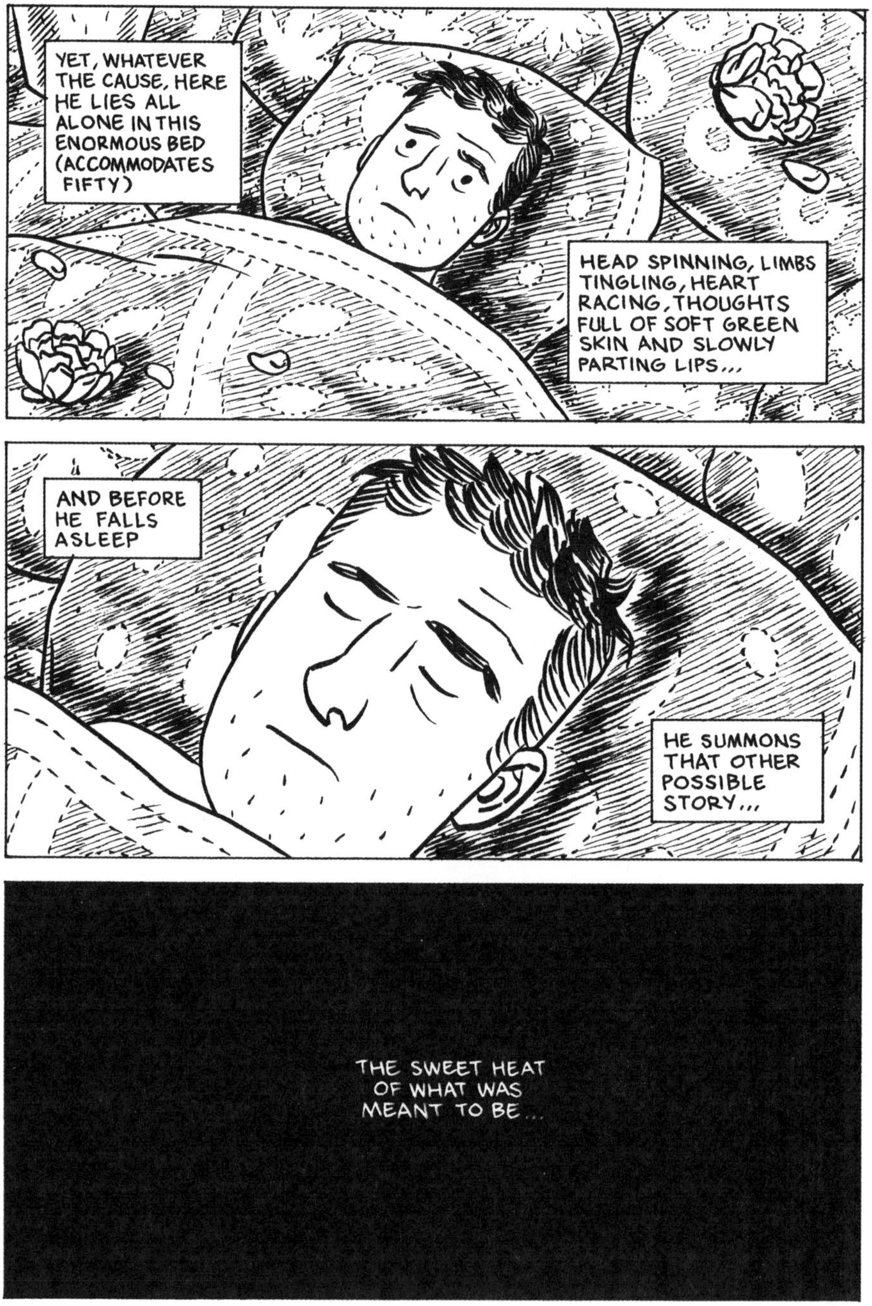

YET, WHATEVER THE CAUSE, HERE HE LIES ALL ALONE IN THIS ENORMOUS BED (ACCOMMODATES FIFTY)
HEAD SPINNING, LIMBS TINGLING, HEART RACING, THOUGHTS FULL OF SOFT GREEN SKIN AND SLOWLY PARTING LIPS...
AND BEFORE HE FALLS ASLEEP
HE SUMMONS THAT OTHER POSSIBLE STORY...
THE SWEET HEAT OF WHAT WAS MEANT TO BE...

Colour a page and a half.

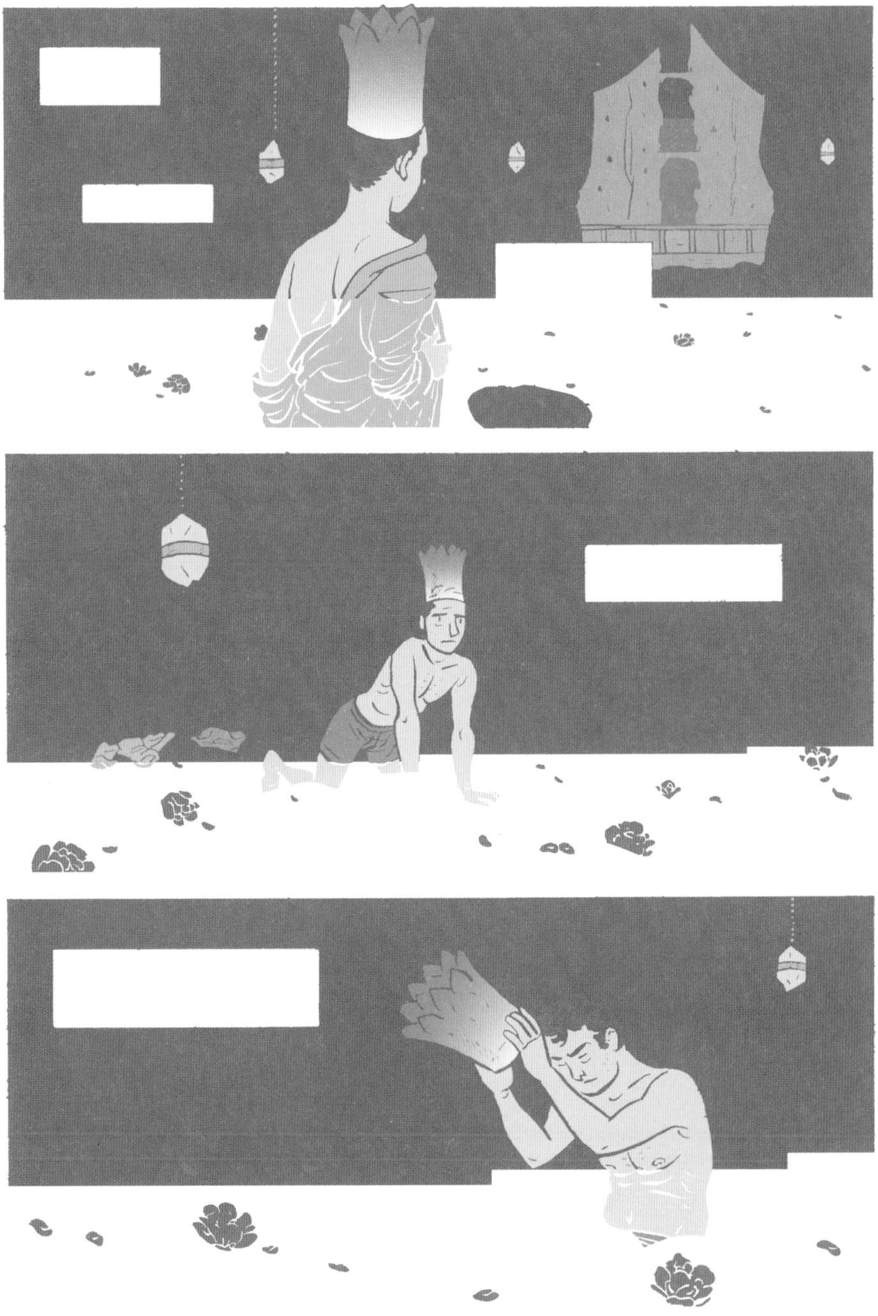

Post page 66 on my website.

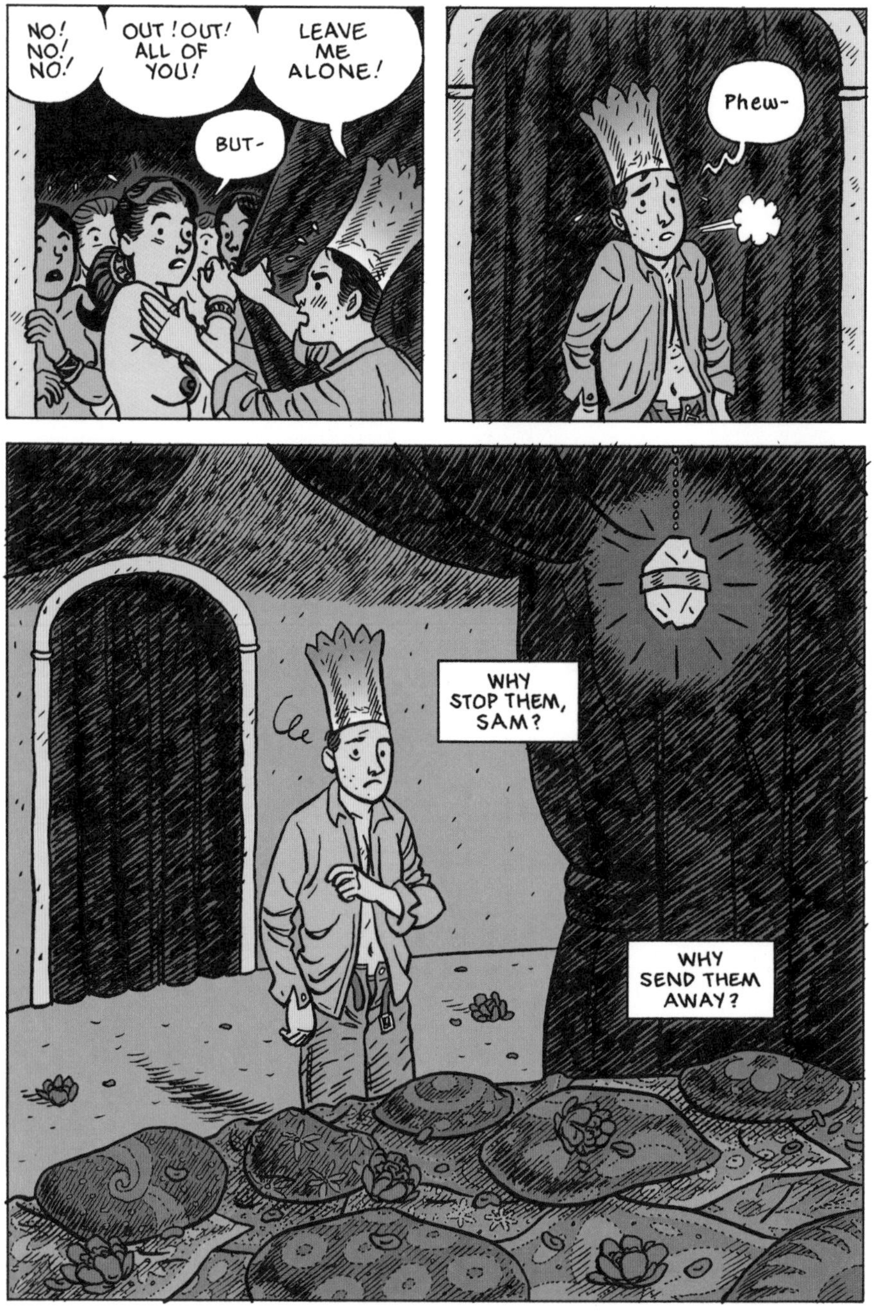
NO! NO! NO!
OUT! OUT! ALL OF YOU!
LEAVE ME ALONE!
BUT-
Phew-
WHY STOP THEM, SAM?
WHY SEND THEM AWAY?

Finish 3 commissioned sketches.

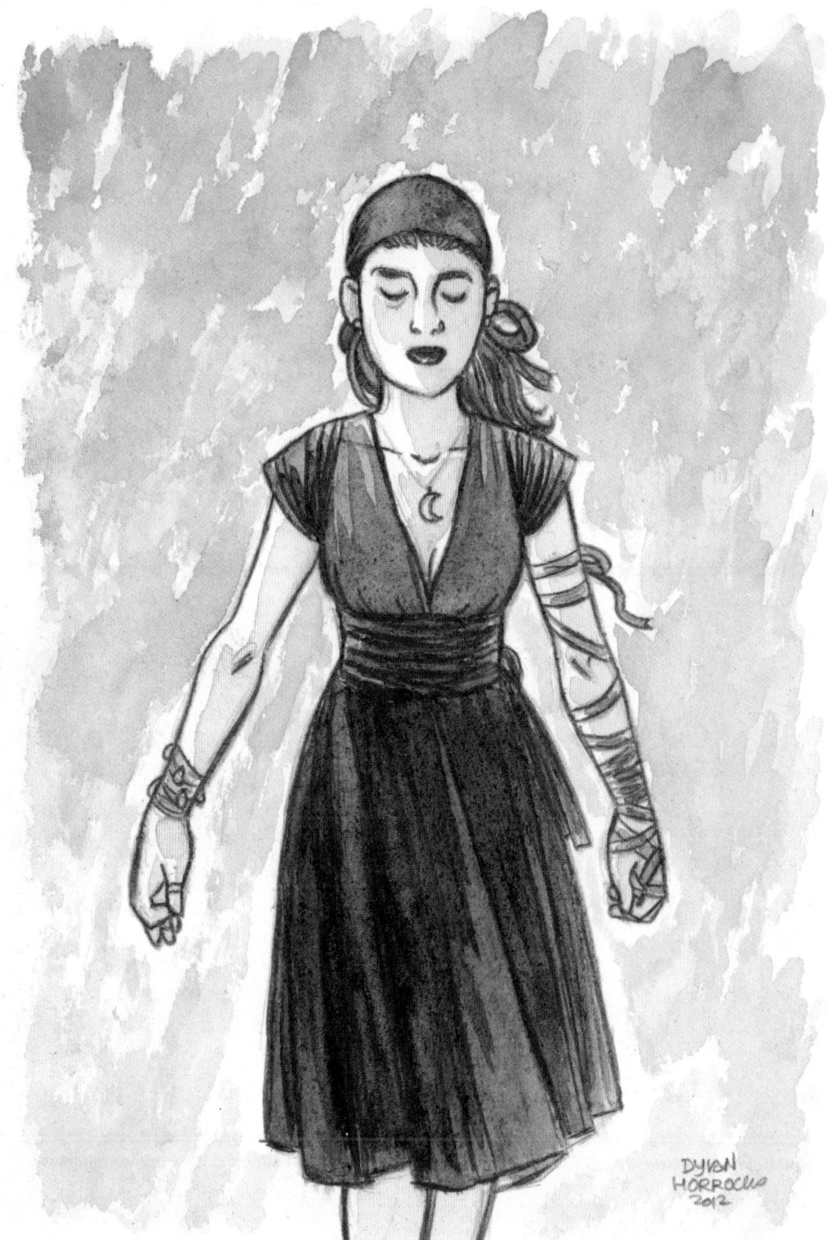
DYLAN
HORROCKS
2012

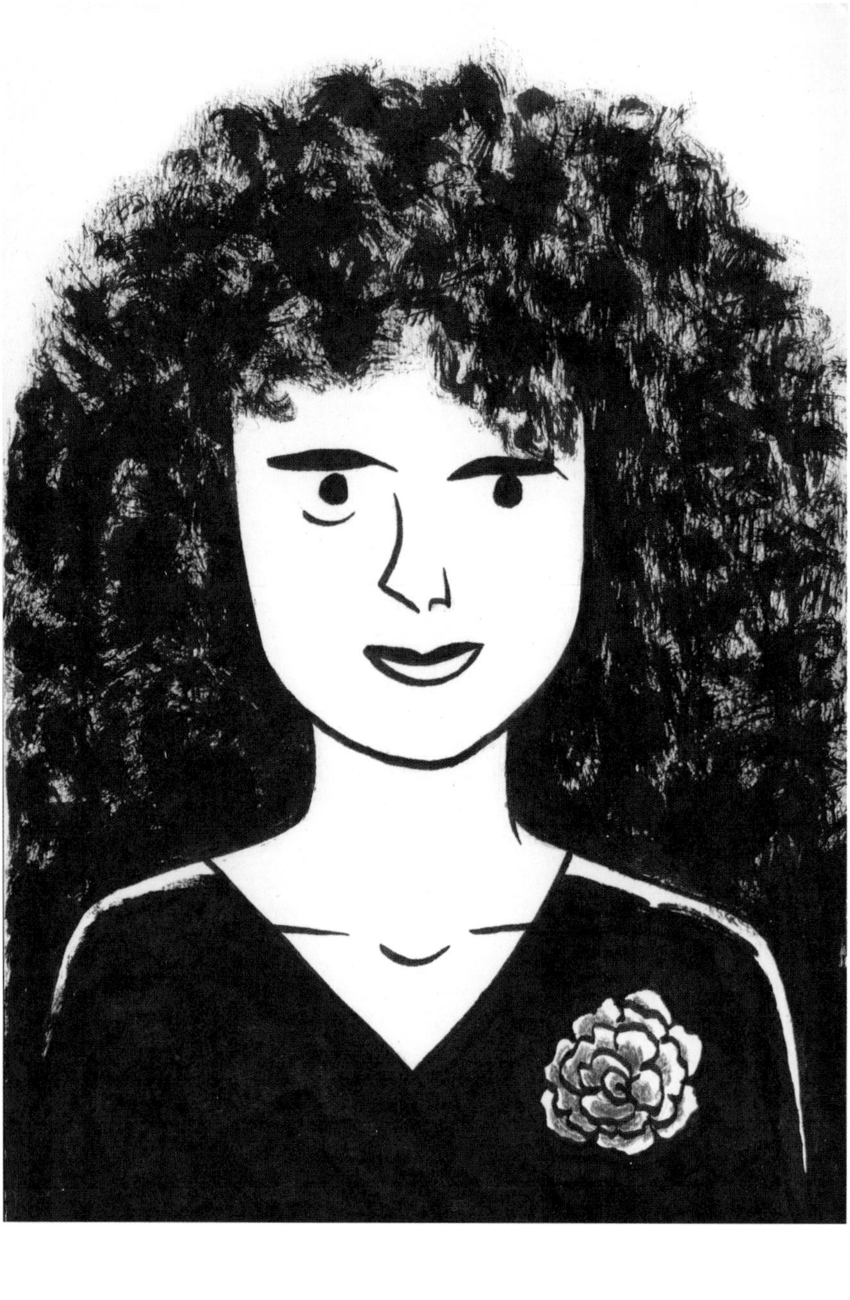

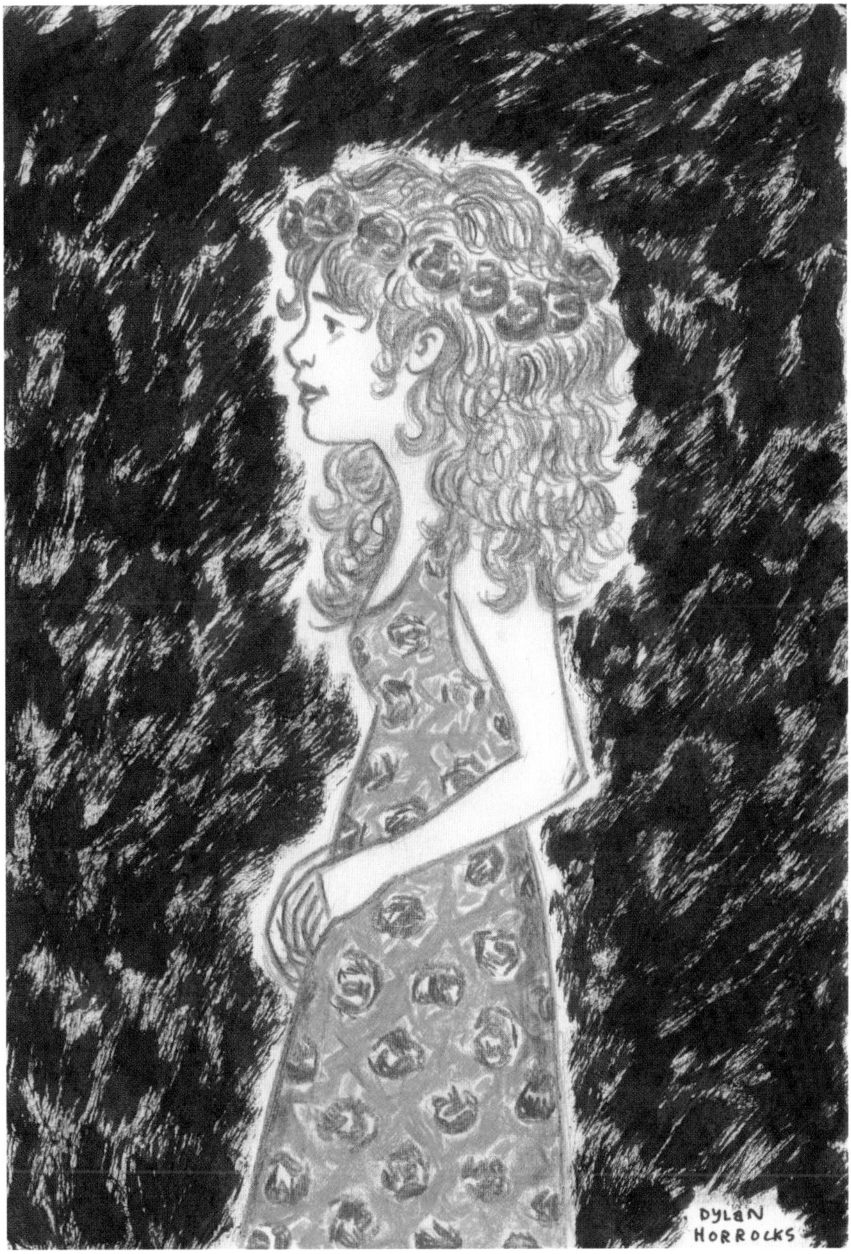
DYLAN
HORROCKS

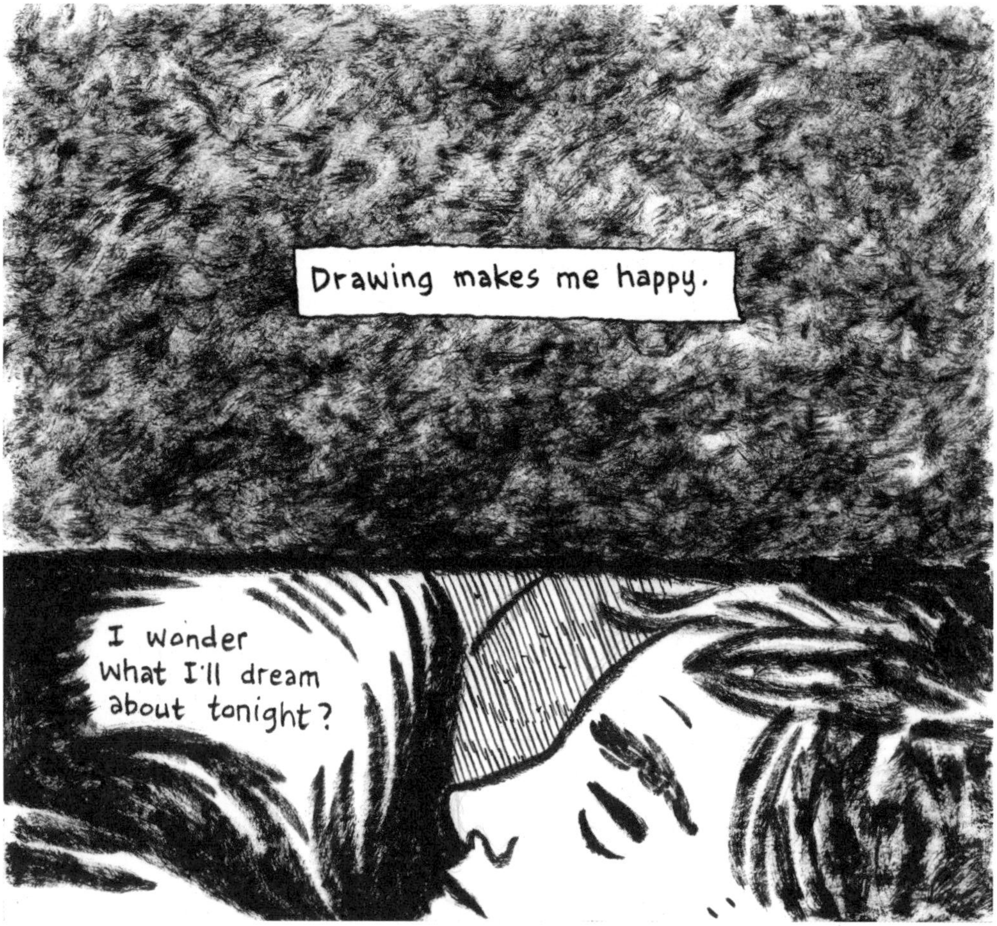
Drawing makes me happy.
I wonder what I'll dream about tonight?

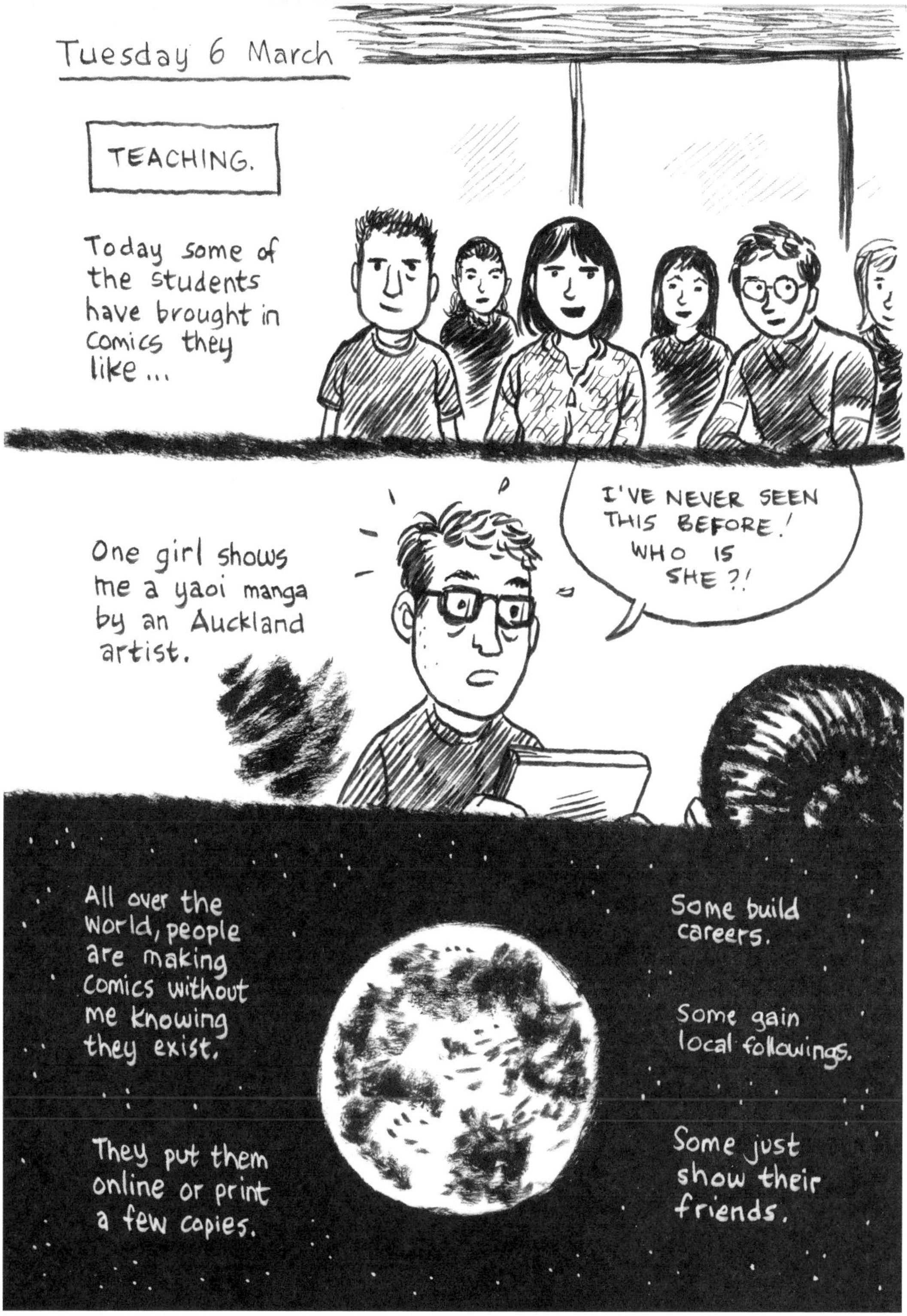
Tuesday 6 March
TEACHING.
Today some of the students have brought in comics they like...
One girl shows me a yaoi manga by an Auckland artist.
I'VE NEVER SEEN THIS BEFORE! WHO IS SHE?!
All over the world, people are making comics without me knowing they exist.
They put them online or print a few copies.
Some build careers.
Some gain local followings.
Some just show their friends.

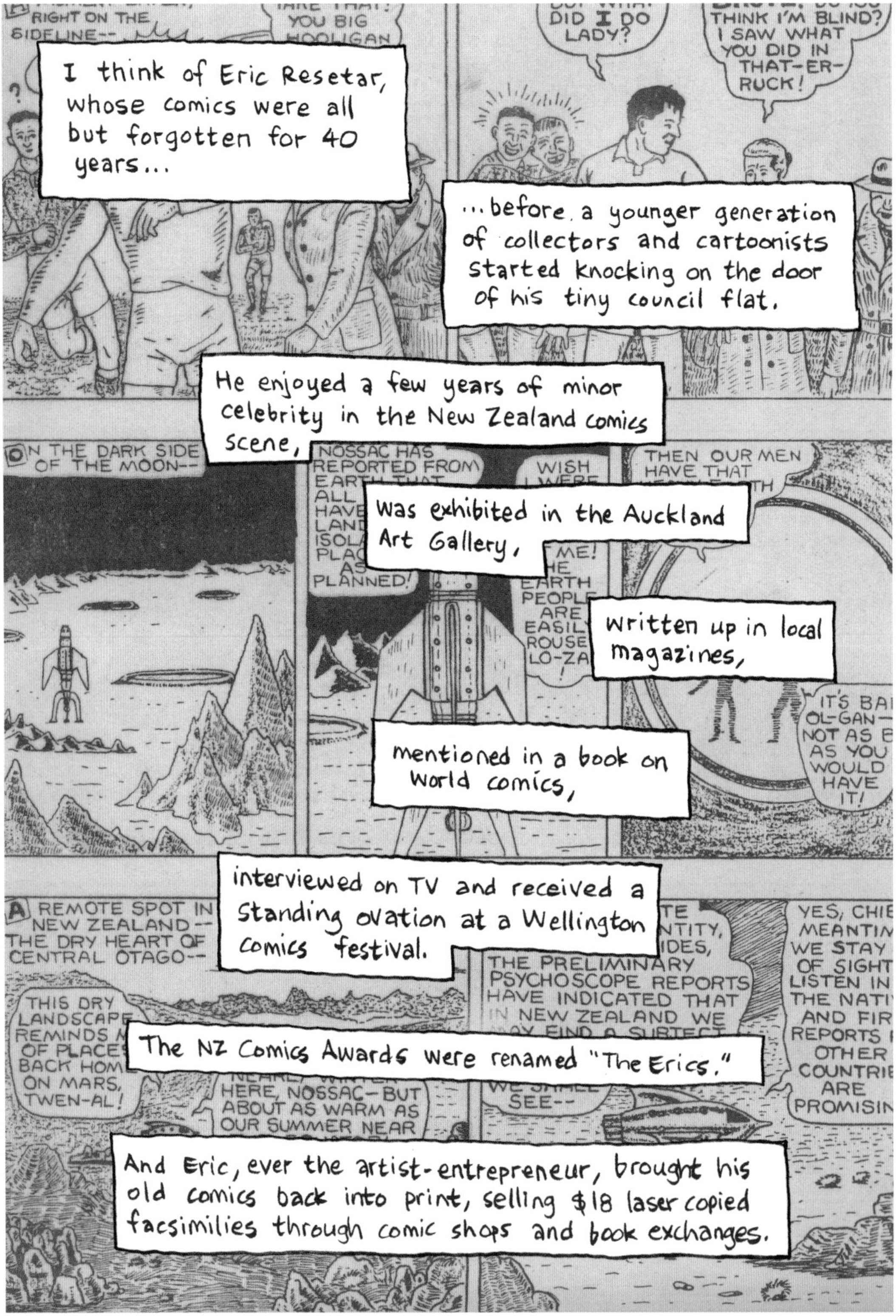
RIGHT ON THE SIDELINE--
DID I DO LADY?
THINK I'M BLIND? I SAW WHAT YOU DID IN THAT-ER-RUCK!
I think of Eric Resetar, whose comics were all but forgotten for 40 years...
...before a younger generation of collectors and cartoonists started knocking on the door of his tiny council flat.
He enjoyed a few years of minor celebrity in the New Zealand comics scene,
ON THE DARK SIDE OF THE MOON--
was exhibited in the Auckland Art Gallery,
written up in local magazines,
mentioned in a book on World comics,
interviewed on TV and received a standing ovation at a Wellington comics festival.
A REMOTE SPOT IN NEW ZEALAND-- THE DRY HEART OF CENTRAL OTAGO--
The NZ Comics Awards were renamed "The Erics."
And Eric, ever the artist-entrepreneur, brought his old comics back into print, selling $18 laser copied facsimilies through comic shops and book exchanges.

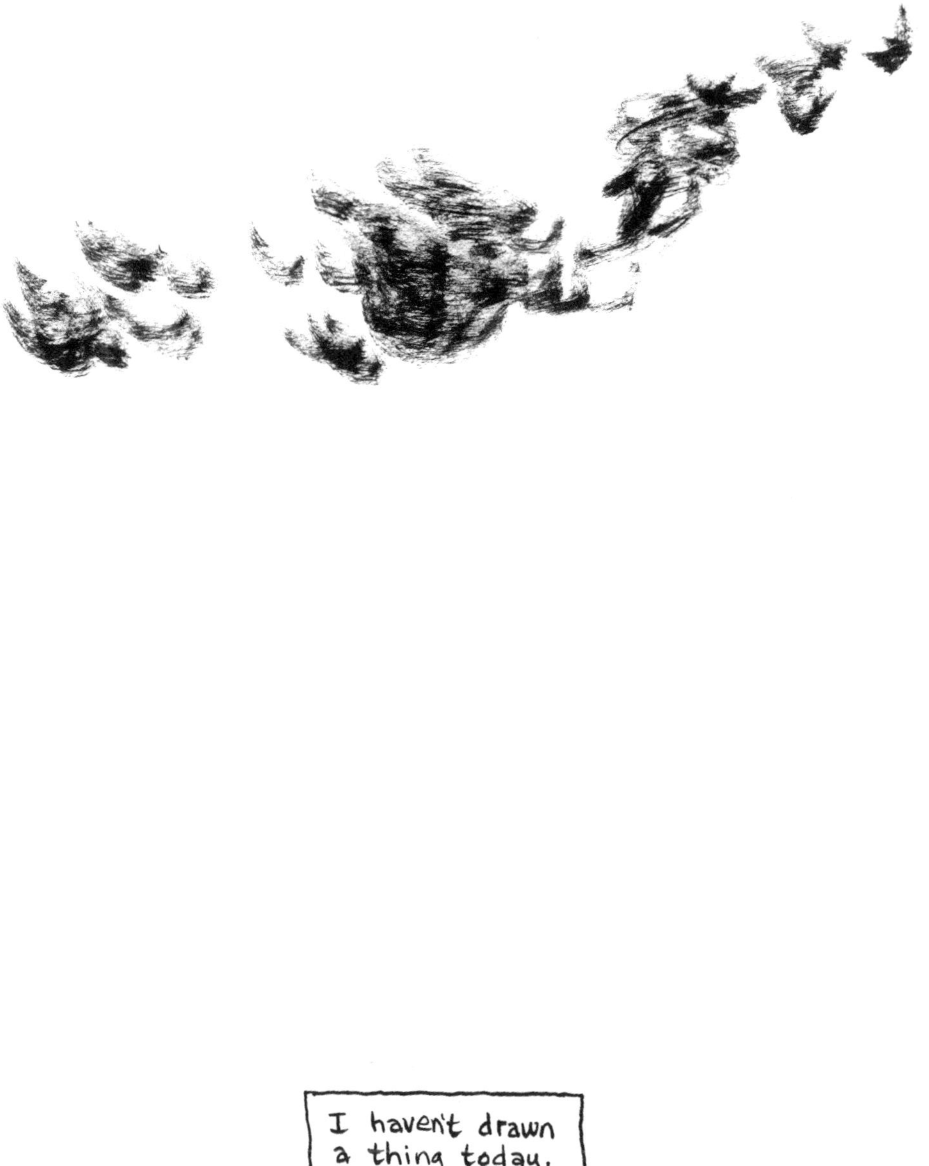
I haven't drawn a thing today.

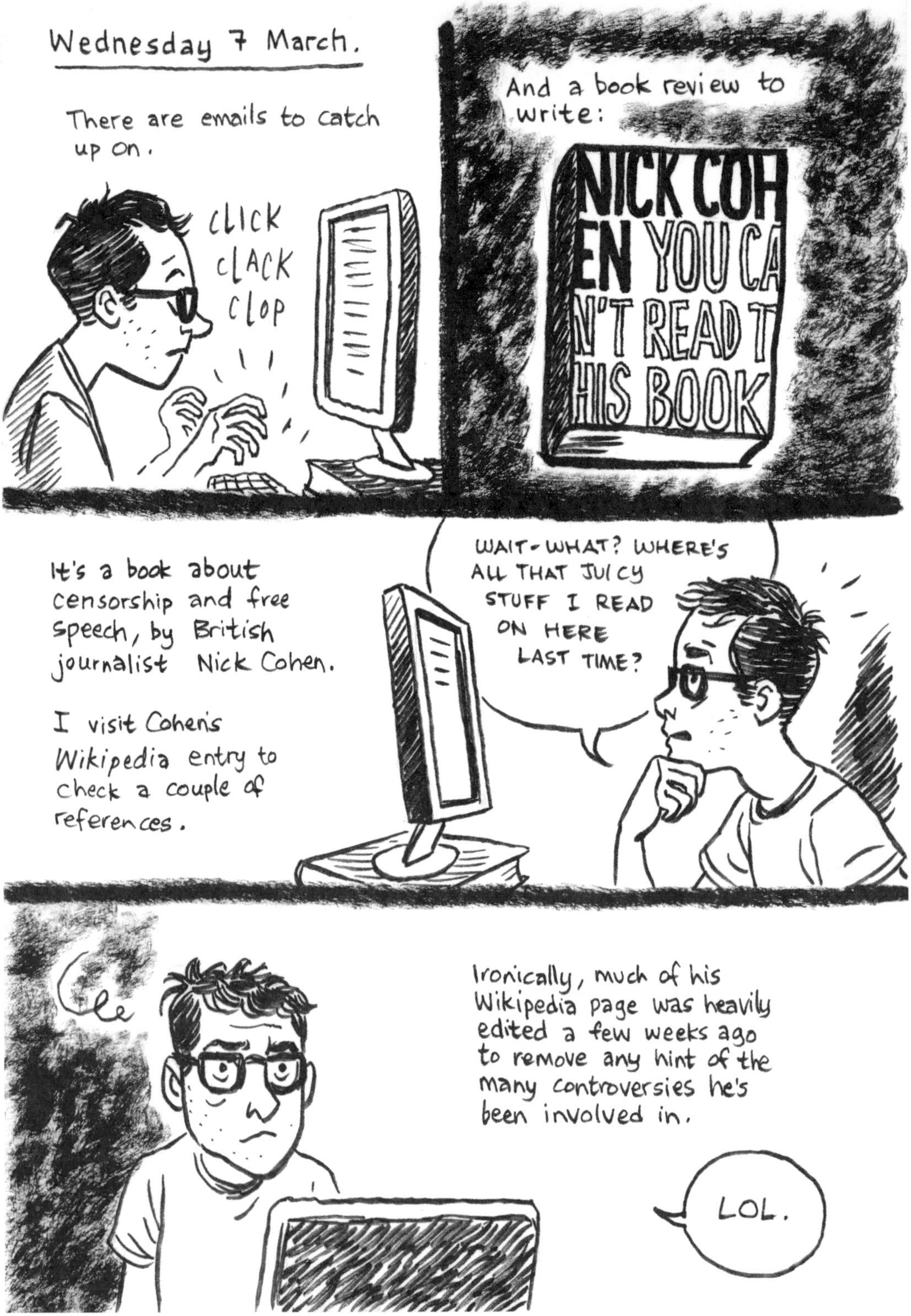
Wednesday 7 March.
There are emails to catch up on.
CLICK CLACK CLOP
And a book review to write:
NICK COHEN YOU CAN'T READ THIS BOOK
It's a book about censorship and free speech, by British journalist Nick Cohen.
I visit Cohen's Wikipedia entry to check a couple of references.
WAIT-WHAT? WHERE'S ALL THAT JUICY STUFF I READ ON HERE LAST TIME?
Ironically, much of his Wikipedia page was heavily edited a few weeks ago to remove any hint of the many controversies he's been involved in.
LOL.

Today I draw this for one of Louis' school friends:

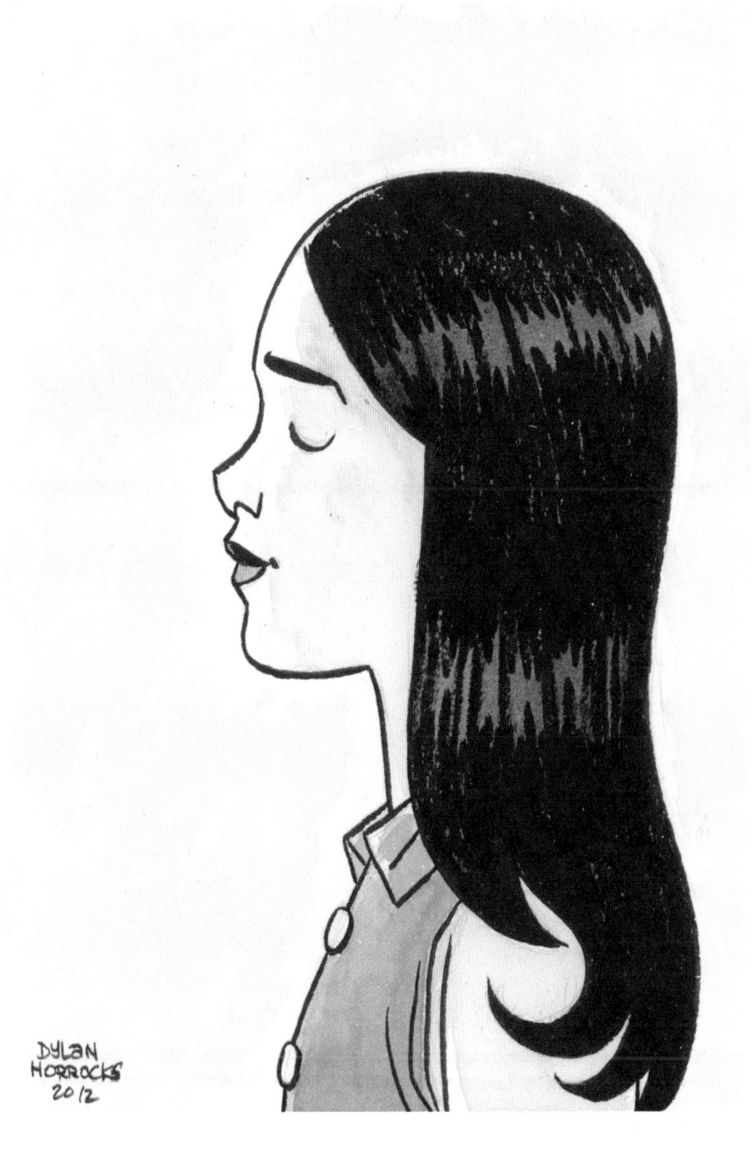
DYLAN
HORROCKS
2012

And this for Abe's birthday dinner tonight:

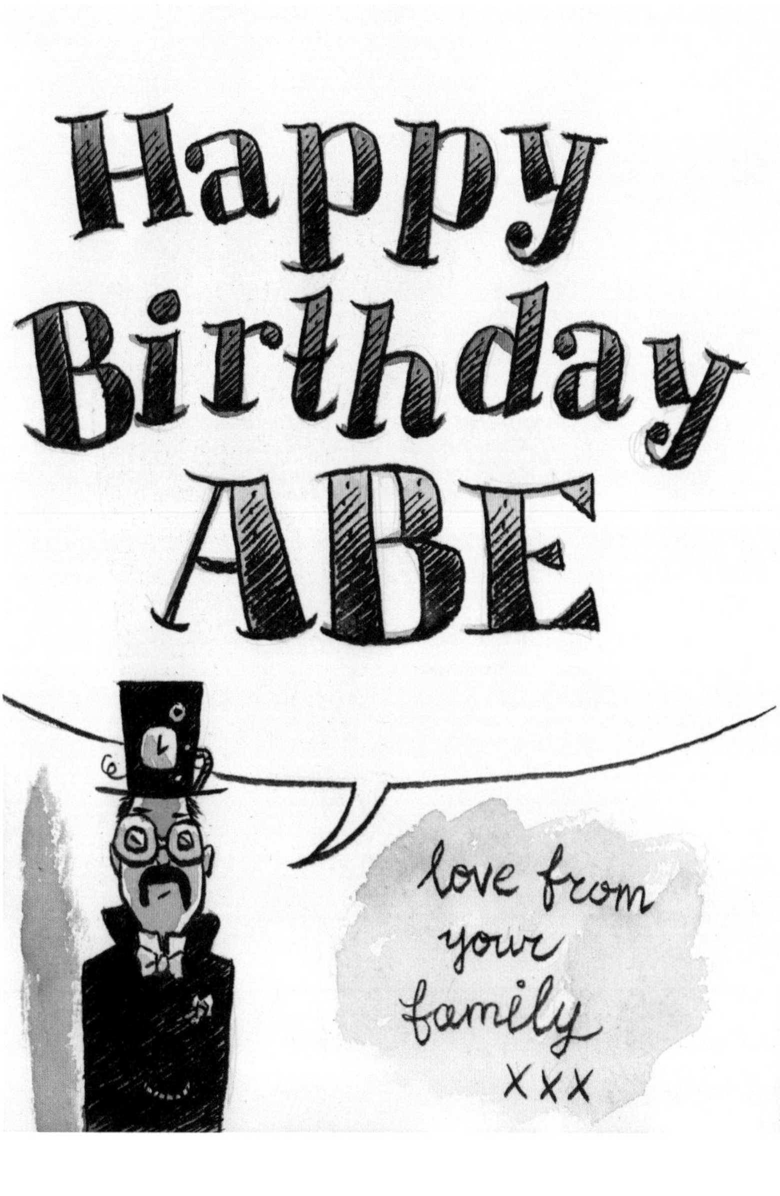
Happy Birthday ABE
love from your family
XXX

I wish I weren't so busy right now. I wish I could spend more time drawing. I wish I had made more comics...

The Magic Pen

But this. We made *this.*

7 March/23 March 2012

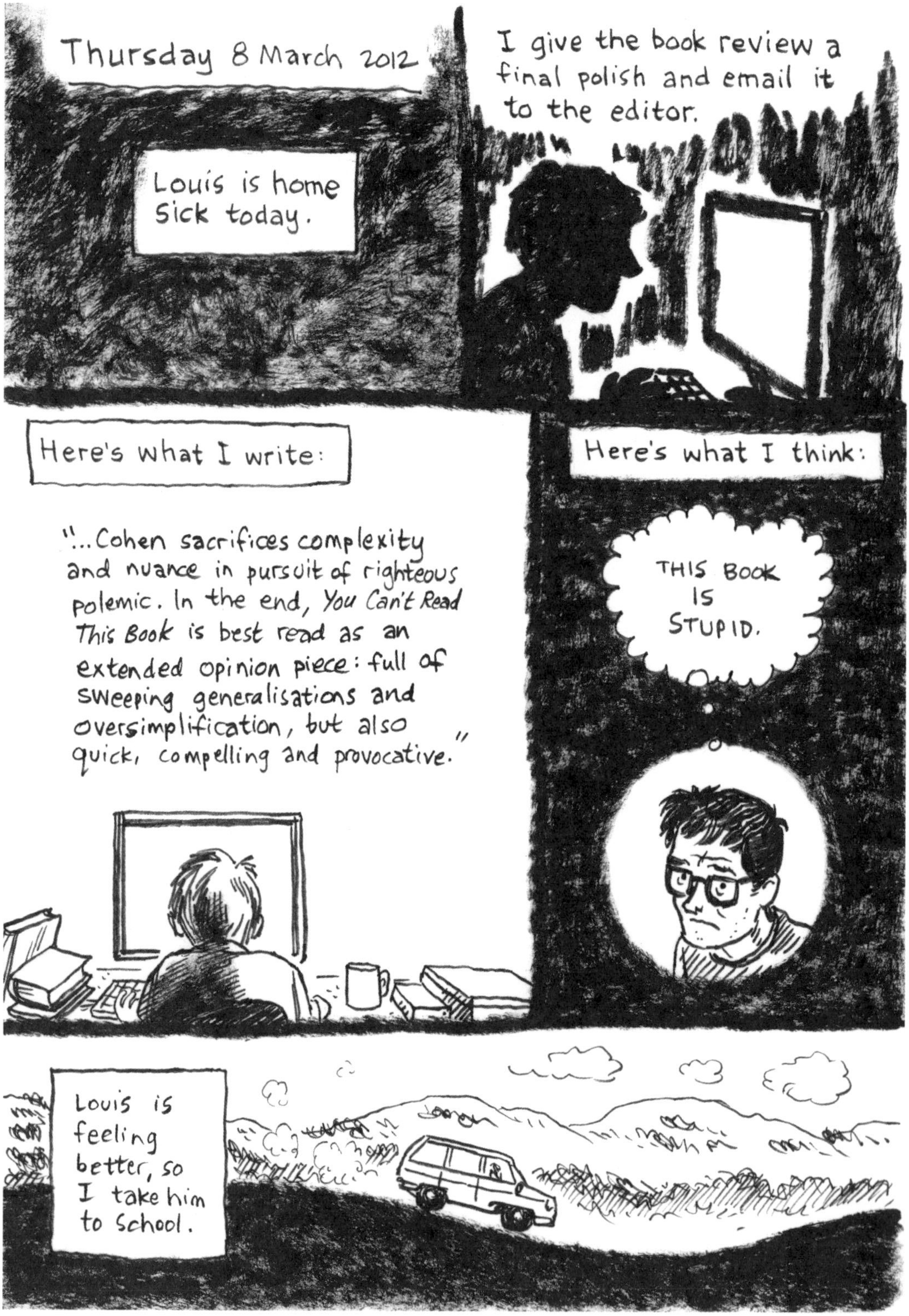
Thursday 8 March 2012
Louis is home sick today.
I give the book review a final polish and email it to the editor.
Here's what I write:
"...Cohen sacrifices complexity and nuance in pursuit of righteous polemic. In the end, *You Can't Read This Book* is best read as an extended opinion piece: full of sweeping generalisations and oversimplification, but also quick, compelling and provocative."
Here's what I think:
THIS BOOK IS STUPID.
Louis is feeling better, so I take him to school.

I draw some more commissioned sketches:

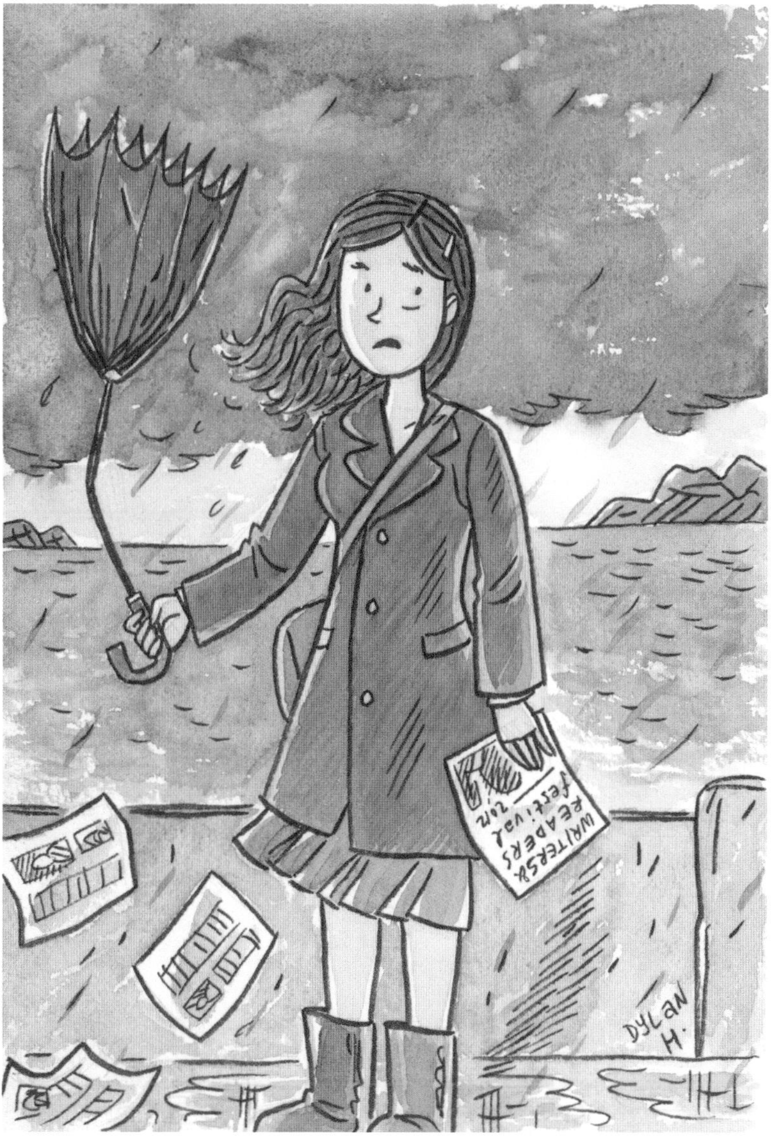
WRITERS&
READERS
festival
2012
DYLAN
H.

Watercolour is a new thing for me. I'm falling in love with it.

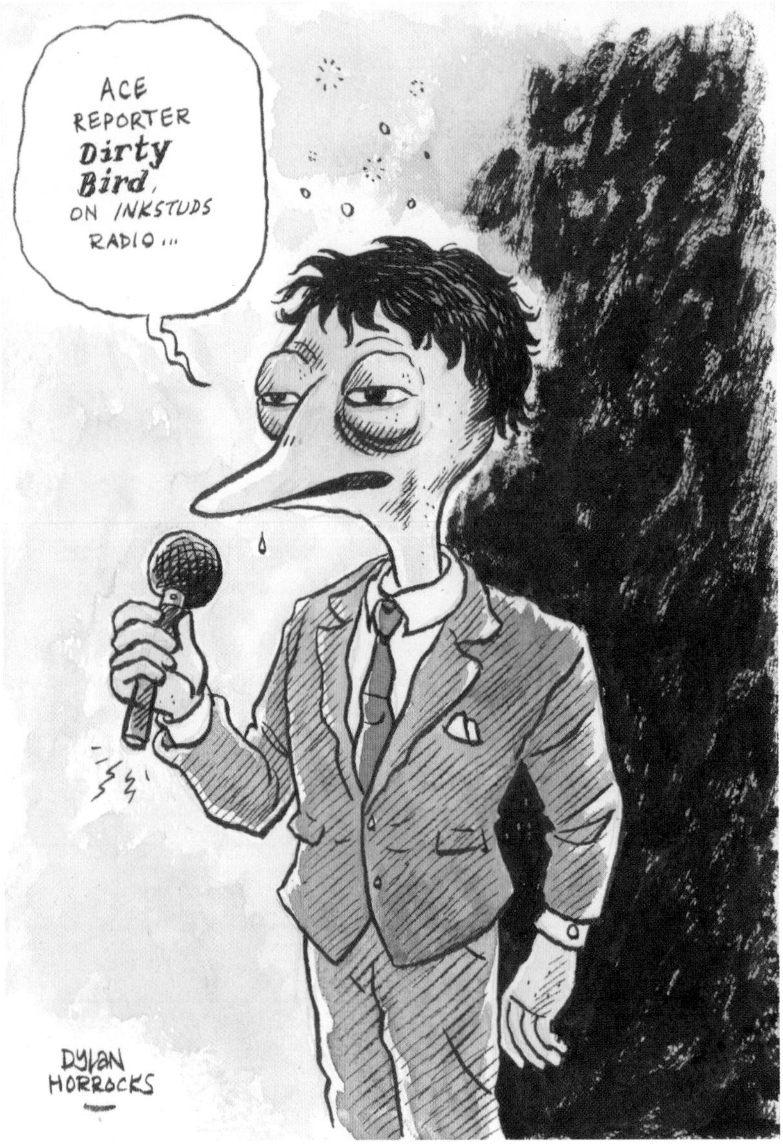
ACE REPORTER Dirty Bird, ON INKSTUDS RADIO...
DYLAN HORROCKS

I've been asked to do the poster for a comics festival:

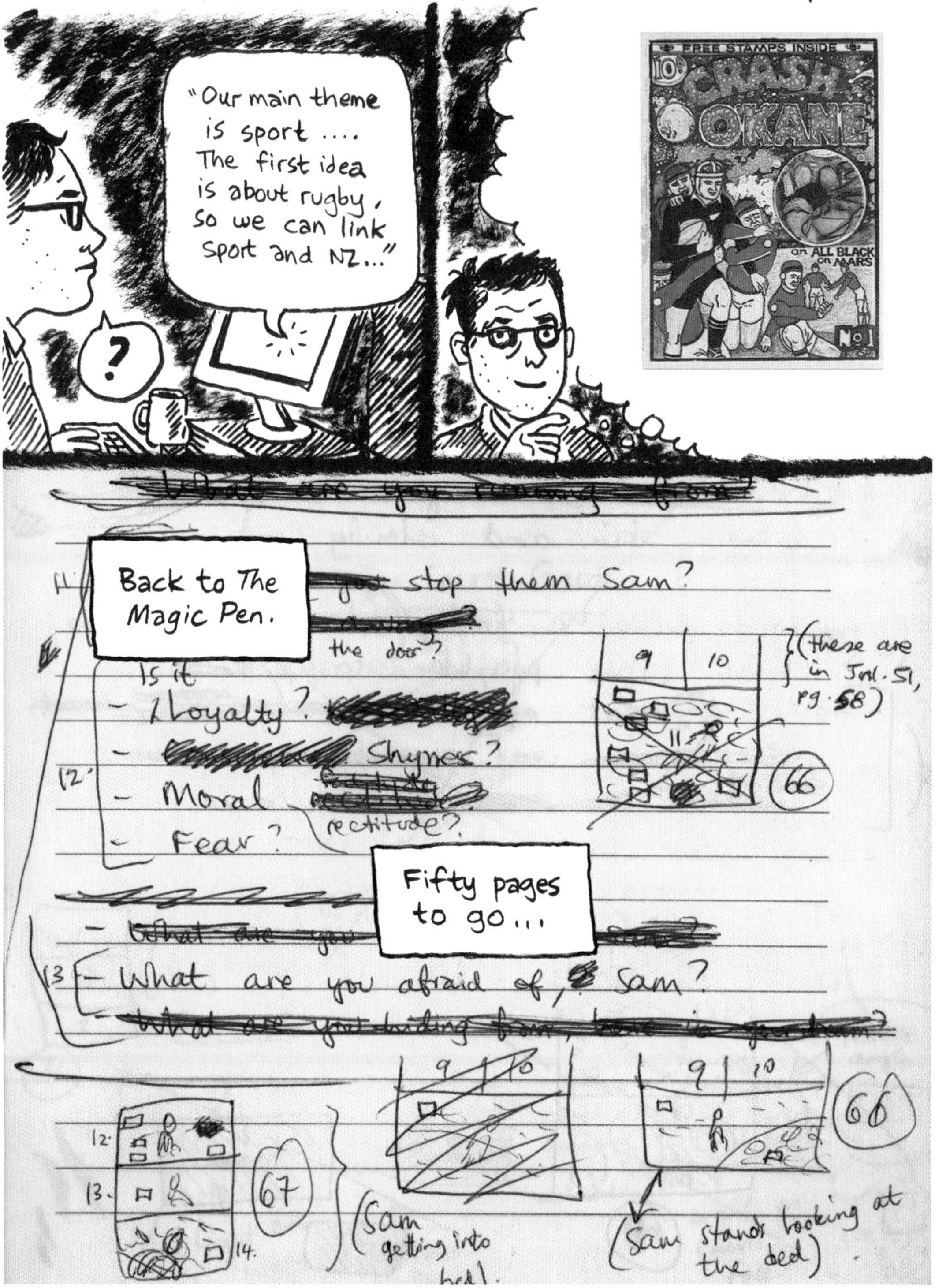

"Our main theme is sport .... The first idea is about rugby, so we can link sport and NZ..."
?
FREE STAMPS INSIDE
10¢
CRASH O'KANE
an ALL BLACK on MARS
No 1
Back to The Magic Pen.
stop them Sam?
the door?
Is it
- Loyalty?
- Shyness?
- Moral rectitude?
- Fear?
(these are in Jnl. 51, pg. 58)
66
Fifty pages to go...
What are you afraid of, Sam?
67
(Sam getting into bed).
(Sam stands looking at the bed).

# NOTES

LITTLE DEATH (1986): first published in *Fox Comics*, an Australian comics anthology. I used Kupe (pronounced "Coo-pay") as a pen-name for several years (on account of it being one of my middle names). In Māori legend, Kupe was the first Polynesian explorer to discover the islands of Aotearoa-New Zealand. The Underground Cafe was a cafe in Auckland in the mid-1980s, which also features in my unfinished graphic novel *Cafe Underground* (serialized in the comic book *Pickle*). I first met Terry while drawing this story, at the now-vanished DKD cafe.

UNWRITTEN STORIES (1987): first published in *Fox Comics*.

MEN THAT PERISH (1989): written for an anthology on images and ideas of masculinity planned by a friend. When that project was abandoned, 'Men That Perish' was published in *Fox Comics*. Includes images borrowed from photographs by August Sander, Robert Capa and others, including some found in a 1930s children's science annual that I wish I still owned.

INCOMPLETE WORKS (1989): first published in *The Dead Muse*, an anthology edited by Eddie Campbell. I drew the last page while staying at my sister's a few days after arriving in London (see 'The Last Fox Story').

THE LAST FOX STORY (1990): mostly drawn in ballpoint pen on memo paper and first published as a 104-page A6 mini-comic, printed on the office photocopier at Waterstone's bookshop on Charing Cross Road in London (where I was working at the time). I began writing it for the final issue of *Fox Comics* (sadly never published), in which contributors were invited to tell stories about their own relationship with comics.

BEATA (1991, 1992): first drawn as a birthday present for my mother in 1991 and later redrawn for my comic book series *Pickle*.

OPPOSITE EQUINOXES (1991): written and drawn in London during the build up to Operation Desert Storm. First published as a 32-page A6 mini-comic.

WESTERN WIND (1992, 2000): the first version of this story was drawn in London for *The Tragedy Strikes Sampler* (a small anthology that never came out). I was saving money to return home to New Zealand and to Terry. The revised version published here was drawn in 2000 and published in *Dark Horse Maverick 2000.*

SUMMONING (1991, 2011): the first version of this story was drawn in London for bilingual French and English anthology *Le Roquet.* Later redrawn in 2011 for Francois Vigneault's anthology *Elfworld* (the version included here).

LETTER FROM CATWOMAN (1991): first published in *Pickle.* Drawn as a tribute to the great English cartoonist Ed Pinsent, after reading his beautiful mini-comic *Illegal Batman.*

CAPTAIN COOK'S COMIC CUTS (1994): drawn while working at the University Book Shop in Auckland. First published in *Pickle.*

TABULA RASA (1994): first published in Tower Records' *Classical Pulse* magazine.

THE STATE OF THINGS (1994): first published in Cornelius Stone's *UFO* magazine, during a particularly bleak winter. New Zealand was going through a long economic slump, made worse by the policies of the right wing National Party government (which included Jenny Shipley as Minister of Health and Bill Birch as Finance Minister, both responsible for harsh cuts to social services), cheered on by free market extremists in Treasury and the Business Round Table lobby group. The opposition Labour Party was in disarray and our most effective left wing politician, Jim Anderton, had just resigned as leader of the Alliance Party after a family tragedy. Meanwhile, Terry and I were expecting our first baby, living in a tiny flat in Mount Eden, spending a lot of time curled up together watching *Northern Exposure* and *Shortland Street,* a local soap opera. We both had a bit of a crush on Nurse Jacki Manu (played by Nancy Brunning).

MAUNGAREI (1995): drawn in a couple of hours for *Black River Chronicle* (a NZ comics fanzine edited by my friend Lars Cawley), when Louis was 5 months old and I was working at the University Book Shop and drawing *Pickle* in the evenings. Our flat was in Ellerslie, at the foot of Maungarei (or Mount Wellington).

HIS LANGUAGE WAS A HISSING SOUND (1997): a fragment from an abandoned *Cartoon History of New Zealand,* which I spent several months researching and writing before the publisher decided not to proceed. The text is based on Te Horeta Te Taniwha's account of meeting the English explorer Captain Cook in 1769.

L'IL AINJIL (1998): a comic about the death of George Herriman, creator of the comic strip 'Krazy Kat' (1913-1944). The two quotations come from *Krazy Kat: the Comic Art of George Herriman*, by Patrick McDonnell, Karen O'Connell and Georgia Riley de Havenon, which is also the source for the comic strip shown below (found on Herriman's drawing board after he died: unfinished and unlettered). At one point I was planning a whole series of comics about Herriman's life, but this is the only one I ever drew. First published in the *SPX 98* anthology.

PICKLE COMICS #1, c. 1945 (1997): drawn for the *Armageddon Expo* booklet and loosely based on *Supreme Feature Comics #1*, a New Zealand comics magazine drawn by Harry Bennett in the 1940s (first shown to me by Wellington-based cartoonist and historian Tim Bollinger).

IF I WERE A POP STAR (1999): first published in Tower Records' *Pulse* magazine, back in the days when comic shops were closing and CD stores were booming. Oh the irony.....

ALMA-LARISSINE'S KISSES (1997): drawn as a wedding gift.

THERE ARE NO WORDS IN MY MOUTH (2000): drawn for *Comix 2000*, a 2000-page book of wordless comics from around the world, published to mark the millennium by L'Association in France.

10-7 (2001): drawn for *9-11: Artists Respond*, a benefit book published by Dark Horse Comics to raise money for victims of the September 11 attacks. The title refers to the date America began bombing Afghanistan. On that day, my family and I were visiting Waiheke Island.

DULL CARE (2005): drawn for *Little Nemo 1905-2005: Un Siècle De Rêves* (Les Impressions Nouvelles, 2005), a book celebrating the centenary of Winsor McCay's famous comic strip. McCay's other creations include the comic strip 'Pilgrim's Progress' (source of the Dull Care case) and pioneering animated cartoon *Gertie the Dinosaur*.

SISO (2006): drawn for *Les Belles Étrangères: Douze Écrivains Néo-Zélandais*, an anthology of stories published as part of a festival of New Zealand writers held in France. 'Siso' was subsequently published in English in David Bradbury's local comics anthology *Pictozine*. The cute animal characters on the first and last page come from *Tiny Folks*, a New Zealand children's comic drawn by Jack Raeburn in the 1940s, photocopies of which I was given by Tim Bollinger.

THE PHYSICS ENGINE (2006): drawn for *Are Angels OK? The Parallel Universes of New Zealand Writers and Scientists*, edited by Paul Callaghan and Bill Manhire (VUP, 2006). This was an anthology published to mark the International Year of Physics and included work by a range of writers responding to conversations with physicists. In my case, I had several meetings with Professor Geoff Austin and Associate Professor Matthew Collett and discussed everything from the physics of clouds, light teleportation, quantum entanglement, the landscape paintings of William Hodge, the silliness of fantasy, the theology of predictability and the role of dice in table top war gaming. 'The Physics Engine' came out of those conversations, along with my own life-long obsession with fantasy role-playing games (see the story's end-notes on pages 137-8).

TO THE I-LAND: THE COMICS OF BARRY LINTON (2007): an illustrated essay on the work of cartoonist Barry Linton, whose work I have loved since first encountering it in *Strips* magazine in the early 1980s. I'm very grateful to Barry for letting me reproduce his work in this essay, which was first published in *Look This Way: New Zealand Writers on New Zealand Artists*, edited by Sally Blundell (Auckland University Press, 2007).

CORNUCOPIA (2009): first published in the special 'Atlas' issue of Australian literary magazine *The Lifted Brow*, which included a piece of writing, art or music for each country in the world. My contribution was dedicated to Cornucopia, a fictional country first visited in *Hicksville* and later explored in the comic book series *Atlas*.

MY WORLD (2009): drawn for *Ctrl.Alt.Shift Unmasks Corruption*, a book of comics put together by Paul Gravett for UK-based charity Ctrl.Alt.Shift (who use online and traditional media and activism to work against global injustice).

THINGS I HAVE DONE AT THE MALL (2010): drawn for a special issue of *Metro* magazine in which writers, artists and photographers documented a single day in Auckland as viewed from various locations.

SOMETIMES YOU FEEL (2011): drawn for *Darkest Day: Comics for Christchurch*, a special issue of *Funtime Comics* published to raise money for the Red Cross following the 2011 Christchurch earthquake, which wrecked much of the city and killed 185 people.

A CARTOONIST'S DIARY (2012): drawn for the Cartoonist's Diary feature on tcj.com, *The Comics Journal's* website.

# THANKS

to everyone who asked me to draw one of these comics for their anthology, magazine, book or website, including:

| | |
|---|---|
| Philip Bentley | L'Association |
| David Vodicka | Chris Oliveros |
| Warren Thomas | Benoît Peeters |
| Eddie Campbell | Les Belles Étrangères |
| Michel Vrana | Dave Bradbury |
| Nick Craine | Bill Manhire |
| Diana Schutz | Paul Callaghan |
| Brad! Brooks | Sally Blundell |
| Francois Vigneault | Ronnie Scott |
| Marc Wiedenbaum | Sascha Krader |
| Cornelius Stone | Paul Gravett |
| Lars Cawley | Simon Wilson |
| Geoff Walker | Isaac Freeman |
| Chris Oarr | Dan Nadel |
| Bill Geradts | |

to Fergus Barrowman (who talked me into this)
and
Kirsten McDougall, Kyleigh Hodgson and Craig Gamble at VUP
my agent Nicolas Grivel
Marc Arsenault and Alternative Comics
Barry Linton, for letting me do a comic about him
everyone involved with Fox Comics, Les Cartoonistes Dangereuses,
Razor
the staff at Waterstone's Charing Cross Rd, 1989-1993
and the University Book Shop (Auckland), 1993-1995
Richard Bird, Sylvie Joly-Langridge
Jeffrey Paparoa Holman, Nigel Gearing
Simone Horrocks
and all my family, friends and former flatmates.

Most of all, love and gratitude without measure to
Terry Fleming, Louis Fleming, Abe Horrocks
xxxooo